MOVE TO MILLIONS®

ADVANCED PRAISE FOR *Move* TO MILLIONS

"Darnyelle's previous books covered a variety of business success tips. *Move to Millions* is the in-depth comprehensive game plan that takes you from amateur level to being a professional entrepreneur ready to unleash your full potential."

—**Omar Tyree**, *New York Times* Bestselling Author and NAACP Image Award Winner

"*Move to Millions* is a must read whether you're already a million-dollar earner or have millions on your mind. Darnyelle is divinely anointed to help purpose-driven entrepreneurs elevate exponentially both financially and spiritually."

—**Patrice Washington**, Host, Award-Winning *Redefining Wealth Podcast*

"I loved this book! If you are a business owner, or want to become one someday, you need to read this book and follow Darnyelle's directions. She's sharing what she's learned on her way to becoming a millionaire, and you can't help but increase your success as a result."

—**Leisa Peterson**, Author, *The Mindful Millionaire*

"Your grandchildren say 'thank you' for changing your life by picking up this book. This book is necessary reading for anyone who wants to scale their business to the million-dollar mark with joy and ease. In this book, Darnyelle flawlessly packages her radical honesty, incredible insight, and sharp ability to coach you from where you are to seven figures and beyond."

—**Charreah K. Jackson**, Founder, Shine Army Media and former *Essence* Senior Editor

"Less than 2 percent of all women entrepreneurs have revenues that exceed one million dollars a year. For the millions of women entrepreneurs who have yet to reach that revenue goal, Darnyelle offers inspiration and sound advice on how to get there. It's a must-read!"

—**Monica S. Smiley**, Editor & Publisher, *Enterprising Women Magazine*

"Darnyelle poured her heart and soul into this book. She knows the principles because she lived them. *Move to Millions* is a transformative guide for small business owners and entrepreneurs looking to take their companies to the highest heights they've ever achieved. This book is a must-read for anyone looking to elevate their business."

—**Raoul Davis**, CEO, Ascendant Group Branding,
the #1 Ranked Minority Owned PR Firm 2021 and 2022

"There is no better person to talk about moving to millions than Dr. Darnyelle Jervey Harmon. *Move to Millions: The Proven Framework to Become a Million Dollar CEO with Grace & Ease Instead of Hustle & Grind* is the book I wish existed before I ever started my entrepreneurship journey! A MUST READ!"

—**Shawn Anthony**, Host of *School's Over . . . Now What? Podcast,*
CEO of Shawn Anthony Enterprises LLC

"*Move to Millions* is one of those books where you can instantly tell the author has walked the walk. Darnyelle has earned the right to write this book and we are the beneficiaries."

—**Dov Gordon**, ProfitableRelationships.com

"The information in this book is gold! I believed I could have a million-dollar business then I implemented the strategies shared in this book. Now, I have a million-dollar business. This book is a must-read."

—**Attiyah Blair**, CEO, The Real Estate Reset

"*Move to Millions* is the truth entrepreneurs didn't know they needed. What I love about this book is that it will have you gasping for air with clarity. Darnyelle is proven, her clients are real, and *Move to Millions* is a diary of entrepreneurial truth!"

—**Aprille Franks**, Aprille & Co | Epic Woman

"Put down all the other self-help books piled on your nightstand and READ THIS NOW! Read it fast, then read it slow—and DO the work! Darnyelle has given you a soup-to-nuts roadmap to become spiritually and financially rich. She shares profound principles and practical strategies for building a business that serves the world AND leaves a legacy for your family."

—**Caitlin Cogan Doemner**, MBA, Founder of the Ecstatic Way

"This book embodies the intersectionality of faith, business strategy, and inspired implementation. It won't just leave you a better business owner, it will leave you a better person."

—**Amy Walker**, CEO, Walker Consulting

"Darnyelle has been given the anointing of magnifying one's potential greatness into financial success. So, if you want to balance that success while maintaining your sanity, this book will give you some of the metrics needed in a transparent and fresh way."

—**Dr. Jatali Bellanton**, PhD, in Neuropsychology

"With many business coaches and mentors spouting the importance of hustle culture, *Move to Millions* is a refreshingly insightful framework that proves that you can make millions without sacrificing what's most important to you. Add this book to your strategic business plan now."

—**Towanna Burrous**, CEO, Coach Diversity

"Darnyelle seamlessly weaves together real-life experiences and real-world experiences to provide a surefooted blueprint to genuine success. As someone who personally knows Darnyelle. and is intimately familiar with the efficacy that her work has in bringing real results to the lives of those blessed to know her, I am excited to see more people able to tap her wisdom and create real lasting legacy in the world."

—**Dan Mangena**, CEO, Dream with Dan

"Darnyelle makes the *Move to Millions* as easy as following her simple, step-by-step recipe. This book reveals degrees of knowledge and wisdom I have rarely seen in writing before.

If you're an entrepreneur, and you read only one book this year, let it be *Move to Millions: The Proven Framework to Build a Million Dollar Company with Grace & Ease Instead of Hustle & Grind*."

—**Allyson Byrd**, CEO, Money Movers International

"Darnyelle is the long-time go-to source for wealth creation. *Move to Millions* is her blueprint of success, which everyone can follow. *Move to Millions* is about creating wealth the smart way. Darnyelle has proven that it's possible with persistent and purposeful actions."

—**Ramon Ray**, Publisher, Zone of Genius.com

"Everyone has a *Move to Millions* story inside of them. Yours will be revealed in the pages of this book. Open it and discover your personal blueprint to your next M.O.V.E."

—**Natasha Joan Haughton**, Business, Life, and Sales Strategist, Vision Manifest, LLC

"Millions-minded leads to millions manifested. This is what Darnyelle so eloquently unearths through principle, process, and practice in this must-have manual for entrepreneurs. Without gatekeeping or watering down what's required, *Move to Millions* is a business blueprint that teaches how to gain leverage and leave legacy without sacrificing or selling your soul."

—**Janice Anderson**, CEO of Significant Life

Move
TO
MILLIONS®

THE PROVEN FRAMEWORK TO BECOME A MILLION-DOLLAR CEO
WITH **GRACE & EASE** INSTEAD OF **HUSTLE & GRIND**

DR. DARNYELLE
JERVEY HARMON

NEW YORK

LONDON • NASHVILLE • MELBOURNE • VANCOUVER

Move TO MILLIONS

The Proven Framework to Become a Million Dollar CEO with
Grace & Ease Instead of Hustle & Grind

Published in New York, New York, by Morgan James Publishing. Morgan James is a trademark of Morgan James, LLC. www.MorganJamesPublishing.com

Unless otherwise noted, Scripture is taken from the Holy Bible, American Standard Version, public domain.

Scripture marked KJV is taken from the Holy Bible, King James Version, public domain.

Incredible One Enterprises®, Move to Millions®, The Move to Millions Method™, The Move to Millions Continuum™, Leverage + Scale™, Leverage + Scale Offer Suite™, Leverage + Scale Messaging Suite™, Leverage + Scale Marketing Suite™, Leverage + Scale Sales Suite™, Leverage + Scale Systems Suite™, Leverage + Scale Talent Suite™, Leverage + Scale Legacy Suite™, Moses Moments™, Next Level Everything®, The Confidence Curve™, The Confidence Clause™, The Confidence Rate™, The Move to Millions Manifesto™, Vision Point vs Vantage Point™, The Millions Messy Middle™ and the Model of Financial & Spiritual Abundance™ are all registered trademarks of Darnyelle Jervey Harmon. All rights reserved.

Proudly distributed by Publishers Group West®

Morgan James BOGO™

A **FREE** ebook edition is available for you
or a friend with the purchase of this print book.

CLEARLY SIGN YOUR NAME ABOVE

Instructions to claim your free ebook edition:
1. Visit MorganJamesBOGO.com
2. Sign your name CLEARLY in the space above
3. Complete the form and submit a photo of this entire page
4. You or your friend can download the ebook to your preferred device

ISBN 9781636981666 paperback
ISBN 9781636981673 ebook
Library of Congress Control Number:
2023933869

Cover and Interior Design by:
Chris Treccani

Author Photos by:
Dave Bullen

Edited by:
Tenita Johnson and Melissa Stevens

Interior Illustrations by:
Rachel Dunham

Morgan James is a proud partner of Habitat for Humanity Peninsula
and Greater Williamsburg. Partners in building since 2006.

Get involved today! Visit: www.morgan-james-publishing.com/giving-back

To my father, the late Robert Joseph Jervey
(September 21, 1952–August 7, 2022),

I will always remember your excitement
for this book in your final days.

CONTENTS

FOREWORD

Move to Millions is the only book that helps you unite God with your birthright. This book guides you through the process of making millions of dollars by impacting countless lives while creating a legacy for generations to come.

I'm Lucinda Cross, President of Activate Worldwide and Activate Your Life™, motivational superstar, and bestselling author. Darnyelle, the queen of powerful messages, asked me to write this foreword. I could not be more honored or thrilled to inspire you to read her book.

Move to Millions is a book of enlightenment and alignment around success in your life and business. It has four parts: the mastery, the operational obedience, the vision, and the execution. Each part is a standalone blueprint for your best life and business ever. It includes data, Scriptures, and her own musings to illuminate the path of making millions of dollars in your business.

What spoke to me the most is how this book relates to my life. I understand the correlation between my business success and faith in God. In order to gain financial success, I had to be spiritually aligned. Any disconnect manifests itself as a lack of confidence.

When you are just starting out as an entrepreneur, if you are disconnected from and lack confidence in yourself, it will be difficult to succeed. The connection you have with God, and the confidence you have in yourself, are directly related to one another. When they align, spiritual abundance is unlocked.

What struck me while reading *Move to Millions* is how intertwined your connection with God and your confidence are, and how they impact your brilliance and competence in your messaging. If you are struggling to convey your message and if the words just aren't flowing, you don't have writer's block. You have a confidence problem. To move back to a place of spiritual abundance, you must repair the disconnect. Otherwise, you can't move forward.

Move to Millions is going to transform your outlook on making millions and impacting the lives of others. This book helps you understand how to surrender to the outcome of your actions and let God lead in order to move toward financial abundance.

We are all gifted. We all have talents to share with the world. I highly recommend *Move to Millions* so you can use your spiritual abundance to next-level your business and change the way you move through the world—with confidence in yourself and a strong connection with God.

While this book is called *Move to Millions*, it's not solely about money and birthright. It's about impacting the lives of others with words. Darnyelle realized God designed her to gather people and foster an environment that unleashes their biggest breakthroughs. And she does just that in this book.

One of the biggest breakthroughs I want you to prepare for while reading this book is the collaboration between your financial success and spiritual alignment.

Darnyelle believes making millions is less about strategy and more about surrender, which is a form of faith and one of the main principles in this book. She has expert knowledge about success speeding up when faith meets business.

Move to Millions is a literary masterpiece, full of enlightenment and alignment around success in your life and business. Darnyelle's "confessions" help guide you through the process of making millions of dollars in one year by impacting countless lives of people and creating a legacy for generations to come. Her stories illuminate the path of understanding so you can truly grasp the idea that "if you didn't come from millions, millions ought to come from you. When businesses make more, the impact is felt by millions."

A book can change your life. The door to movement and alignment only opens from within. This information cannot be taught, only caught. Make a conscious decision to open the door to wealth! Make a conscious decision to make yourself better by finding reasons to increase your value, instead of finding reasons not to. That, my *Move to Millions* partner, has made a world of a difference in my life and in my business.

Who has the next move? Checkmate!

Lucinda Cross
Chief Activator
Forbes Next 1000 | Motivational Speaker & Women Leadership Trainer | Verizon's Comeback Coach for Small Business | Media Personality | at Activate Worldwide, LLC

PREFACE

Now We're *Here*

Have you ever stopped and listened to Drake's "Started from the Bottom?"

I have.

I must admit, I love it *here. Now.*

Today, I am . . .

Here, running a multimillion-dollar company.

Here, building a legacy of wealth for my future children and great grandchildren.

Here, starting our foundation to create a massive impact in the world.

Here, making my ancestors proud.

Here, giving God something to bless.

But *here* hasn't always been a place that I loved.

I remember:

The *here* that happened after I called off my wedding three months before the big day because my fiancé got an older woman in our church pregnant.

The *here* of two more failed engagements followed by questioning if I was even lovable at all.

The *here* when I was holding "high-end" events at Howard Johnson motels.

The *here* that wondered if I should go back and get "a real job" because I couldn't figure out how to earn enough to call myself "self-employed."

The *here* that included watching my car be repossessed.

The *here* that followed filing bankruptcy and almost living in my car.

The *here* when my diet consisted of alternating ramen noodles and peanut butter and jelly sandwiches for breakfast, lunch, and dinner because that's all I could afford.

Like Drake, I started at the *bottom*.

My mom going to jail when I was eight was my *bottom*. When I was ten years old and in the fifth grade, I was blessed to have a teacher named Mrs. Dixon.

Mrs. Dixon was my savior. Mrs. Dixon loved me so much that she was also my sixth-grade teacher. (Yes, she changed grades just to have more time with me. That's my story and I am sticking to it.)

Because of Mrs. Dixon, I didn't become a product of my environment.

Because of Mrs. Dixon, I didn't have babies in my teens or the word felon on my CV.

Because of Mrs. Dixon, you're reading this book right now.

At ten, I was a hot mess. My mom had been in jail for a few years. My dad was marrying a woman whom I'd overheard say that she wished my sister and I weren't there. I was angry.

Scratch that. I was *pissed*.

And Mrs. Dixon could see it. She decided that she couldn't let it marinate. As I write this book, I am so grateful that, when she looked at me, she didn't see just another angry black girl. Instead, she saw a girl with promise and potential.

One day before recess, she called me over and asked me a question: "Darnyelle, have you ever heard of a journal?"

I looked up at her and shook my head no.

The following words started the trajectory of my first defining moment: "Child, you are so angry! But you are also so gifted. And if we aren't careful, your anger will make you miss your potential. Not on my watch. I want you to take this journal, and every time you get angry, I want you to write about it."

Mrs. Dixon knew that we'd get *here*. She saw it then.

I don't think Mrs. Dixon was expecting me to fill that journal as fast as I did! Two weeks later, I couldn't wait to get off the school bus and run to Mrs. Dixon. I had to show her that I had not only filled my first journal; but, more importantly, I'd found my purpose.

As I slowed down to run into her arms, I screamed, "Mrs. Dixon! I think I found my purpose!" She had been teaching us about purpose in class.

"What is it, sweet girl?" she said as she smiled down at me.

"I want to use my words to help people change their lives," I said, smiling back at her.

"I see that for you, child. And you're going to be the best at it."

From that day forward, at ten years old, my mission was clear. I wanted to use words—both written and spoken—to change the lives of others. I didn't really know how it would manifest back then, but I knew for sure that, someday, it would be clear.

And now we're *here*.

Here, writing best-selling books.

Here, selling out live events.

Here, getting standing ovations.

Here, making more in an hour than many make in a year.

Here, hosting a life and business transformational podcast.

Here, using words to transform lives.

I am Darnyelle. My name means "the secret place where dreamers go to dream." I am a disrupter. A status-quo-crusher. A belief-barrier breaker. A child of the Most High God. His favorite daughter. The CEO of my own company and the co-creator of the Move to Millions Movement.

It's taken some time for me to go from my bottom to *here*. This book is my memoir—and a methodology for you.

I don't know what your "*here*" looks like. I don't know if you're at your bottom or hustling your way to the top. But, right now, you're *here*, with me.

Like Mrs. Dixon, I can see your potential, probably more clearly than you can.

I'm not looking at where you are now. I see where you are going.

Making millions.

Moving millions.

Leaving millions.

It's not just your dream; it's your destiny.

And it's my prayer that this book shows you a faster, more aligned way to get there, with more grace and ease and no hustle and grind.

INTRODUCTION

I t's not lost on me that you picked up this book thinking that it's all about money.

It's only *partially* about money. And truthfully, it's about something much deeper and bigger. Now, don't get me wrong; we are all conditioned to hold a set of beliefs about money that really don't serve us. So, yes, we will talk about money. We have to talk about money. Money is a lesser thing that most entrepreneurs make a major thing. You can't talk about millions without talking about money. But money alone isn't the reason I wrote this book.

I wrote this book because I see you and I hear you. I wrote this book because I have been where you are, trying to get to my next level with the conflicting information on how to do it damning my soul. I wrote this book because I want you to finally have a proven blueprint of how you can build your own million-dollar company without having to hustle and grind in the process. I wrote this book because I want to see you step into the purpose for which you were born.

This book is about birthright. And deserve level. And significance. And leveraging and scaling your business in a way that serves you financially and spiritually. It's about realizing that you deserve to make, move, and leave millions, and that your business, the one you have right here, right now, can bring that into your life experience.

I believe that success in business is as much about strategy as it is surrender. This book will prove it to you. Don't get me wrong, I'll share plenty of strategies. But I am also going to share what most books don't have the guts to share: what it really takes to have a million-dollar company without sacrificing your faith, family, freedom, or fun in the process.

If you're reading this book, more than likely you're already an entrepreneur. You already have a business that is successful, and you are already making money. If you're reading this book, your success isn't the question. If you're reading this book, you're millions minded. You've got your business to a point that has put millions on your radar. And it's not a pipedream, either. It's legit. You may not know what day or time you'll cross the million-dollar mark, but you're on it. You know that it will surely come. It's what you desire. And you're not afraid to say it out loud.

And just so we are clear, the Move to Millions that we are speaking of in this book is about making one million dollars in cash or more in one year from impacting countless lives through your business. No disrespect to those of you adding up several years to get to millions. That counts, too, and I celebrate you for achieving that milestone. But this here book is about getting to the milestone of making one million dollars in cash—revenue, not sales—in one calendar year. If you haven't done it yet, you're not alone. This book is about doing what many haven't done. And if you are a woman or a person of color like me, that list just got much smaller.

At the time of the writing of this book, statistics published by American Express say that the average firm owned by a woman of color only makes $24,000 a year, and the average for all other women-owned firms is $142,900 a year.[1] There is a huge gap amongst women-owned small businesses. I don't know how in the world you feed the average family size on a business that is only making $24,000 a year. The same report shares that one in five firms that generate one million dollars or more a year is led by a woman. Only 4.2 percent of firms have revenues of over one million dollars a year. Further, if we consider all women-led firms, that statistic diminishes because only 2.35 percent earn in excess of one million dollars a year. And lastly, if we look exclusively at black women-owned firms, that percentage diminishes again to less than 1 percent.[2]

These statistics burn my biscuits. The truth is that I am writing a book that, according to the reported statistics, won't move the needle toward the million-dollar mark for you unless we find a way to bridge the massive gap that is currently in place. A gap that, although we didn't create, we have to deal with. A gap that often shapes identity and calls into question purpose, destiny, and value. A gap that, with the help of the framework shared in this book, will close.

I want to see more businesses make millions of dollars in one year. I want to see more CEOs of small and microbusinesses become millionaires who create and leave financial legacies that shift generational trajectories. I also want to see those same business owners become philanthropists and angel investors, giving a leg up to someone else because they're leveraging the framework I share in this book. I am already working on it. Over the last eight years, I have created thirty-eight million-dollar CEOs. That means that thirty-eight people who've worked directly with me and my team in the last eight years have leveraged strategies we teach to become a million-dollar CEO. Many of those CEOs broke the money mindset barrier that almost kept them from the million-dollar mark in their business. Today, these CEOs have also become millionaires.

Just to make sure we are all on the same page, a millionaire is one who has accumulated at least one million dollars in assets: cash, property, investment portfolios, insurance, business valuation, etc. My whole body is one fat goosebump right now just thinking about what I have helped thirty-eight CEOs achieve. And that is not counting the nearly one thousand others who we have helped get to six and/or multi-six figures. The truth is, until 2020 when God gave me the mission that I am happily on, Move to Millions, I wasn't even focused on creating million-dollar CEOs. Watch me work now that my mission and movement are crystal clear. In the first year of this new mission, we created ten million-dollar CEOs through our work. As I write this book, we just added another eight to that number at the end of 2022, for a total of eighteen in the last two years.

I get excited thinking about the possibility of leaving my great grandchildren enough money so that they can choose to go to college, buy or build their first home or start their own company. As I get excited about it for me, you better believe I am excited about the possibility for you, too.

While I don't want to diminish the significance of having made millions over a period of years, that's not what this book is about. Truthfully, this book isn't even about the millions of dollars that your business makes in one year. This book is about the principles and business growth strategy that will allow for leveraging and scaling the company that will make the millions of dollars you want to leave to your children's children and enjoy right now. It's also about putting millions of dollars away to be used to establish a legacy and create generational wealth long after your sun has set. This book is about the movement that God kissed me with. It's about a simple realization that you don't have to choose.

You can love God *and* make millions.

I answered the call to start this movement, and to write this book, because it's time that our companies truly fund the life we crave today and the legacy we desire to leave tomorrow.

When I was a junior in high school, ready to start applying to college, my dad sat me down. He told me that if I desired to go to college, it was on me. He didn't have anything saved to help start me on my way. If you recall, my mom had spent eight years in jail. So, she hadn't set any of her commissary money aside to help.

I will never forget how that made me feel.

At the same time, I vowed to never say the same to my children or grandchildren. In fact, I am clear that my grandchildren will know my name because of how I heard it said recently. I am the prototype. Because I dared to dream beyond the projects I was born in, my future heirs will not experience lack. I am literally a belief-barrier breaker and a generational-trajectory shifter.

And you can be, too.

Before I knew that I would lead a movement called Move to Millions, I secretly knew that one day, not only would I have them, but more importantly, I'd be able to leave them to others. For me, it was never about where I was from—dirt poor parents who did the best they could with what they had, although they didn't have anything left over to send me on my way. It was always about where I was going—to impact the lives of others with my words and resources.

That is what I want for you, too, as a result of picking up this book.

Before we can jump into what I really want to share with you, it's story time again.

It was 6:15 a.m. on the third day of my annual live event. I was fresh from the shower. It's in the shower that my CEO and I have our daily board meetings. That's right. God is the CEO of my company.

"You know this is the last time you're going to call it this, right?" Holy Spirit said.

Before I go deeper into the story, let me do a quick sidebar. God does this to me all the time. And as life would have it, these massive shifts always happen during one of my live events. I realized early in my business that I was made to gather people and to create an environment for their biggest breakthroughs.

This time around, we were at Breakthrough in Business Live. Our theme was Next Level Everything®, based on the last time God dropped a gem that wrecked my whole plan . . . in a good way.

[sidebar] I was literally driving down the road adjacent to my home when God told me that He would let *them* live on whatever level *they* settled for.

I had to pull my car over.

God literally said that He would let entrepreneurs live on whatever level they settled for. So, you know me. I said, "Let's settle for Next Level Everything!" I decided to take this nugget from God and turn it into the theme for my live event.

[Back to the story] I made it over to my hotel bed before He spoke again. I was sitting on the edge, putting lotion on my legs, waiting intently for Him to finish His update.

It felt like ten minutes went by before He said it.

"Move to Millions."

I'm not going to lie. I immediately felt chills cover my body. This was always my sign that not only was God near, but He was giving me something life changing.

I leaned into it.

I said it out loud: "Move to Millions." I loved the way it rolled off my tongue. I felt like I finally had my "movement" just as God spoke again.

"This is your new mandate," He continued.

"You make millions move," He said next. Then, He was done. It was over as soon as it began. Except, it wasn't. This was just the beginning.

With no additional directives, my goal was to hold my peace until God shared more. But I immediately found myself feeling the most insatiable feeling of worthiness.

Confession time: I didn't always *feel* worthy.

Even though, in this moment I did, that didn't stop me from having a "Moses Moment™." A Moses Moment is one of those moments when you question if you are really who God is sending for in this season. If you know the story of Moses from the Bible, then you know that Moses felt unworthy and inadequate for all the reasons (being abandoned, killing, his stutter, all the things). And as a result of what he did and what he had been through, he questioned the call on his life. Moses actually tried to bargain with God. He outright suggested that God should send someone else, his brother Aaron, all because he didn't see himself the way God saw him. And yes, we will talk more about this later. For now, let's just say, not seeing yourself the way God sees you will mess with your millions.

I questioned God immediately. Maybe He intended to give this movement to someone else. Maybe He was just running it by me to see if I liked it. It couldn't be for me because, well, I questioned if I could pull it off. I hope you don't mind my transparency. If you follow me online, or if you're in one of my programs, or we've connected in some way over the last twelve years, this could come as a surprise. But it's still true. I have done my fair share of questioning if I am the one to fulfill the big dreams I hold in my bosom.

You have also likely had your fair share of Moses Moments on this journey called entrepreneurship. One thing is for sure: when you experience one, you want to give yourself the time and space to remind yourself of who you are and what you have already accomplished.

Something you need to know about me right off the bat is the only outcome I am attached to is the one where God gets the glory. When I'm uncertain if He will get the glory, I shrink back. Now, I am getting better. But this book is about the good, the bad, and the incredible of my journey, and I have to tell you all of it. Part of the problem with the sensationalism of having a million-dollar business is that people are acting like they woke up like this (cue Beyoncé). Like they grabbed their laptop, headed down to the beach, and voilà, a million dollars popped out of their customer relationship management or sales software. But the truth is not a single million-dollar CEO woke up like this. All of us have Moses Moments. Those moments go on to define us and make us great, or they distract us and make us weak.

Now. I got my Moses Moments honestly.

You see, I am not supposed to be here. I was in my twenties when I learned from my highly sedated mother during one of her many trips to the hospital that I almost wasn't.

As she continued in her stupor, she began to apologize profusely. "I didn't know," she said.

She was referring to the fact that she didn't know that she was carrying me, and as a result, she got high on a regular basis (it was her way of coping with her life, but that is another book for another day). By the time she learned that she was nearly six months pregnant, the doctors feared the worst.

"If this child survives, they may never know life like a child born without an enormous amount of drugs in their system," the doctor told my mother.

She stopped getting high immediately and prayed.

God heard her prayer.

A month later, I was born. To every doctor's surprise, there was nothing cognitively wrong with me. There were no indications that there had ever been any recreational drug use while I was in the womb.

But God.

When there is a purpose for your life, there is nothing that can keep you from fulfilling it.

She named me Darnyelle because she heard God say "this child will exist in the world differently." She wanted me to have a name that would immediately stand out.

My name means the secret place where dreamers go to dream—something else we can thank Mrs. Dixon for. In the sixth grade, we had an assignment to find the meaning of our name. Since Darnyelle isn't like Sarah or Amy, we had to do a lot of digging. But we finally found the root name, Darnell, which meant a secret or hidden nook. By adding that *y* we found another indication of my purpose: the hidden nook became the secret place where dreamers go to dream.

Oh, and by the way, if you ask my sane, coherent, very conscious mother if she ever got high while pregnant with any of her children, she will profusely deny that she did. But I wasn't sedated when she told me what she told me. Every once in a while, she belligerently reminds me that she never got high with any of her children. And in those moments, I pretend as if she never did.

* * *

As I replayed God's message, I became overjoyed because I had finally found the movement to propel my purpose forward.

"Move to Millions," I said again. My whole body vibrated at the next level.

I have to be honest. When I look back over what my life has been like up until this point, I didn't see this coming.

About a month later, God gave me my next download. "Oh, and this is an acronym," He said.

Ooh, how I love acronyms!

"I know," He said.

Well?

"Mastery, operational obedience, vision, and execution to and beyond millions."

I sat with those words.

"Oh, and this isn't just about the money," God continued. "Sure, it includes the money. Money is essential for moving millions. This is also about the impact and legacy. In my Word, it says that a wise man leaves an inheritance to his children's children. Your job is to equip entrepreneurs and small business owners to be able to do so. Your job is to focus on helping them increase their income and their impact. This has to be a generational movement. What they do today will impact tomorrow, and the impact of tomorrow will shift the generations. Got it?"

Got it?

Yeah, I got it and I also got nervous.

That was a lot. Heavy. Like could I really pull this off?

I sat with the words again. Mastery. Operational Obedience. Vision. Execution.

Sure, at first glance this seemed right. Seemed like what it would take. But I still felt the weight of the assignment.

Mastery. Operational Obedience. Vision. Execution. I repeated each word to myself.

It's always been in the big moments when the weight of the enormity of what I have been tasked to do that overwhelm creeps in, and I start to question who I am.

Only temporarily.

But in that quick minute, I felt like Moses. I tried to come up with excuses as to why I wasn't the girl for the job and why He should send someone else. My desire to have the spotlight not turn on me was because I was often afraid of my own power. When I look at the anointing on my life, sometimes it's scary.

Not only do I desire to not miss God, but I also desire to be the impact that I know I was called to be. That meant I had to take a step back, take it all in, and then listen for my next set of instructions. I decided to close my eyes and take a deep, life-altering breath.

What came next both shocked and excited me.

As I closed my eyes, I saw it. All of it. This book, the programs, the docu-series, the live event, Oprah's Garden and Super Soul Sunday, the stages, all of it. And I also saw that it was time for a massive up-leveling. But I wasn't ready for all that yet, so I ignored the vision and kept focusing on my current assignment.

A few months later, I woke up feeling startled. All of a sudden, I felt out of sorts in my business. If you followed me prior to getting a copy of this book, you are probably familiar with my old logo. There was a purple lady everywhere, like a little bit better than clip art purple lady. And in this moment, it became painstakingly clear that my purple lady felt out of place. Like literally just a month or so before I woke up feeling like it was time for her to go, I had a new Move to Millions logo created with her in it. She was so engrained in who I am. From the moment I left corporate America, I got the purple lady. As I shake my head thinking back to that moment, I'm in awe of how our suite of brands all had that hideous purple lady tying them together. Suddenly, I was clear.

The Move to Millions was not a journey she could take.

I had to kill the purple lady.

I know that sounds both harsh and drastic, but it was the only way I could let her go. She had to suffer a death, an unearthing, a realization that not only was her time as my brand icon over, but her life was ending as well. She represented the recently released corporate version of myself - you know, a little corporate and a little free. Instead of wearing a suit jacket to my home office, I wore just a skirt and top. The version of me that remembered her training and decided not to depart from it.

That lasted four years. The first purple lady didn't even have hair! I guess it was implied that her hair was in a corporate bun.

By 2015, she got swag. While she was still there, her confidence had increased, and she was ready to take on the world. She let her hair down, put her hands on her hip, and we went for it. We had just crossed the million-dollar mark for the first time, and she was ready for our next level.

That lasted another five years.

But now she had to go. Lock, stock, and barrel. She needed an RIP instead of prime real estate on our website, logos, social media profiles—everything. It was an upending in every way. While I was ready for her to go, she also represented stability.

I grabbed my laptop and opened up a fresh Word document to ask myself a series of questions, which began with: Why am I ready to help others make and move millions?

It took me no time to fill up several pages with why me and why the time was now. For instance, I didn't want anyone to suffer what I suffered when I first made the move back in 2014. Amongst the biggest tragedies of my first million-dollar year, I paid nearly $400,000 in taxes that year. I immediately questioned why I ever wanted to have a million-dollar business if I was going to have to give it all, or at least a lot of it, to the IRS.

No thanks. You can keep your million-dollar business. This million-dollar business thing turned out to be everything that Biggie said it would be. It was more money and more problems, and they could have it all. I'm not going to lie. I still have a nasty taste in my mouth when I think about that year. While I will share more of the story later in this book, what I can share now is that I was in the wrong tax filing status and legal entity.

From there, I asked myself, "What do we want to be known for? Who do we want to serve in this next season? What is the transformation we offered better than everyone else in the marketplace?" Before I knew it, I had rewritten our brand story, brand promise statement, mission and vision, ideal clients, and our entire key messages document. Now, I just needed the look and feel to accompany this new message.

I wanted our clients to know that they were in for an experience. I wanted them to come to expect the level of excellence that we provide without question. I didn't want there to be a question or surprise when it came time to make the investment that would change their life.

And I'm sorry. The purple lady couldn't be part of this.

I wanted a visual experience that never called into question my brilliance and why I was the only, and obvious, choice for their next level. I was clear. It was about to go down.

And I immediately knew that not only was I the woman for the job, but I *was* ready.

The following Monday, I reached out to one company, the company I felt was the company to personify this redirect, this refresh. I was clear. The company name wasn't changing. I was also clear that we were going all in on moving low multi-six-figure business owners to millions.

For years, I straddled the fence. I would say I didn't work with startups, but then I'd take a set of clients who I knew weren't ready for me. [insert face palm] I did this because I kept running my business with one foot on the gas and one foot on the brake at the same time. I wanted to coach the big dogs, but I was afraid that they wouldn't see me as the obvious choice. I got comfortable playing small even though I told myself that I was playing big. I was playing way too small.

That was then.

Now we're *here*.

Now I am ready. The recent set of clients we enrolled were perfect, and the results we helped them get were next level. And I knew this was just the beginning.

I am ready.

Even with all that certainty and confidence, it is scary. But I am doing it afraid. I know that answering the call on my life is bigger than my fear to stay in my small bubble, serving just a few dozen clients a year and making my own millions. I know it's time to share the blueprint that I have created and laid out with our clients who knew they were called to millions.

For me, it's about getting to the million-dollar mark sustainably. Without the increased stress and overwhelm. That takes time. I estimate it to take three years to make the move in a way that serves and supports you as the whole CEO, give or take, depending on what you have set up when we meet.

Year one is about getting your foundation set, including the right strategy, offers, pricing, messaging, marketing, and sales. We focus on the first four Million Dollar Assets™ and bringing on a full-time executive assistant. We will explore the assets fully in this book's section two.

Year two is about tightening the foundation and building the next three Million Dollar Assets. We also begin to build out your full team. We are literally preparing for rain in year two. And in year two, you significantly reduce showing up as a service provider so you can be the CEO. I know that is hard to conceive, but I will share exactly how to do it.

Year three is about refining and amplifying. This will include pouring on the scale and building the final Million Dollar Asset™. We will explore the final asset in the final section of this book.

Before you ask, yes, you can hit the million-dollar mark in one year. And yes, I will share that with you as well.

For nearly a year, we have been working on a brand refresh to bring God's vision for the next season of my company into fruition. This book is a culmination of that vision, the rebirth, and the rebrand.

What started out as three simple words from God's spirit to mine has become a mantra for my life and career. I believe that we were born abundant. God is calling us to step back into that abundance, and He is using entrepreneurship to do it.

This book is a direct reflection of this movement, what it means, and more importantly, the success clues and truth bombs that are essential for you to claim your own Move to Millions. I should also mention that the move is just that—a move, a series of actions predicated on taking a journey to wholeness financially and spiritually. I believe on this move everything about you will be called into question and action. This isn't a simple anecdote to "get rich quick." This is a lifestyle, a recipe for living your life and scaling your business at Next Level Everything because you decided you want to walk into your birthright.

xxxvi | *Move* TO MILLIONS

This book will unfold in four parts, one part for each step in the acronym God gave me: mastery, operational obedience, vision, and execution. Each part is a standalone blueprint for your best life and business ever. Each section will highlight principles, assets, and legacy.

As I share the principles, assets, and legacy, I will share data, Scriptures, client success stories, and my own musings to help you undergird the knowledge that if you didn't come from millions, millions ought to come from you. When businesses make more, the impact is felt by millions.

As a business coach who works with millions-minded entrepreneurs, it's important for me to share the whole truth, not just the warm and fuzzy laptop on the beach part you see when you scroll through social media. I'm going to tell you about the doubts and fears, the hiring and firing, the cash flowing in and the cash flowing out for payroll, equipment or consulting, and coaches like me parts, too. I'm going to share the challenges you'll face at home, if you're not grounded and careful, and how to be the best version of yourself for your spouse and children. I am going to get into all of it. You need to know. When I hit this amazing life-changing milestone, there was no book to read, community to join, or event to attend.

But that won't be your story.

A big part of the reason I do this work is the education piece. Back in 2014 when I did the first million, I paid enough to feed a small village for a year in taxes, and I allegedly had a "million-dollar mentor" at the time. I say allegedly because one would think that if the coach had already been where I was heading, there would have been at least a warning like "You might need to get a CPA and tax strategist because you're making way more money," or something like that.

I got nada.

But you won't have to say that because this book is designed to hip you to the million-dollar business game so you can prepare. When you make the move, you can be excited that your dream came true, unlike me when I felt like I walked into my biggest nightmare—one I couldn't wake up from, by the way.

We need to normalize talking about money. I know in order to do that we need to have a firm understanding of how money works. If you look like me, more than likely you were raised in a financially illiterate home. As a result, the decisions you make today are based on a lack of information. While that is important, this is not the book where we will get into all of that. However, I will share enough about it for you to become dangerous enough to move your life and business forward financially.

There's a balance that comes with the whole truth of business ownership. My mission is to tell the truth.

As someone who has done millions with grace and ease, I will happily share that perspective in this book. And as someone who has also done millions the hard way, I will share that, too.

It doesn't have to be "hard." But you have to be clear, aligned, and present. Getting to seven figures isn't just math. Even though you can pick up a five-dollar calculator and figure out how to make millions, that is not enough. We have to throw out the tired, outdated thoughts, feelings, and beliefs as well as the actions you've been taking that aren't getting you to the result you want. We have been taught that you have to work hard for money. But the truth is that working harder doesn't make you more money; it just makes you tired. When I learned about the importance of living the right principles, like alignment and surrender, my money moved more. And yes, I will go deeper on that soon.

In 2021, we did $2,100,000; it was the easiest financial growth I've ever experienced. And I want to pass the lessons I've learned in the process on to you. That grace and ease took us all the way to the coveted Inc. 5000 list, ranked 1,209, in the top 25 percent of the fastest growing companies in America.

Happy reading.

CHAPTER ONE

My First MOVE

"Living life at your next level is about mastering the principles."
—DARNYELLE JERVEY HARMON

When I was a little girl, I was fortunate enough to spend time with my Aunt Ida. Aunt Ida was my paternal grandmother's sister. Aunt Ida didn't play. She taught me very early in life that everything had principles. *Everything*. So, naturally when I started unpacking this mandate and the assignment God gave me, I, too, went looking for the principles that would guide this project and, more importantly, the next phase of my work.

One weekend in particular, my sister and I went to spend time with Aunt Ida. We were helping her in the kitchen, and she taught us a valuable lesson. Aunt Ida could cook anything by memory. But before she ever started, she first made sure she had all the necessary ingredients for what she was cooking. She sent us to look in her pantry for specific items. When she was out of one item, she said, "Girls, don't ever try to make a recipe if you don't have everything you need. Some things you can't substitute. You need what is called for."

As I sat down to write, Aunt Ida's words came flooding back.

"You need what is called for."

When it comes to leveraging and scaling a business that will earn millions, you need what is called for. And here's the thing: few people are will-

1

ing to share what is really called for to have a company that makes, moves, and eventually leaves millions. Since you're reading this book, you will be one who learns what it will take because I vowed that my life and business acumen would leave success clues. Getting to the place that many are praying to reach and not sharing how you got there is selfish, especially when what you share doesn't take anything away from you while helping others to get to their next level.

If you desire to figure out how to make and move millions in a way that serves and supports all that you desire to be, you have to understand the principles first.

Principles are what's called for.

In your life, and most definitely in your business, principles guide you every step of the way. Just like your business will be built on a set of guiding principles, the source of all that is—God—also has a set of principles. Because God is principled, we can access a blueprint to success in every area of our lives. I will be honest; it took me a few years to realize the principles that would come to govern my work. I started my business in a silo. Its purpose was simply to do what I felt I was called to do and make money while doing it. It didn't take long, however, to feel hollow. That wasn't enough to work for. After my first stint at the million-dollar mark, I realized that establishing core values (principles) was essential so that my work went deeper than making money. Making money is not reason enough to impact the lives of others.

The first time I made millions in my business, I was not following any principles. I'm not exaggerating. I was much too busy trying to make a dollar out of fifteen cents at the time. I had to get to the million-dollar mark to validate my existence. I had been so forced to hear repeatedly how I was not worth the skin that held me together as a child that I questioned everything about myself. Even when I grew into womanhood, I was still saddled by the belief that maybe I wasn't good enough. It's why I was addicted to success. It's why I found a way to show people that I mattered every chance I got. It's why I worked harder than most for longer than most.

When I started my first "real" job in corporate America, I bought into the belief that my peers told me. I put in "facetime," and no I am not talking about that feature on your iPhone. I was living the truth that I had come to believe: you have to work hard to make money. That's all I was focused on. When you've been without for so long and someone tells you the answer is to work more and, while you're at it, harder than everyone else, you come to believe that is the key to having more money. I convinced myself this was right because watching my parents was definitely not the answer. Let's not forget to mention that my dad reminded me of the hard work required to have the necessities. I knew that if I wanted to have more than that, I was going to have to work hard.

I had to prove that I could make it, too. You may not have been there when I walked out of my six-figure corporate job, vowing to never return to the workforce. But I was. And every day, the sting of regret haunted me. So, I hustled harder. Except working harder doesn't make you more money; it just makes you tired. But that didn't stop me from hustling and grinding. I think that is why I am so adamant about not doing either these days. Back then, I felt justified. I was trying to do all that I could to make enough money to avoid living in my car.

When I sent my pink Cadillac back to Mary Kay Cosmetics in 2008 and gave my full attention to my business, it was already too late. I didn't have a plan when I decided that I was moving on to the next thing. As a result, I was not taking a principled approach to getting to my next level—unless the principle was "by any means necessary," that is.

I was doing anything to make ends meet. Anything. And I still couldn't keep up. So, eventually, the bottom fell out. I had to file bankruptcy and go back to work. It was the only way to avoid figuring out how I was going to live in my car with the contents of my four-bedroom home. I learned a powerful lesson that day, although I wouldn't have been able to tell you the lesson until many years later. The way you see money is about the way you see yourself. I wasn't convinced that I added value to anyone deep down. I was a walking fraud, the queen of "fake it 'til you make it." I was so out of integrity that I started to believe my own hype.

The shame that went along with realizing that, only a few years before, I had vowed that I would never work for anyone else again was debilitating. Yet here I was, unable to pull it off. I was fortunate enough to find a job quickly. That job was a life saver, even when I was not living any principles. God was still looking out for me.

The job that I took was running a women's business center's entrepreneurship program. Funny, right? I still smile when I think of the irony and serendipity of that position. I literally got paid to figure out how to build my own impact-filled company.

Because the early years weren't filled with a principled approach to life nor business, I found myself chasing the elusive seven-figure mark. To be honest, I cannot even tell you why that was the number, other than the fact that making $143,000 that first year full-time again in my business is when I quickly realized that it was not enough.

I struggled massively with comparison when I first got into the marketplace. I was good for comparing my day one to "their" day fifteen thousand. At the time, there weren't many—and I mean any—black, women million-dollar CEOs in the coaching space. I quickly decided that I wanted to be the one. Unfortunately, that was a pure ego-driven decision. Because it was only backed by ego, it didn't stick.

Write this down: When you know your why, your what creates momentum and impact to live your why.

Because I didn't have a reason, it was short-lived and never sustainable, which is a big part of the reason it was the equivalent to a pipedream.

Even though we deserve more money, it can never be about the money.

I chased the number for several years. No matter what I did in my business, I never came close to hitting that goal. It was like no matter what I tried, because my approach wasn't principled, it fell flat. Every single time. No matter what I achieved, the carrot was still farther away.

It tanked my self-esteem and made me question my purpose. However, the truth was it was never about the action. It was always about my thoughts, feelings, beliefs, and, most importantly, how I saw myself. I didn't see myself as wealthy, as impactful, as strong—as whatever you think you should look like to impact the lives of others with income and influence to match. I had this ever-present fear that, one day, people were going to learn the truth about me: that I was not as good as I claimed to be. As a result, I never got close to the goal because it might cause too much attention.

Interestingly the year I finally hit the goal, I had a big breakthrough. I realized that I did deserve to make that kind of money. It was largely because I had recommitted myself to deepening my connection with God. In so doing, I got to hear from Him how He saw me. I sat with a decision to get clear about why I desired to earn at that level. As a result of getting clear about my why, it was like my why paved the way for my actions to bring me what I decided I was worthy of.

You have to see it first. You won't see it if you don't believe it's possible for you.

You have to see it to see it, so you get to experience it.

It works this way: your thoughts are immediately impacted by your feelings and beliefs, which affect the words you speak, the actions you take, and the results you achieve.

Thoughts → Feelings and Beliefs → Words → Actions → Results

Ever heard of the phrase "You bring about what you think about?" It's not just a saying; it's the truth. It works in the case of everything you can think of, including your health, your relationships, and most definitely your business and money. This is why you think something and immediately talk yourself out of it. Then, you don't do what could have produced it in the first place.

Your actions and results will always follow your beliefs. If you are anything like I used to be, you feel unworthy, guilty even, of having *that* much money. So subconsciously, you stifle, self-sabotage, and shift from exactly what could create the windfall. If you've ever said, "I just need . . ." then you know what I am talking about. *Just* is a limiter; it gives us permission to play small and think of ourselves as less than we were created by God to be.

It took *years*, intense years of self-study, mental health support with my therapist, and relationship with God to flip my script. I had to unlearn comparison as a yardstick for success. I had to unlearn working hard for money. I had to unlearn doing more to justify my existence. I credit my first and long-standing therapist with all of the discoveries that have us now *here*. Thank you, Michelle.

When I finally stopped thinking about myself as small and saw myself the way God has always seen me, I got the courage to double all of my rates, and everything shifted. It started with just the courage to do so. The courage put me on a trajectory to alignment. Honestly, I didn't realize that I had come into alignment with who I really was. But once I did, it was on like Donkey Kong (if you were born in the mid-seventies or early eighties, you'll get that reference). Interestingly, I didn't know that the catalyst for earning at that level was based on how I saw myself. In fact, I can go so far as to say that most problems are because of one of two things: how you see yourself or how you see money. That's why almost immediately after hitting the milestone, I backslid. Those feelings of inadequacy came flooding back, making what should have been a dream come true the longest nightmare ever. I went on to kill that million-dollar business because, well, it wasn't right for me. I was angry, stressed, easily triggered, and overwhelmed. Every time I thought of Proverbs 10:22, I felt like it wasn't my time to make millions.

"The blessing of the Lord, it maketh rich, and he addeth no sorrow with it."
Proverbs 10:22 KJV

I should probably bring you into the full story of my first move to millions so that this makes more sense to you.

It was 2014, and we were about eight weeks from my annual live event, Unleash Your Incredible Factor Live. After a session with my then business coach, I did something I had never done—and wouldn't advocate anyone else to do. I compared myself to my coach and grabbed my calculator. I asked myself, "If I charge what she has the balls to charge, what will my income be?" While I was afraid to see, I was also intrigued. When I added it all up, I would already have a million-dollar company if I was priced like she was. Comparison is a slippery slope. I do not recommend that anyone compare themselves to anyone else. It's a distraction that will cripple your confidence and your cash flow. By no means should you price your services by comparison. I will share some of my favorite pricing strategies with you in chapter 2, but I will spoil it for you now: comparison didn't make the list.

When I realized that I could already be a million-dollar CEO, I did it. I raised all of my rates and met with my team to advise them of the new prices that we would roll out during the live event in two months.

My team at the time was on board. They definitely felt that I had been doing what many women entrepreneurs do: undercharging but overdelivering. You know, overcompensating for our disbelief that people would willingly pay us *that* much. Everyone was on board with our newly doubled rates. We created the order form, sent it off to the printer, and called it a day.

Initially, I was more excited than I was nervous. I knew that I deserved to charge that much. The voices in the back of my mind didn't outpace the rationale of what we delivered even back then in our programs. So, it was settled. Our two programs would double. We got confirmation from the printer that the form was ready to go, and that was it.

Until it wasn't.

That night, I had a dream—well, a nightmare really—that no one signed up for our programs. And I'm not going to lie. I panicked. So much so that I woke up early that morning so that I could go into the office and change all of the prices back to the ones that made me feel comfortable, but also kept me stuck at six figures, before the rest of the team arrived. I wasn't ready to admit to them that in my moment of panic I shrunk back. There is a reason why people say you should never make important decisions when you're emotional. Any time you're hungry, angry, anxious, lonely, or tired (HAALT), you should decide not to decide. I didn't take that advice. Instead once they were all changed, unbeknownst to my entire team, I hurriedly sent the order form back to the printer and prepared to go back upstairs to get ready for the day.

I didn't even get out of my office before the phone rang. It was the printer, informing me that, in spite of his best efforts, the new order form was corrupt. He couldn't print it. Worse yet, I couldn't do anything about it. Clearly, my tech-savvy limitations were in question. After the big speech I gave the day before, I couldn't dare tell my team that I didn't *really* believe any of it and that I'd reduced all of our prices back to make sure that we had some clients come out of the event.

Instead, I was "forced" to pretend as if my dream wasn't a bad omen and go with the original documents that had been sent with the doubled rates.

Forced.

Yeah, right.

I hadn't been forced; God had stepped in to keep me from backing down on my birthright. I have always believed that the definition of salvation is to be snatched out of harm's way. And on this day, I was saved. If I had my way, I would have made a life-altering mistake that I may not have been able to recover from.

Months later when I made the offer at the live event, we were all surprised to watch three times more clients enroll in our programs, and I became an instant million-dollar CEO.

An instant million-dollar CEO.

Does that sound like an oxymoron to anyone else besides me?

I've never met anyone who was an instant million-dollar CEO. The truth is, even when the manifestation comes quickly, the work to get to that point took years.

Years.

And lots of them.

I had done it; I had crossed the elusive seven-figure mark. Where was the confetti? The trumpets? The late breaking announcement interrupting *Jeopardy* and *Wheel of Fortune*?

They didn't happen.

That's the thing. Hitting a milestone like this is as significant as you are when you hit it.

And because I was afraid, confused and overwhelmed by my instant increase, it was also short-lived. Sure, during the 2014 event, we made $1,300,000 in three days. We went on to generate $1,800,000 that year and $2,300,000 the following year. But by 2016, I had fired the clients and the team. I was back to my small, manageable, mid-six-figure ($600,000 to be exact) business.

I know Oliver Wendall Holmes said, "Man's mind, once stretched by a new idea, never regains its original dimensions." But a business sure could.

The truth is millions seem overrated. It was everything that Biggie said it would be—it was more money and more problems. I had paid more than $400,000 in taxes. I had hired fast to try to keep up with the fact that I had gone from about thirty to 270 clients overnight. I was overwhelmed, and I had simply created just a good paying job for myself. They could have it.

All of it.

I didn't want millions if having millions meant I had to work longer and harder. I didn't want millions if I couldn't see straight long enough to enjoy what I had created. I didn't want millions if it meant I had to give up my soul, joy, and purpose in the process. This is the part that entrepreneurs seldom talk about, but I'm committed to telling the truth about this part. There are far too many people painting a picture that making millions is easy, and all you need is a laptop and a beach to make it happen. The truth is it takes all the principles I am going to share with you throughout this book. In fact, I can boldly declare that it will take a true move of you and God—mastery, operational obedience, vision, and execution—to hit the million-dollar mark. It will take a whole lot of belief. In fact, I will go so far as to say that millions start in your mind long before they land in your bank account. Unless you challenge your own personal beliefs to access them, they will remain at bay, even though you have been earmarked to have them.

The truth is I needed to define my principles. The principles by which I would live my life and run my business. The principles that would be my guiding light in the times of uncertainty. I needed to surrender my company to its true CEO (more on that later). I vowed, because I knew that I would make millions again, that when I did, I would do it in a way that served and supported me. Now that I have, I am committed to allowing my success to leave clues for you.

In 2021, my word of the year was obedience. I quickly realized that this wasn't about the definition of obedience in the traditional sense. This would become about surrender as the CEO of my own company. I have come to realize that real CEOs aren't in control. They are acting in obedience to what their Creator, the true CEO of the company, is telling them to do.

I also quickly realized that the whole MOVE concept was a double entendre—that it would be impactful in life, as well as business. Mastery relates to living the principles of surrender, alignment, and obedience as much as it does having the right strategy, sales infrastructure, systems, support, and success mindset (you'll come to know this soon as the Move to Millions Method). Operational obedience is as much about doing what your spirit tells you to do in integrity, and for the greater good of those you serve, as it is about making sure that your company is built to run without you. Vision is as much about seeing yourself the way God has always seen you as it is about determining the course and path that your business will take to significantly impact your team, clients, and community. Execution is as much about giving God something to bless as it is about taking the right strategic actions each day to move your company forward. The bottom line? The Move to Millions is a pilgrimage that you and God will take together. You'll have to work on the spiritual principles while you tighten the business principles.

The first section of this book covers *mastery* and will dive deep into the seven Million Dollar Assets. This section will share the tangible strategy required to move to millions. We will talk about each area of your business. If you haven't started to think about them all yet, no worries. By the time we are done, you'll know what you'll need to master. Remember, we are after mastery. So we are going all in on each, one asset at a time. In this section, I will also chronicle client success stories, highlighting a few clients who, in leveraging the assets, made a move to millions along the Move to Millions Continuum. The end of each chapter will include a chapter action plan so that you know where to focus as you start working towards your move.

The second section of this book covers *operational obedience*, where we will go deeper into each of the spiritual principles you will need to master in order to solidify your move. Now, most people don't realize the role each principle we will discuss plays in your move. But trust me. Not only do they matter, but they are the catalyst to sustaining the money you desire to come into your life and business. We will cover faith, confidence, surrender, alignment, embodiment, and forgiveness.

The third section of this book covers *vision*. We are going to get into one of my favorite topics: vision point versus vantage point. We will also delve into the "millions messy middle" and how to navigate this difficult period on the move. We will end the vision section with the Move to Millions

Manifesto—your soul's new battle cry and guidepost all the way to the mil-lion-dollar mark and the legacy blueprint.

The final section of the book covers *execution*. We get into an action plan for pulling it all together with more flow and less flex. We will also discuss your accountability and implementation plan, leaving you with the charge to go forth to make, move, and leave millions.

This book is the book you've been waiting for as a millions-minded entrepreneur. I know you will be happy that this book isn't just theory, but it's also actionable insight and strategy you can begin to apply *now* to see results. Also, we have created a resource guide for this book. You will be prompted at times to head to our resources page to grab a download to further illustrate a concept I am referring to in this book. You'll find that at https://www.movetomillionsbook.com/resources.

My sincere hope is that this book will become your guide to your first million-dollar business milestone.

CHAPTER TWO

The Move to Millions Continuum

"Success in business demands a posture change."
—DARNYELLE JERVEY HARMON

"There's levels to this, Darnyelle."

I rolled my eyes because I wasn't trying to hear that.

The scene was lunch with my mentor when I worked in corporate America. I had requested a meeting with him because I had been passed up for a project that I knew I was born to lead. When they chose a white man to run lead on a project about recruiting more women of color, I about lost it. Between you and me, that was when I started to plot leaving. I wasn't ready to just "pick up my mat and walk," but I was starting to look into alternative career opportunities. Also between you and me, entrepreneurship wasn't yet on my radar. When he reminded me that there were levels to the hierarchy of any structure, I decided to learn how to play the game, but with a twist. The game I was playing was for me and my next level. It became crystal clear that I had to first determine the level I wanted to be on. From there, I could chart the path to bring it into my reality.

Similarly, after having worked directly with a thousand clients and having impacted more than twenty-five thousand people through speaking to audiences at conferences and events, I had seen it all. I immediately noticed that an entrepreneur's ability to understand clearly what would be required at any level determined their ability to get to the next level. Years later, once I decided to go all in on working with entrepreneurs and small business owners who had achieved the six-figure milestone, I remembered this lesson and designed what today is the Move to Millions Continuum.

The continuum was designed to chart the path to making, moving, and leaving millions. I have come to realize that often we get stuck on one rung or another because no one has ever laid out clearly what it takes to move to the next level.

That stops today.

There are five levels on the continuum. The levels are momentum, mastery, millions, majesty, and monumental. Let's walk through each level, one by one. I will define the level, where you are likely experiencing challenges, and what you need now to move to the next level.

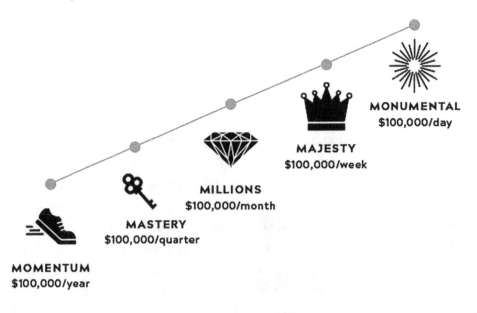

MONUMENTAL
$100,000/day

MAJESTY
$100,000/week

MILLIONS
$100,000/month

MASTERY
$100,000/quarter

MOMENTUM
$100,000/year

Momentum

Momentum means that you have successfully achieved the first milestone on the Move to Millions: $100,000 in a year. This is a big deal. Congratulations. I don't want you to celebrate too long, however, because it's a milestone, not a stopping point. As you will hear me share often, $100,000 is small-business poverty. Ouch! But it's true. I know we all dreamed of getting to the six-figure mark, and when we did, oh the life we would live! I got to the six-figure mark as an entrepreneur in 2010. My excitement was short-lived. Making $100,000 is really about $40,000 a year when you add in your self-employment tax, income tax, and basic business expenses. For me, there was not enough left over to live the life I had written about in my journal. I was very disheartened to have gotten to the place I had dreamed of, only to feel like someone slipped me a Mickey.

In full transparency, you can "oops" your way to $100,000 in a year. It is truly not hard. It will require a shift in money mindset, but outside of that, it's simple. Twenty clients or less paying you at least $5,000 for your transformational program. That's it. Even though it's simple, you can probably cosign that doesn't make it easy. If so, it wouldn't have taken either of us so long to get there (if you're actually there as you read this book). It took me nearly three years to hit $100,000, although with my help, many of my early clients achieved this milestone before I did. For me, it was my money mindset that messed with me.

You see, I could easily collect a salary that added up to that amount, but to be solely responsible for making that much went against everything I had been taught about money. If you're struggling to hit this first milestone, you likely too grew up in a financially illiterate family. It's okay. You're getting the education you need now, and it is truly better late than never. I was deep into my thirties when money started to make sense. I had my bankruptcy to thank for it. I was required to take a financial literacy course as a part of my bankruptcy recovery. Thank you BKO laws!

At the $100,000 a year mark, you are likely working by yourself in your business. You are in all departments: customer service, customer delivery, marketing, sales, IT, admin, and customer retention. You might even be housekeeping and laundry. That means that you are tired, and you aren't spending enough time in your zone of genius, which means that the best of you isn't present day in and day out in your business. This probably has also created some form of resentment that you are trying to grow a business in. I recall when I was trying everything in my power to hit six figures. It kept eluding me. Its elusive nature was the reason I ended up going back to work and filing bankruptcy. I couldn't confidently articulate my services being worth more than a few hundred dollars. Even that was a stretch. As a result, I couldn't earn enough to escape the feast or famine cycle of my business. And eventually, the famine won.

More than likely, if you're in the momentum stage, you are a business owner who is still trying to figure things out and find your groove. You may be doing the most. You have too many offers and too many specialties for your clients and prospects to take you seriously. You are clear that you have work to do to create a business you can get truly excited about. More than likely, you've got a few clients now, but you haven't found your groove yet. So, new clients are welcomed sporadically instead of like clockwork. It's possible that your business was born out of a layoff, necessity, or desperation in search of something better than sitting behind someone else's desk. You feel that "start and stop" energy of not really having a clear vision, plan, and acumen to achieve what you dream about for your business.

You're not where you want to be and you're working harder than you should, without as much traction as you'd like. You'd like to fill your practice and get more money coming in. You want to ramp up as quickly as possible with goals in the next few years to go to multiple six and then seven figures in your business.

At this point, you're starting to take your business seriously, largely because hitting six figures wasn't all you thought it would be (if you've hit it). Spoiler alert for those of you on your way: Don't stop there! Keep going! Perhaps you've had one month where you exceeded what's normal for you. You know that if you can implement the right plan, you can really make this business something special that adds value to your life, your clients' lives, and, most importantly, your checking account balance.

While you know that you want to do millions in the future, right now your biggest struggles tend to be finding the consistency in working *on* your business. Sometimes you're on top of the business. Other times the business is on top of you. It's likely because your strategy isn't clear. Even though you're not there yet, you're already thinking about what it will look like to shift from six-figure years to six-figure quarters. Just thinking about growing your business to this level warms your heart.

Right now, you're feeling both the discouragement and the anticipation of getting to the next level in your business. You're also likely still charging your clients based on what you earned when you were an employee, and you already know that you can't keep that up. As an entrepreneur, you actually have way more costs than you thought you would.

To get to the next stage, you need strategy. You need to get clear about who you are and what you really do to help your clients. You need to focus on one clear pinnacle client with one clear problem to which you offer one clear solution. You need to think about the transferrable result you offer, so that you are not seen as a commodity, but an asset. As an asset, you will be able to raise your rates into the $10,000 to $25,000 per program range, which will increase your business to mastery and six-figure quarters. You also need to start looking at more than the next week in your business. Ideally, you need to look at one quarter at a time. Learning how to set real, actionable goals, and knowing that there is nothing in the way—mindset, messaging, marketing, or sales—is key to you actually achieving your goals.

At this point, you really need a better, more defined strategy that will lead to more clients, which means you need clearly defined offers, *and* you need to raise your rates. If you were serving more people, you'd be able to stabilize your income. With more income, you'd have more confidence to make a bigger splash with your marketing and to bring on at least your first team member. Strategy for you will include your packaging and pricing, your positioning, and your promotion plan.

To do this, you need help with your key messaging. You also need to identify the right marketing strategies and learn how to sell. The good news for you is that the mastery section of this book will help you to make powerful shifts that will lead you to the mastery stage.

It's time to think about tightening your infrastructure and establishing some real goals and assets to get your business to your next money milestone in the next six to twelve months.

Mastery

Mastery means that your business is achieving $100,000 or more per quarter. You should feel so excited and proud because that means, on average, you're experiencing $35,000 months in your business. At the mastery stage, you have seen some clarity and confidence in your business. You're coming into your own. While you know who you are and who you serve, you're still not quite confident enough to charge what you know you *really* should be charging (think about adding a zero to your current offers). You justify not charging more as not being able to help those you are called to serve, and you settle for enough when you were created for more. Or you keep your prices lower than they should be because you equate higher prices with more work. At this stage, your success is not in question. You are successful, and even with a clear knowledge of that, you yearn for your next level.

So, here's the thing: while $35,000 a month is amazing, if you are hustling and grinding and selling from a wide business model (lots of offers in lots of price points), you can't celebrate for real. You more than likely have several offers, and you're trying to focus on selling all of them at the same time, except you already know that you can't chase two rabbits and expect to catch either one (let alone the five, seven, or nine that you are chasing right now). This is not the way to scale your business. Highlight this: Scale happens with simplicity. At the mastery level, simplicity most looks like focusing on a signature offer (more on that in chapter 3). Simplicity also looks like focusing on the Incredible Ones™ (more on that in chapter 5). Simplicity looks like mastering your sales tool, too (more of that in chapter 6.)

Because you have money coming in, you placate and feel like you've hit the holy grail. But let's be honest. You are working way too hard to not be seeing millions. You've gotten to the six-figure quarter mark (or very close) by playing it safe. But you are not-so-secretly tired of hiding and being a best-kept secret. Since we are being honest, you're overwhelmed and finding time to expand is a challenge. There's no time and no more of you to go around. You are officially the bottleneck. Sure, you can brag about the fact that you have thirty or forty clients, but you're the only one serving them all, likely one-on-one. We both know what that means: you feel like a hamster on a wheel. You're working harder, but more isn't showing up. You are committed to growing to multiple six figures, even seven figures. But the idea of growing more makes you worried that you'll lose even more of your control and freedom. You have money coming in, but you're working really hard, holding tons of conversations to bring it in. You need help with streamlining and simplifying your sales. Just by shifting how you sell and gaining leverage in the sales process, you'll start to make more consistently. You'll also leverage your sales tools and stop working so hard to earn.

Your pinnacle clients come to you in waves. You don't know if it's going to be a $30,000 month or a $5,000 sales month. Because you're not leveraging the right sales systems and automations, you live the feast-or-famine cycle month after month. As a result, you're finding yourself living the hustle and grind that is often glorified on Instagram. Trying to scale with low ticket offers has you too busy working on the day-to-day instead of the big picture. That must change *now*. *Let's be honest. Low ticket doesn't transform; and you, Incredible One, were created to transform every life you come into contact with.*

It's time that you, once and for all, get the courage to position your business for your true greatness. To get to millions ($100,000 a month), it's time to tighten your business's sales systems and automations, and your mindset.

For millions to happen for you soon, you need to develop your Million Dollar Assets. That means you'll have to streamline your offerings so that each gives you: (1) leverage [no more working one-to-one]; (2) the power to serve your clients fully [they aren't worried about how much time you give them because they are getting consistent results]; (3) a scalable solution [you can easily serve one hundred just like you serve ten without breaking your business], all at an investment level that brings bigger money into your business and requires your clients to show up for themselves through this investment. You'll also need to tighten your key messaging to appeal to your pinnacle client (which lets you rise above the noise and become their only and obvious choice). Note: You have to tighten your message at every stage of the continuum.

Millions

The millions stage on the continuum means that you are successfully having $100,000 cash months and your company generates $1.2 million a year in gross revenue. Talk about game-changing income! You're literally making in thirty days what few are making in a year, according to statistics. Some people think that the millions stage is the place to be. Except, because you are there, you know that it's not all it's cracked up to be. Sure, you're making more money. But you're making it the hard way. You're likely starting from scratch instead of having the right systems in place to get to the next stage. To be at millions, you definitely have a team supporting your efforts. No, your virtual assistant won't cut it. After all, you're on target for, or just hit, your first million-dollar year. Having a team without clear systems is almost like pandemonium.

At this point, money is not the problem. You have a signature offer that sells consistently for $10,000 to $29,999 or more. You have a clear strategy that you're leveraging to hit your monthly revenue, and you have plans to uplevel again. At this stage, you likely are still working too much *in* your business. You need to start pulling away from service delivery, slowly but surely. You may have started the journey to bring on your first talent team members, but they're still looking to you to participate in the client service delivery and to tell them what to do. You haven't slowed down enough to create the systems they'll need to take this off your plate. So, that makes the problem *time*. You're not free to work on, and strategically preside over, the business. You're likely the CEO, COO, and CMO even though you have a support team in each of those areas. You are the only one driving strategy and decisions. This is hard for anyone, but especially for you. You are making consistent money, but the money isn't solving the problem.

To stop the drain you feel at this level, you need systems. Systems will not only make your success predictable, but they will put you on a trajectory to hiring the right management team so you can get to majesty ($100,000 a week). You need systems for everything; and yes, we will talk about all of the systems you need in chapter 9 in your Leverage + Scale Systems Suite.

Majesty

Majesty means that you are generating $100,000 a week. Whew! This is something to see! That means that at the end of the year your company has the potential to generate $5.2 million in gross revenue. At this level, you have strategy, sales, systems, and some support working for you. Experience tells me for the clients we serve at this level, like Marquel and Herman, that you need more higher level and management team support. Your team is still likely really lean, so you have people performing multiple functions (or multi-tasking), which means that you are not getting the best out of your team. Or you have almost all contractors, so your payroll is high, well above the recommended 30–40 percent of revenue, but you're still not fully covered. Your team is not fully vested because they have their own businesses to run while also working in yours. At this level, you have more than enough income to create the dream team, but you've yet to pull the trigger because you're afraid of the weight of having employees. You don't want to relive your corporate horror of managing people. I'm sorry to be the one to tell you this, but it is a myth that you can have a business that generates multiple millions with a virtual assistant! You're also telling yourself the story that you have to be present for the business to run. You are probably dealing with the guilt that prevents you from effectively replacing yourself because, at this point, you might not even want to be your company's CEO.

More than likely, you feel like your business is "your baby." So, you hold onto it for dear life, thinking that if you aren't there something will go wrong. Or you think people will stop enrolling. I only know because this is where I was when we hit majesty. Feeling guilty about "pawning" my clients off on my team. Except, I wasn't pawning them off because my team is the bomb dot com. It was because of my own story. I believed I had to be present at this level of investment, which traces back to one of the core lessons my dad taught me: you have to work hard for money. Except, that's not true.

The truth is at majesty you shouldn't still be working *in* your business *at all*. This is the point that your clients are hiring your company likely because of your impact on them, but not because you're still the lead service provider. You should only be working on your business. You need to be available to be in the rooms where the deals are happening and the check-cashing connections are being made. You need to be out there making connections, increasing visibility, and trusting that your capable team can hold down the fort while you're creating new opportunities. Your org chart will shift massively as you approach and hit majesty. You'll go from one team with one goal to three to four teams with goals that roll up into one goal. We will get into your support at this level in the chapter about your Leverage + Scale Talent Suite.

Monumental

Monumental is just what it sounds like. At this level, you're making $100,000 a day. This means your company has the potential to generate $36.5 million a year. In full transparency, we have had several $100,000 days, but we do not make $100,000 a day every day. It's important for me to be honest with you. I don't believe in spouting theory. Our goal is to generate $100,000 a day when we are in a launch, and we have done that successfully. What I can share is that, in order to produce each $100,000 day that we've experienced, it took strategy, sales infrastructure, systems, support, success mindset, and leadership. I'm going to place the emphasis on leadership because our last $100,000 day was done without me! My team was able to step up and create a launch that went over extremely well. Yes, I prepared them; but they showed up fully. This is why leadership is so important. You have to create a culture that permeates each team member down to their core so that they work like they own the company. To do this, ego will have to be low, and a sense of achieving the mission and vision will have to reign supreme.

Monumental days are not challenging to accomplish when your strategy, sales infrastructure, systems, and support are all working together. This is what we recommend you focus on if you want to see one or more $100,000 days in your business's future. This will take a focus on launching and taking the time to make sure each launch asset is developed, tested, and proven to achieve the result you desire.

Monumental days are a true leadership play. Picture Hannibal Smith from the hit show *The A-Team* because plans are coming together, consistently. For that to happen, you have to first have the right team and crystal-clear objectives for the role every member of the team plays. You'll need leaders, not just doers. People who can think and reason at a level higher than what is required for their role on the team. People who want to show up that way for you. That will require development and time. Personally, our entire team has a coach so we can make sure we develop them and their skills, and we adequately equip them to lead like they own the company. I also believe in empowering your people. Sure, you must have a protocol in place for them to follow. But within that protocol, each team member should have some autonomy to perform without having to be micromanaged. Now to get here, it will take work, time, and trust. Just as I advocate to hire slow and fire fast, developing leaders is about calculated strategy and not rushing simply because you need the role filled. I made that mistake back in 2014 and 2015. After crossing the million-dollar mark almost overnight, I scrambled and hired to fill the demand. But I never trained, developed, or empowered the people. It was a complete nightmare instead of what I had been dreaming about for years.

I will share more lessons when we get to the chapter on leadership and legacy. But for now, know that a desire to achieve your next milestone marker is pretty monumental in and of itself.

Now that you understand the Move to Millions Continuum and see yourself in it, what is your next step on the continuum?

CHAPTER THREE

The Move to Millions Method

"Seven figure earners don't reinvent the wheel.
They find a framework that is proven, and they work it."
—DARNYELLE JERVEY HARMON

don't know about you, but I have read the staggering statistics and they made my head hurt. Small businesses with no employees have an average income of $46,978.[3] Only 10.35 percent of service-based business owners cross the six-figure mark.[4] Even less, 4 percent, cross the seven-figure mark, which turns into less than 1 percent if we are focused on black woman-owned businesses.[5] We now also know that the average black woman-owned business only makes $24,000 a year.[6] If we've ever needed a book like this, we need it now.

In my company, we work with service-based business owners who have been stuck at six figures, and we help them to leverage and scale their businesses toward the million-dollar mark in less time, with less grind and more grace. Right now, I am working with fifty men and women (98 percent black) in my Move to Millions Mastermind. As a part of our curriculum, we share our Move to Millions Method with them. As a result, many of them hit their next move to millions milestone in a year or less. As recently as the fourth quarter of 2022, our mastermind clients generated $5,433,816 in revenue for an average of $155,251.88 in quarterly revenue per business, based on the thirty-five clients who reported their numbers in time to be featured in this book! These clients are generating more than $24,000 a month, week, day, or hour in their businesses, defying the statistics that are shared by American Express. Here's a quick look at the method:

THE MOVE TO MILLIONS® METHOD:

A proven formula to scale to 7 figures and BEYOND

SALES
Choose the sales tools that make millions easy

STRATEGY
Price, Package, Position, Promote (includes PR)

Success Mindset

SYSTEMS
Tighten the 7 systems to 7 figures

SUPPORT
Build & lead your million dollar team

Over the last twelve years, as I have been tweaking and tweaking our framework, I've become clear on one thing: what got you to six figures won't get you to seven. We see entrepreneurs try repeatedly to achieve their goal without upleveling the key areas of their business: strategy, sales, systems, support, and success mindset. For those who hustled their way to six figures, getting to seven will require that they leverage the power of systems and automation. For those who could get by with desperate sales energy, seven figures will demand that they require more from their clients and raise their rates. For those who built their brand on low-ticket offers, we implore them to develop their Leverage + Scale Offer Suite. I know firsthand that six figures will have you sitting in overwhelm while trying to deliver your services to your clients. We show clients how to create a Leverage + Scale Delivery

System so that the move to millions doesn't burn them out. We've watched clients who have not yet reached six figures (when we worked with clients at this level) switch their strategy like they changed their underwear. Now, we marvel at watching our mastermind clients focus on one strategy for one client for one year and cross the million-dollar mark with simplicity!

All of this is about sustainability for me. As a result of reading this book, I want you to look back at your business three years from now, five years from now, and even ten years from now, and say that this book was a defining moment for you. There are tons of coaches out there teaching you marketing and sales strategy, getting you through your next launch. But I am offering you an opportunity to build a company that will be sustained over time as you learn tried-and-true strategies to move your life and business forward.

The bottom line is that if you desire to create a sustainable million-dollar company, you'll need five things. Here's an overview, because we will go deeper into each in the subsequent chapters of this book:

Strategy

Strategy is about your packaging, pricing, positioning, and promotion. You can't do any of the former without first identifying the problem you solve for a client who has been unsuccessful at attempting to solve the problem on their own. Without strategy, businesses fail when they should scale. As a service-based business, the key to your business's continued growth and development is strategy. We like to define strategy as the infusion of packaging, pricing, positioning, and promoting. Essentially, your strategy must include your offers, your value-based pricing, your messaging, and your marketing. Having a big-picture strategy for your company is the difference between doing six figures the hard way and doing seven figures with grace and ease. Once your strategy is clear, you'll develop your first three Million Dollar Assets, which are the key to leveraging and scaling your company: your Leverage + Scale Offer Suite, your Leverage + Scale Messaging Suite, and your Leverage + Scale Marketing Suite.

Sales

As a service-based business owner, you have options on how you sell your services. When it comes to sales, we help our clients create their Leverage + Scale Sales Suite. There are five different sales suite options that we will go deeper into in the sales chapter. Each of them is about a leveraged sales approach so that you can go from one yes at a time to many yeses at a time.

Typically determined by whether you work business-to-business (B2B) or business-to-consumer (B2C), your sales suite is the key to scaling your business quickly. The cool thing is that, regardless of your sales suite, you are still leveraging the seven phases of the sales conversation! The ultimate goal is to create an evergreen enrollment process so that nothing stops you from bringing on new clients every day, if you so desire!

You're the CEO. That means you need a clear framework that you can teach *your team* to use to keep the sales coming into your business. Your job is to strategically preside over the sales process, not to get caught up in it. Focusing on sales may not be the best use of your time if you want to cross the million-dollar mark with grace and ease. Anywhere you need to focus may cause bottlenecks and capacity issues.

Systems

Systems make millions predictable. To scale your company to and beyond the million-dollar mark, you need to have seven core systems operating consistently:

- Operations—your key to the day-to-day management of your entire business
- Financial—your key to managing the receivables and payables for your business
- Legal—your key to managing your Intellectual Property and other legal management
- Marketing—your key to managing your messaging and marketing systems
- Sales—your key to managing your sales cycles
- Client—your key to managing client progress and service delivery
- Talent—your key to managing happy, productive team members

When you have each of these systems set up and working optimally, the Move to Millions will happen quickly.

Support

To scale fast, you need to organize your team into three sub teams: operations, talent, and marketing and sales. Your ops team keeps the day-to-day running with a focus on customer service. Your talent team creates the client experience and focuses on service delivery. Your marketing and sales team focuses on lead generation, pipeline or funnel management, sales, and topline revenue. Thinking of your company in this way is a game changer.

I purposely share all of the tactical components of the method first. That is what you all think it will take to make, move, and leave millions. You'll come to learn once you start this journey, if you haven't already, that the strategy is the *easiest* part. The real work happens in the final part, the part that runs through each of the others: the success mindset. To be clear, no one thinks they have a mindset problem. Most think that there is just something that they haven't learned and if they learned that thing, then, *voilà* they'd be making millions. As my client and friend Attiyah Blair says, "Most people are addicted to information and allergic to what really creates the shift: execution."

Success Mindset

Tightening your Move to Millions Method will be *useless* if you don't believe you deserve to earn the money coming your way. The Move to Millions requires an incredible shift in mindset as well as a realization that making millions requires more flow and less flex. And truthfully, your mindset runs through everything. How you see yourself based on how you were raised and taught all impacts your success mindset.

I have learned over the years that I cannot teach anything if I am not teaching about what I like to call your inner seven-year-old. When we are born, we are born with only a subconscious mind. Your subconscious mind takes everything you present to it as if it's the truth. So, from birth to the age of seven, your parents and other family are downloading into your subconscious mind to create your conscious mind. Yes, that means that all of the fear, lack, chaos, and confusion that clouds your judgment today and keeps you from taking the steps that truly bring you closer to your goals are inherited from someone else. The truth is that you came here as abundance. As your mother pushed or the doctor pulled you out of the womb, your abundance began to diminish. Now, your parents could only teach what they had learned, so this isn't about them or placing blame on them. But to do better, you must know better. Part of that comes in realizing that most of the things you hold as beliefs are lies. There is literally a lie in the word *belief.*

If the reason you picked up this book is because you are stuck at six figures, it's because one or more of the five areas covered in this quick chapter is currently a gap in your business. Your gaps could be the gateway to your first million-dollar year. As you read this book, we will go deep into each of the potential gaps in your business. For now, following this overview, I recommend a quick self-assessment to determine where your biggest gap lies: strategy, sales, systems, support, or success mindset. Ask yourself these questions:

- **Strategy:** Do I have an offer suite that is highly leveraged and scalable? Is the foundation of my business (packaging, pricing, positioning, and promoting) strong enough to start my move? Does my messaging consistently attract and convert my most ideal clients? Which marketing strategy can I credit for 85 percent of my lead generation?
- **Sales:** Do I have a sales script that, when leveraged in my sales suite, brings me new clients consistently? Have I mastered how to shorten my sales cycle so I can better predict revenue? If I have others supporting my sales efforts, can they close without me, or do I constantly have to jump in? Are they enrolling people every day of the week and keeping results consistently?
- **Systems:** Have I already begun to create the processes, playbooks, and procedures that make my success duplicatable and predictable each month in my business? Are there any of the seven systems that are nonexistent in my business? Do I have standard operating procedures (SOPs) and processes for each of the seven systems?
- **Support:** Do I have the right support so that I am not the bottleneck in my business? Have I developed the right leadership skills

to effectively manage the efforts of others on behalf of my goals to continue to scale this company? Have I thought through my organizational chart to have a sustainable million-dollar company? For the team I have, are they clear about their role and key performance indicators (KPIs)?

- **Success Mindset:** Are there any limiting beliefs that threaten to derail my next level of growth financially and spiritually? Do I *truly* believe that I am worthy and deserve to operate a business that makes and moves millions?

Now that you have processed the questions you need to ask yourself as you read this book that is designed to change your life, business, and bank accounts, let's jump into part one: mastery.

Part One:

Mastery

CHAPTER FOUR

Mindset for Millions

"Hard work won't make you millions. Alignment will."
—DARNYELLE JERVEY HARMON

W hen I was growing up, I thought we were poor. The truth is we were middle class. But the way my dad saw money made me feel poor. There never seemed to be enough. *Ever*. We didn't talk about money and wealth, unless you count those moments when my dad was upset because some rich "cracker" (as he would refer to white people) did something he deemed to be asinine. I learned as I got older that the way my dad saw money meant that access to money wasn't for us; we were only meant to have enough to get by. And the money we did have, we had to work twice as hard to get. He reminded me often when I would ask for money that we didn't have a tree out back that he could just pull money from. For him to give me money, it meant he had to labor for it.

I shake my head every time I think back to those early years. But I can't blame it all on my dad. We went to live with my father when I was eight upon my mom being sentenced to sixteen years in prison. My dad and mom got divorced when I was two. From age two to eight, living with my mother showed me signs of poverty, too. My mom was a "rob Peter to pay Paul" kinda mom. Don't get me wrong. My mom did her thing. She held it down; she held us down. We were never hungry, and we were the best-dressed kids in the projects. She did whatever it took to make sure we were cared for. We were her pride and joy. But she never mastered money. Money was always something that there was never enough of, no matter how hard she hustled. Money was like grains of sand on the beach. It always seemed to slip through her fingers. I used to hear my mom make deals with people for money. She also taught me that having money wasn't in the cards for us.

My father actually made pretty good money, but he was an addict, so his money went to his addiction, which left scraps for us. So, again, there was never enough money. I started working when I was thirteen, just to be able to have more than what my basic needs required. I still remember writing in my journal that I would always have money even if that meant that I had to sacrifice something in the moment to never feel poor. I carried these sentiments into adulthood. Working for the bank, my Mary Kay business, and even the early years of Incredible One were saddled with these beliefs about money that didn't serve me.

Truthfully, the way each of my parents saw money and passed their money stories and beliefs down to me wasn't *their* story either. It came from how they were raised and what they were taught about money. Each of their parents were poor and lack-minded. They came from a long line of hustlers who never seemed to get a break when it came to money. No matter what, there was never enough. My paternal grandparents were direct descendants of slaves in South Carolina, just two generations from field slaves on the Jervey Plantation. My maternal grandparents were descendants of slaves from Maryland and Virginia. While I do believe that they got their beliefs honestly, it's a big part of the reason that I am so adamant about teaching people about money and how it works. We have to break the cycles of financial illiteracy and open up the possibility to live wealthy.

Oh, and I can't forget the television shows I grew up watching. Shows like *Dynasty*, where the rich people really were evil, and *Good Times*, where they tried to make being poor seem fun—like you were somehow more entertaining if you didn't have money. Church made it seem like being poor meant we were more holy than if we were rich. After all, Mark 10:25 says, "It's easier for a camel to pass through the eye of the needle than for a rich man to enter the kingdom of God." The stories about money were everywhere.

I've come to realize that money is spiritual. The way you see money is really about the way you see yourself and your relationship with God. Through this filter, as I look back on my parents and their relationships with money, I can clearly see who they believed themselves to be and why money impacted them the way it did. When they were married, I recall hearing my mom and dad fight incessantly about money, or the lack of money, to handle our basic needs. We struggled. They were always fighting loudly and physically because my dad smoked the money and my mom had to go steal just to make ends meet. There was a time in my teens and early twenties when I resented both of my parents and money, specifically because of money. Today, I realize that resenting money caused so many of my own issues as a young adult and business owner.

I often tell the story of when, at sixteen, I got home and opened my bank statement to learn that my dad had nearly emptied my bank account. Fifty percent of every paycheck I had earned since I was thirteen went into that account, and it was enough money to buy me a car when I got my license. By the time I was sixteen, there should have been nearly $7,500 in that bank account. Yet as I read the bank statement, there was $234.19. When I confronted my father, his response was "living under my roof has never been free." So with that traumatic experience, I gained a new money story: money can be taken from you without your consent. I truly did believe at that time in my life that money, and access to it, was just so hard. I heard on a weekly basis that we were lucky just to have the little that we did. Over the years and into my thirties, I kept telling the stories that had been handed down to me. "You have to work hard for money. Money is only for what you need. We are lucky to have enough; don't expect more. Black people aren't meant to have money. We are supposed to struggle like Jesus. We are just lucky to be here and not still slaves. My money is already spent." I think you get the point.

I was never taught anything about money, but I certainly caught what money came to mean to me. I basically grew up financially illiterate. Whenever I had access to money, it never felt good. As a result, I made bad decisions and poor choices. By the time I was an adult, my money was so funny that it wasn't funny. I was a hot mess, and I was struggling with my two money personalities. On the one hand, I was a miser. I was so afraid of going without money that I would hoard it. I would deny myself what I wanted, and I only spent money on things I had a defined need for, except for when I was binging. In those moments, my spender was front and center.

She spent money I didn't have in the form of credit cards to feel validated, safe, and as if I mattered. When my spender showed up, I went broke. I had seven credit cards by the time I was a sophomore in college. While I went to college on a full scholarship, I had enough credit card debt to have paid student loans twice. I had no idea that having credit cards was not always a good thing, especially if you didn't have the money to pay the bill when it came. I will never forget walking the quad and seeing one credit card vendor after another. I didn't even know what a credit card was, until a dormmate happily shared that having a credit card was like having layaway that you got to take home now and enjoy.

I understood layaway. Every school year and Christmas, we used layaway to get clothes and basic items. There wasn't enough money to just go to the store and purchase.

My money personalities, like many of the entrepreneurs who become my clients, never served me. They were created out of an unclear understanding about what money is and how it works. Truth be told, were it not for me filing bankruptcy in my midthirties, I still might not know what money really is. But because I was required to take a financial literacy course to understand money, and I was introduced to the book called *A Happy Pocket Full of Money* by David Cameron Gikandi, I learned the truth about money.

A Happy Pocket Full of Money was the first book on money to change my life.

Money is energy, and it is always available. Money isn't a new construct; it's been around since the beginning of time. In fact, God talks about money more than 2,300 times in the Bible. God talks about money so much because He wants us to master it. God sees money as a "lesser" thing, something that we as creations in His own image should have dominion over. Unfortunately, most of us haven't got that memo. So, we see money as evil and something that is unattainable. But the truth is that money is spiritual; access to it is birthright. Now that I am aware of that, money will never be my problem again. I also realize that desiring money doesn't make you greedy. It, as Jen Sincero says in her book *You are a Badass at Making Money*, is a desire for life. Jen goes on to remind us that desire means "of the father" in Latin.[7]

Let's look at the parable of the talents in the book of Matthew in the Bible. Allow me to remind you with the Darnyelle version of the parable. The master is going away, and he leaves each of his three servants with money. To one, he gives five; to another, two; and to the last servant, one. The master is testing the servants to see whether or not they will leverage the money to increase it or allow fear to keep them from accessing more wealth. Two of the three servants doubled their master's money. The last, in fear, buried the money, earning nothing extra. Upon the master's return, he checked in with the servants to learn what they did with the talents. The moral to the story? Money is nothing to fear! It's an energy to double! When you fear money, you won't get the reward, recognition, or responsibility you seek. The two servants who doubled their talents were made "masters over more." The one who buried his talent was stripped of the one talent and banished from the master's property. In this parable, God is showing us that money is a "lesser" thing that we must master in order to get access to major things.

What would happen in your business if you looked at money this way? What would happen if you mastered money and didn't allow it to master you?

At least twice a week, I have a conversation with a prospective client who is like the third servant—afraid of money. And as a result, they are not making as much as they'd like in their business. They aren't aliens. Most people struggle with money—the concept of it, how to earn it, how to keep it. And it's because they, too, were raised in financially illiterate households. They got it honestly, as I like to say.

Remember earlier when I mentioned your inner seven-year-old? From birth to the age of seven, who we are is formed. When we are born, we come into the earth realm as vessels of light. Then, we meet our parents, and unfortunately that light begins to dim. As we try to navigate those early years, we are looking to our families to teach us everything we need to know. We are only born with a subconscious mind. Remember that your subconscious mind takes everything you present to it as if it is the truth. That can be a good thing; but in most cases, it's a bad thing.

Our conscious mind is formed based on what we see, experience, are taught, or what is caught. We literally come into our families as a sponge. We soak up all their lack and fear, and we make it our own. By the time we are seven, we have seen so much lack, fear, desperation, and settling that we build a life around it. Then we grow into adults. We go to work in corporate America. We decide we aren't meant to sit behind someone else's desk and leap face-first into entrepreneurship. This could be a good thing except, we don't have a good relationship with money. So, we start businesses, charging pennies on the dollar and charging by the hour. After all, an hourly rate is all we know. But hourly rates won't get your business to the million-dollar mark—at least not without putting in a lot of billable hours.

One of the main things I learned about money is that it's not about the money. It's about who you become on the journey to having access to more. That is why God talked about money so much—to normalize access to it so that our character wouldn't be impacted by having it. Once we realize that access to money is about becoming, everything changes. I like to refer to the Model of Abundance[8] to explain this concept:

Who must I **be**

To do what I desire to **do**

In order to have what I desire to **have**

Be. Do. Have.

You have to be it to become it, and you must be it first. What I have realized is that the model of abundance really looks like this:

Who must I **be** [What is my identity?]

To do what I desire to **do** [What actions must I take?]

In order to have what I desire to **have** [How do I experience the feeling of security?]

Your abundance is your identity. God established it for you in Genesis when He said that He was making you in His image to have dominion. God's biggest desire for each of us is that we become more in order to live into the identity He approved for us before we were formed in our mother's womb.

The key to abundance is the journey and who you become on the journey. Stepping fully into your abundant birthright is what seals your identity.

I really wish I understood this when I started my business, or even when I was stuck and struggling at the six-figure mark. It would've saved me *years* of frustration. It's why I am so adamant today about teaching money mindset everywhere I can. I truly want for everyone to walk into their abundant birthright. Most of us were raised to believe that we have to do something to have access to money. But because money is an energy, we just have to be in alignment with it. We have to believe that we are worthy of access to it.

"If you hold the belief that you must work hard to make money, then you cannot make money unless you are doing hard work. Your actions will always follow your beliefs. No success hinges on hard work. All success, including success financially, is realized through alignment."
—Darnyelle Jervey Harmon

This realization changed my life. It started me on the path I now teach from. I get booked frequently to share my signature keynote, Mindset for Millions. This is my most requested topic because most people quickly realize that until they work on the six inches between their ears, they won't feel seven figures between their fingers. And interestingly, what holds us back from seven figures are the stories that we tell ourselves. Some stories we tell out of our own recollection and experience. Others we tell because we were taught, or we caught the stories from our elders.

Several years ago, when I first started speaking, I would start a presentation with an exercise I called the Box of Limitations™. The box was really a way for me to conduct some market research. I would ask the audiences to give me their limitations so that they would be free to live their best life. I had a pretty box up front, and I would have them write their limitations down in regard to fear and money. They'd then place them in my box. When I did my TEDx talk in 2017 called Burn the Box, it was based on this premise.

When I would get home following a talk, I would unload the box. The stories I would find! There were so many limiting money beliefs that I actually created a worksheet to capture the more than one hundred I saw consistently. This also became the backdrop of my own learning so that I would be equipped to help others overcome the meanings they had for money that weren't accurate. If you want to shift into the mindset for millions, you're going to have to come face-to-face with your limiting stories and dismantle each of them, so that you can stop holding yourself accountable to those fallacies. Which money mindsets and limiting beliefs have you bought into?

No matter the belief, here is how to dismantle it:

- **Clarify the origin of the belief.** Who is responsible for you believing this? Where did it come from? How have you seen it play out? Is this your own experience or are you counting on someone else's recollection?

- **Ask, "Is it possible that this belief is not true?"** By questioning the belief in real time in your current reality, we often find that it is possible that it's not true. And in this case, all we need is a shred of possibility to begin the process of dismantling the limiting belief.

- **Ask, "Is there current evidence to validate that this is something to fear?"** If there is no current evidence, then it's not a real fear. It's a projection.

- **Determine what is waiting on the other side of the belief.** When you get into what's possible by pressing through the limiting belief, you open up your feelings and emotions specifically around positive belief and expectation. That will get you into an energy of abundance.

- **Write down what you would do if you didn't hold this limiting belief any longer.** Being able to get past the limiting belief long enough to vision cast what is possible is a sign that the limiting belief is losing its power.

- **Reframe the limiting belief into a positive affirmation.** You can literally take the limiting belief and recreate a positive life altering affirmation. For example, let's say you currently hold a belief that there is never enough money. You can reframe that belief by saying, "I am so happy and grateful now that I am surrounded by the abundance of money whenever I desire for it to show up in order for me to access what I desire in that moment."

- **Take the first action in the direction of what you'd do if you didn't hold that limiting belief.** Movement/action is always the fastest way out of the stuck place you're in. Even when you don't know all the moves, take the next move you know to take. As Rumi says, "When you start to walk on the way, the way appears."[9]

Limiting beliefs have one purpose: to lead you to believe that holding onto that belief is for your protection. Once you realize that the beliefs you hold aren't actually serving you, you have the potential to enter a mindset of abundance. This is the mindset for millions. The realization that the beliefs you held were actually working against you, instead of propelling you toward the abundance that you were created to experience, is a growth mindset. In her book, *Mindset*, Carol Dweck states, "In a growth mindset, challenges are exciting rather than threatening. So rather than thinking, oh, I'm going to reveal my weaknesses, you say, wow, here's a chance to grow."[10] When it comes to money, opening yourself up to a growth mindset is the fastest way to shift your money. Just offering yourself the possibility of a growth mindset around money will put you on the trajectory to gaining access to millions. I tell my clients all the time that money is mental before it is movable.

It's also possible that the hold up for you with money is because you are experiencing one of the most common money blocks: unworthiness, fear of getting too big, fear of abandonment, the burden or responsibility of success, or unforgiveness. Any of these have the potential to block the flow of money into your life experience. Each of them shows up differently based on how you were raised and what you were taught or caught about money.

Which is yours?

Mine was abandonment. When I was eight, my mom's home was raided, and she was taken to jail. I have struggled with abandonment ever since. When I first started speaking professionally, I was fortunate enough to get on some powerful stages. I was often the only woman. The men speakers would celebrate me, telling me that I could "bring the heat" and hold my own on any stage with any man. They also informed me that this skill was going to make it nearly impossible to find a man who would be "willing" to stand in my shadow. If you know anything about me, you likely know that the one thing I wanted more than anything was someone to love me, *for real*. After my mom went to jail, I went to live with my father. Because of my father's work schedule, my sister and I were left with my stepmother most of the time. We heard my stepmother on the phone with her mother or a friend, sharing that she "wished Jeannie would come get her kids!" The thought, as I grew into a young woman and eventually an adult, that I would one day have a husband who would love me unconditionally, is what saved me in those moments when I questioned my existence. Hearing these men so confidently express this made me shrink back. I wasn't going to make lots of money if that meant I was going to be alone. Remember I said earlier that what holds us back are the stories we tell ourselves. I forgot to mention that the stories *others* tell you that you believe hold you back as well. For years, I bought into those lies. For years, I didn't earn at the level I was born to. For years, I didn't have a successful romantic relationship either.

In the event that you are struggling with any limiting money belief that is blocking the flow of your money, I just want to remind you that none of those lies you've been telling yourself are true. The truth is God desires wealth and abundance for you. As I already mentioned, He talks about money, wealth, and possessions more than He speaks of Heaven or Hell. That is because He desires that you be wealthy. Here is one of my favorite Scriptures to reinforce God's desire for you to be wealthy:

Proverbs 10:22 KJV says, "The blessings of the Lord, it maketh rich and he addeth no sorrow with it."

This means that not only should you be wealthy, but you shouldn't have to hustle and grind to experience it either!

There are tons of Scriptures that express similar sentiment, but this is the one I want to leave with you at this moment. Yes, you can have millions of dollars, and no, it doesn't make you evil. Listen, I get it. I grew up misquoting that Scripture and a host of others that led me to believe that being poor was holy and that somehow God rewarded the struggle. I believed that I was more like Jesus if I was broke. But as I shared with the parable of the talents, fear of money is not a reward.

Once I realized that money was an energy, and it is always moving, I started playing what I today refer to as the Money Moves Game. Once you've shifted your mindset to see money as an energy, the rest is simple. To make money move, you have to do two things: invest and be investable. That's it. Here's what I mean. You have to make money move by releasing it to someone or something else in the form of an investment. Once you release the money, you need to be investable so that someone else can release money to you. Because money is an energy, it is always circulating. When it is circulating, you stay in the flow by investing and being investable, or said differently, releasing and receiving.

A few years ago, my husband and I were building our dream home, a Toll Brothers home. After visiting the design center, where we chose all the upgrades, we realized that the deposit on our dream home's options was $50,000 (20 percent of the total amount of options). My husband immediately wanted to take items off the list. He promptly stated, "We can't afford that." Instead, I reminded him that we make money move, and we could afford whatever we desired. To show him better than I could tell him, we decided to play the Money Moves Game to create the $50,000 deposit. Highlight this: When you're an entrepreneur, "I can't afford that" need never be in your vocabulary or come out of your mouth. You can create the money you require. As entrepreneurs, if we need money for something, we can create an offer to access it.

As entrepreneurs, we solve problems for profit. That means there is never a day we are without money, as long as we are able to solve a problem. I told my husband that we could create it. That is exactly what I did. We needed $50,000, and although the money was in our savings account, I wanted to reinforce to my husband that we could always create the money. I sat down first and thought about my ideal client and a problem they had right now. I wanted to be able to take all of the money and apply it to our deposit. I knew that my offer need only cost me time. If it was focused on me, I wouldn't have to pay my team to fulfill it. So, I decided that I was going to be the offer. I sent three emails to my list announcing that I was offering a one-time only ninety-day unlimited coaching opportunity with me for $5,000, and I had ten spots. My husband gave me two weeks to create the money. I created it in seven days. By the time the second email was sent, all ten spaces were filled. After the credit card processing fees, I had $48,500 in cold hard cash, which I added $1,500 to so we could make the deposit.

Why was this so easy for me? I realized that abundance is my birthright and that it will stay in my life when my thoughts, beliefs, words, and actions are in alignment. I knew I could create the money. I believed I could create the money. I spoke out loud that I would create the money. I believed and didn't doubt that I could create money. I was clear that there was no block standing between me and the money I desired to create. I had a plan to create the money, and therefore, I created the money.

The reason this is the first chapter in the Mastery section of this book is because you have to master money and your money mindset if you intend to make, move, and leave millions. If your story is anything like mine, the thought of having access to millions of dollars might scare you. And if you feel the fear of success and responsibility creeping up on you, it's okay. You now know how to handle those fears. Your money mindset will be predicated on your money backstory and the stories you recall as you attempt to leverage and scale your business. Listen, I am not judging you. I am hoping that by being transparent about my own journey and how I am today a multi-millionaire in cash and assets, it becomes an example of what is possible for you as well.

A big part of my money success today is because I forgave my money past. I wholeheartedly believe that forgiveness is the gateway to experiencing flow in every area of your life, especially your money. I had to be willing to travel down memory lane and answer some questions about money: How has money let me down in the past? Who was responsible for how I saw money? What would it take to forgive money and them? I had to retrace it all—how my parents behaved around money, what they said about money, what they showed me about money when they weren't speaking, all of it. I even had to look at my friends and centers of influence and get clear about the impact those relationships had on how I related to money. As hard as it was to relive these experiences, they made a significant difference in how I see money today. They all opened me up to realize that I do deserve it and I am worthy to have more money than I can give, spend, invest, and save.

By dealing with my money fears, looking at how I acted when it was time to pay bills, and honing in on my thoughts, feelings, and beliefs when I was presented with an opportunity to invest in myself, I got to the root of my money issues and mastered the reality about money. The truth is money wants the best for me. Money is always available to me. Money is a tool that I can use to access what I most desire in my life and my business. Money respects me. Money loves being in my presence.

In order to get here, you will likely have to complete an exercise I have our clients do. Trace your money patterns. In full transparency, I learned this from my therapist. She was the one who helped me understand the patterns I live in. As I already shared, we all have an inner seven-year-old. Because we were only born with a subconscious mind, everything we learned, observed, saw from birth to the age of seven became our set of patterns that repeat every seven years. I know for a fact that, until you learn, and therefore break your patterns, they will replicate every seven years.[11] That means that you are living in a holding pattern, and the seven-year-old version of yourself is really calling the shots.

To complete the assignment, take a sheet of blank paper. Turn it horizontally and number it from one to your current age in seven years per column. Then you want to trace back as far as you can recall for the first time you experienced and came into an awareness that there was something called money. Write down positive and negative occurrences. For example, I was six when I realized that there was a thing called money. I was in the grocery store with my mother, and I decided that I wanted a piece of candy. So, I slid it up onto the checkout lane. My mom, upon seeing it there, met me with a backhand slap and quickly told me that we didn't have money for that. She gave me the first limited belief I held about money: that it was only for what you *need*. To this day, I have to catch myself between a need and a desire so I can access what I most crave in any given moment. Every time I think back to that memory and the limited belief that my mom created for me at six, I recognize a negative pattern that includes a traumatic experience with money. Case in point, I was thirty-four (year six of my 29 to 35 cycle) when I filed bankruptcy. That is just one of the money traumas that came from my first encounter with money. Since I've learned how to break this pattern, I am grateful to say that money traumas no longer impact me.

When money isn't flowing for you, there are three things to check:

- **Check to see if you're hoarding money.** Now, I'm all for having a rainy-day fund, as long as your fund doesn't have you holding your breath in lack when you should be breathing the big moments of life in. In the parable of the talents, which I will refer to a few times throughout this book, the servant who buried the money was shunned. Money has to move. If yours is stagnant because you fear that you may have a great need later, money can't move. This was a big mindset shift for me.

- **Check your unforgiveness.** Holding on to how someone has hurt or wronged you will impact your money significantly. While I will go deeper on unforgiveness in section two of this book, it needs to be said now. This is one of the biggest blocks to accessing more money that I have found in my work. I always recommend checking your heart if your money starts to get funny.

- **Make sure that you are using what is in your house.** I love the 2 Kings story of the widow who visited Elisha when the debtors wouldn't stop calling and threatened to take her sons. Elisha asked her simply, "What is in your house?" She replied, "I only have a little oil." He told her to borrow as many empty jars as she could get from her neighbors and to fill them with the oil. He also said that the oil wouldn't stop pouring until there were no jars left. After all the jars were filled, he told her to go *sell* the jars to pay her debts. What's in your house (your wheelhouse/gift) is marketable, desirable, and available. It can be sold to your "neighbors." If you know the story, then you know that she borrowed jars from her neighbors. Then, she went back to them with their jars and her oil, and they gave her money—more than enough to pay her husband's debts and live with her two sons.

As a result of coming boldly into this realization, I shifted the way I thought about money. I went from thinking about it in terms of what it costs, and I started thinking about access to it as the ability to invest. Remember, investing and being investable is what makes money move. I decided to take personal responsibility for the good and bad money decisions I've made. I also started to give myself an enormous amount of grace when it comes to money. I stopped holding it to be the end all be all in my life. That took away the power I had given it and allowed me to take power over it. I realized that God wasn't holding anything back from me. That is why money became an ally instead of a foe.

This is what I hope you come to believe and feel, too. I know that moving into this kind of relationship with money will position you to make, move, and leave millions.

Chapter Action Plan

1. Identify your definition and, therefore, your relationship with money.
2. Journal about how money has impacted your life and shadowed your beliefs, especially in your own business.
3. Determine what you desire to believe and what you decide to hold true about what money is instead.
4. Create your money beliefs.
5. Confirm your biggest money block.
6. Write your new money story.
7. Celebrate by making a purchase of something that makes you feel wealthy.

Remember: Information without action is just a waste of time. So, make a plan to implement now so you are one move closer to your first million-dollar year.

Client Case Study

Meet Attiyah Blair, RESET

I first met Attiyah Blair back in 2012 when she was ready to transition out of her position as a TV producer at NBC in Philadelphia. A mutual friend introduced us, and we met over lunch. By the end of that lunch, Attiyah had registered for my $497 Get Paid Intensive where I was going to show her how to package, price, and sell her Incredible Factor. Immediately following that workshop, we started working together. We had some early success in that business. In our work, Attiyah was able to raise her prices and attract some better paying clients. Eventually, however, Attiyah began to resent her business and she closed it down. She didn't leave entrepreneurship, but she reset and started to focus on real estate exclusively.

A few years later, in her new business, she returned for support adding a coaching line of business to her real estate investing business. Together, we built her coaching business to seven figures. We leveraged the power of live events to give her an entirely different stream of revenue. She built a digital course and a $10,000 coaching program. One of the things I love about Attiyah is that she is very self-aware. She started to become bogged down by her coaching business and she decided that keeping it wasn't worth it. We spent some time creating the plan for her to close the coaching side of her business.

Even though she's no longer coaching today, she is still running a multimillion-dollar business. Attiyah has been enrolled in most of my programs over the years, most recently in the Move to Millions Mastermind, where six-figure months became her new normal:

"Working with Darnyelle has been a game changer for me! Strategy—tight. Sales—tight. Systems—tight. Support team—tight. In the last year, I've crossed a major threshold and now I'm a million-dollar CEO! Darnyelle is the GOAT, and I'm telling you: your life will NEVER be the same if you get into her space!"
—ATTIYAH BLAIR

Her Continuum MOVE:
From Mastery to Millions in year one in the Move to Millions Mastermind.

CHAPTER FIVE

Leverage + Scale Offer Suite

"People will pay you more than you think for the right offer that has been packaged and positioned well."

—DARNYELLE JERVEY HARMON

Since 2008, I have had the pleasure of working with tens of thousands of entrepreneurs at every stage. First as a Mary Kay Cosmetics independent executive pink Cadillac sales director with five hundred women in my unit at one point. Then, as the director of the Center for Women's Entrepreneurship in the state of Delaware. Now through my own company, Incredible One Enterprises, which I came back to full-time on January 1, 2011. Regardless of the level of the entrepreneur, there is this overwhelming sense that getting your business to the million-dollar mark is solely about strategy. It's as if entrepreneurs truly believe that all you need is the right strategy and voilà—millions will start falling from the sky. Yet according to the Small Business Administration, 89.19 percent of all non-employer entity businesses never make $100,000 in gross receipts.[12] Clearly, it can't be just a strategy that allows a business to make more money. If it were just strategy, the statistics would reflect that every business was profitable and creating jobs! Since I started my own entrepreneurial journey and found success while growing my company by at least 50 percent each year (most years well over 100 percent growth), I realized that there was a formula that helped me to get to the growth I've grown accustomed to and helped our Incredible Factor University clients experience as well. Back in 2009, I called this formula the Leverage Your Incredible Factor System. Today, we call it the Move to Millions Method. In both formulas, I paid close attention to what it was actually taking for me and my clients to see success. Here's a hint: It wasn't just strategy. You've already been introduced to the method, but here it is again:

THE MOVE TO MILLIONS® METHOD:

A proven formula to scale to 7 figures and BEYOND

As you can see, it takes more than strategy to become a million-dollar CEO. I've proved it, and the clients I will be introducing you to in this book have proved it as well. What I have learned is that strategy, sales, systems, and support, albeit important, are nothing without the success mindset that runs through the middle of this formula. Take Kim Kendall, as an example. Kim is a master of her craft. She is amazing at interior design. There wasn't anything that I could teach her about design. However, as much of a master as she was with design, she didn't take her business to the next level. It was working with me and working through the full formula, with a lot of emphasis on success mindset, that was the turning point. Kim had an aversion to real money in her business. She said she wanted to make it, but she showed up in her business in a way that repelled it until we started to work through her mindset. Upon doing so, we watched her revenues grow from $8,000 a month to $60,000 a month easy! In just eighteen months, Kim's $100,000 business became a $500,000 business. Were it not for her desire to slow down and focus on family, we would have made the Move to Millions together. This is the power of mastery.

When you understand what it will take, and you have the support and accountability to take it on, mastery is the result. And it's the result quickly. Throughout the method, there are seven assets that are created to help our clients, and now you, leverage the power of mastery to make, move, and leave millions:

Strategy:
- Leverage & Scale Offer Suite
- Leverage & Scale Messaging Suite
- Leverage & Scale Marketing Suite

Sales:
- Leverage & Scale Sales Suite

Systems:
- Leverage & Scale Systems Suite

Support:
- Leverage & Scale Talent Suite
- Leverage & Scale Leadership & Legacy Suite

I will keep reminding you that every asset requires a success mindset. You'll also see that play out as I share client case studies and success stories with you.

When I started working with clients privately back in 2010 and 2011, I found that every single client I worked with was struggling with the same things. After feeling like a broken record for saying the same things, sharing the same strategies, and creating the same templates and guides as when I ran the women's business center, I formulated what became my signature framework and methodology with an emphasis on marketing. I was convinced back then that all you needed was good marketing to make more money. Yet even with all of my good marketing, I still ended up filing bankruptcy in 2010! I now know that it's not just good marketing. It's changing the way you think, act, and reason. It's looking at your business like a company so that you can focus on building assets. Once I came back into full-time entrepreneurship, I focused on becoming unemployable. I knew that the way to pull that off was to create assets that would add value to my work. That was the game changer. Today, you get to benefit from the assets I created that have made me a multimillion-dollar CEO and millionaire.

asset: property owned by a person or company, regarded as having value and available to meet debts, commitments, or legacies[13]

Our first asset is the Leverage + Scale Offer Suite, which is all about your packaging and pricing. Many falsely believe that in order to make millions, they need many offers in varying budget levels. That actually couldn't be farther from the truth. I recently saw a news clipping of a story highlighting how Payless Shoes launched a new high-end brand, Palessi. This brand sold the same shoes you could find in your local Payless shoe store when they were open; except now, they had a much higher price tag. Influencers, celebrities, and stylists were invited to their grand opening, and they perceived that these once $10–$40 shoes were now worth $500 or more![14] Because I had been let it on the joke, as I watched influencer after influencer remark at the quality and craftsmanship of the shoes, I immediately realized how true the statement I have said every time I have talked about packaging and pricing since 2011 was. *People will pay more than you think for the right program that has been packaged and positioned well.*

Packaged and positioned well.

When you learn how to create offers that are better and more aligned than what you have been offering, you will automatically position yourself above the noise in the marketplace, and people will cease to question the investment to access them. Pricing is only an issue in the absence of perceived value.

Now, you can't come right out of the gate and just focus on your packaging. It is important to note that before you start working on your packaging, there are a few things that I recommend that you do.

Tighten your relationship with money.

If you don't believe that you can earn it, you won't. While you can make millions the hard way—with tons of small, low-end offers—I don't advocate for that. I believe that when you understand the problem you solve, you have a responsibility to offer access to the solution at a price point that demonstrates the value to be received for years to come upon accessing the solution. It will be challenging to do so if you don't understand money and have a strong, powerful, and positive relationship with it. Remember, money is energy. They don't call it currency for nothing; it is supposed to flow.

There is no shortage of money, only a shortage of personal belief, confidence, and connection to the energy that brings what we crave into our life experiences. Getting to this understanding about money and realizing that I do deserve to have more money than I can give, spend, invest, and save, is why I am a millionaire today. Yes, I made some sound investments. But it started with a belief that I deserved to defy the definitions of money my parents taught me. Since I now see money for what it is, there is never a shortage of money in my life or business. I can even go so far as to say that money will never be my problem.

Before you start to package your solution, you, too, need to understand that you are deserving of earning more in one transaction than you may have made when you worked in corporate America for a year. I still remember my client Jasmine's, who is a former schoolteacher, recent $249,000 launch. She was able to accomplish it because she understood that she could create money at the rate of her personal belief in her own worthiness. Because she tightened her relationship with money, she literally made more in one launch than most people in the country made in a year—in a matter of days!

Up-level your ideal client.

There are 7.888 billion people in the world[15] and a portion of them are your most ideal client, or pinnacle client, as I like to refer to them. When you reimagine your packages and ultimately price them based on the value and not your time, you'll have to be sure that you are doing so with a specific client in mind. Just like there are Kia's and Bentley's on the road at the same time, there are many who have the problem you solve. But not all of them will be ready, willing, and able to invest at the level accessing your solution demands. (Hint: You should be the Bentley.)

By going through the exercise to up-level your ideal client, you'll be able to take every asset and design it for those you desire to serve. When it comes to your ideal client, you think of them in three "buckets" or scenarios: those who just realized they have the problem you solve, those who have been dealing with the problem for a period of time, and those who are ready to do anything to eliminate the problem. Even within these three buckets, you'll quickly see how each has a varying level of commitment to solving the problem. Depending upon their level, they may feel that they have time to try out solutions instead of getting right to the one that will make the problem dissipate.

Part of the reason we give our clients a fifteen-page ideal client worksheet is because you have to know everything about your client so you can eventually use the words that will resonate with them and cause them to seek out your solution. Without adding the full worksheet in here, there are a few things you'll need to know about the types of clients who are ideal for your high-end offer, including:

- Who would they say they are?
- What would they say they are struggling with?
- What would they say they desire instead?
- What do they need to stop struggling?
- What beliefs are your ideal clients willing to do anything to protect?
- What are the biggest fears your ideal clients hold that threaten to keep them from the solution they seek?
- Where are they gathering in large enough numbers for you to gain traction in confronting them about their problem?

Answering these seven questions through the lens of demographics and psychographics will help you to create a pinnacle client profile so that you can speak directly to them in your marketing. We will delve deeper into the messaging in the next chapter.

Clarify your business model.

A business model is the process you utilize to make money in your business. Spoiler Alert: There are tons of business models, and they all work. The key is in finding the right business model for you. Business models fall into two categories: deep or wide. A wide business model is a model where you offer multiple products and services, typically seven, that range from free to the highest end. As you can imagine, inside of this business model, there will be a lot of offerings, often too many to keep track of in a way that will yield profit. Wide models have become famous as a result of online or internet businesses that take cold traffic and synthesize it into sales and eventually clients. They take the long road, selling smaller, Band-Aid offers to warm new prospects up for their higher-end, more complete offers.

Wide business models aren't ideal because they require lots of options in lots of price points. As the saying goes, you can't chase two rabbits and expect to catch either one. So, we typically recommend that instead of spending your energy on a wide business model, you develop a deep one. A deep business model is developed to equip and eliminate the full problem that your pinnacle client is currently aware of and looking to resolve. Deep models tend to offer longer, more robust solutions compared to their counterparts' Band-Aid offers. The offerings are made up of one complete solution and it is designed to honor your expertise at the highest level. With a deep business model, you will be able to truly solve your pinnacle client's problem and create an environment for them to experience release and elevation.

Most people think that wide models are easier. The truth is you're expending the same energy, but it will take longer to hit the point where you are able to cash in substantially. Typically, a wide model requires tons of traffic, most often in the form of advertising, which means that you are often barely breaking even from your lower-priced offers with the hope that they will turn into longer-term clients. The problem with this rationale is that often the prospect gets tired of the Band-Aids and goes in search of a real solution—especially once they realize that they will end up spending the same money, or more, if they started in a wide business model's ecosystem.

I'm going to save you the time of trying to develop the wide model and give you the cheat code to set up a deep business model. You'll serve your clients more deeply from the onset versus hoping that you'll bring in enough lower-ticket clients to make millions. By just doing the math, you can see how much faster your move to millions could be. When you take the time to get extreme clarity for your first million-dollar year, it will pay off dividends because you'll be able to simplify to multiply!

Up-level your signature business move, a.k.a. your signature system.

Your signature business move, or signature system, as most of the personal development industry calls it, is the key to being able to package, price, and position your offers so you can quickly get to your million-dollar milestone. Thinking about the process, framework, and methodology that you use, then thinking of the ideal client for it, will create an interesting dynamic for you to do your best work with your pinnacle clients. To start up-leveling your process that makes success predictable for your pinnacle client, get clear of their true desires and how you help them get exactly what they crave as fully as possible.

I remember when we updated our signature system. The Leverage Your Incredible Factor System had twelve steps. Twelve long steps. In full transparency, when people purchased our do-it-yourself program, they seldom made it all the way through the system to get the results—not because the system was flawed but because the additional steps caused people to feel discouraged. Therefore, they would stop working the system prior to the result showing up. That defeated the purpose. So, as we worked directly with our clients in one of our coaching programs, we could easily see where to cut some of the steps out or shorten the amount of time spent in an area. As a result, we noticed that we could condense the process without impacting the outcomes. After having taken more than one thousand clients and students through it, we realized that we could simplify the framework. When we did, those twelve steps became the four phases of the Move to Millions Method. By simplifying the framework, we've been able to get our clients to the result much quicker. Each year 10–20 percent of our clients have their first million-dollar year and the other 80–90 percent grow along the Move to Millions Continuum.

Since we noticed how simplifying our framework accelerated client results, we've begun to recommend that our clients undertake a similar process, which is why our curriculum includes a module on up-leveling your signature business move. We have clients retrace the steps of their system to identify those areas where they can simplify or deepen key components to improve results. Starting this for yourself will be simple.

Close your eyes and seeing the end results or outcome that your clients will achieve if they follow your process. Write that down. Then, take some time and journal on what it will be like for the client when they reach this result. Once you can see the end result, you simply back into the steps that help them to arrive there, one at a time. Look at documenting the steps this way: Now that you can see where you want your pinnacle client to end, what is the first step they must take to arrive at your end point? And the second? And the third? Fourth? Fifth? Sixth? Seventh?

Where possible, you want to try to get your system to seven steps or less. Seven steps make it palatable, and people can see how completing the steps will make their lives easier. It also gives them hope as we think in sevens naturally—seven days a week, seven dwarfs, and seven wonders of the sea. For those of you who understand the role that numbers play spiritually, seven means perfection and completion. Our goal is for your pinnacle clients to complete your system and experience the result that you are known for helping them achieve.

If you don't have a signature system yet, that's okay. Yes, you can get to the six-figure mark by accident, without your signature system being well thought out and ready to transform lives. Depending on where you have been prior to picking up this book, I want to be clear that to get to seven figures, you'll need a signature system. It's important that you think through the process you use *every time* with a client to make their success predictable. This system will become the foundation of your first seven-figure year.

Have documented results.

You'll have to have helped your clients get clear results that not only transformed some area of their life, but was also worth more than you charged them to access the result. Later in this chapter, we are going to talk about pricing. Your ability to raise your rates hinges on the value you can offer to those who choose you to solve their problems. I am absolutely, unequivocally not one of those coaches who says "charge what you're worth." No one could afford you. So, as we will walk through in a little while, your pricing has to be about the value you can provide and clearly articulate with a demonstration of proven results that you have helped others to achieve.

Once these five prerequisites are complete, you're ready to start thinking about your offer suite. Building high-value, high-end offers come from developing a solid Leverage + Scale Offer Suite. An offer suite is an important part of a deep business model. While there are several types of business models that work well in the deep model spectrum, we typically find that our pinnacle clients who are consultants, choose from one of three: live events, certifications, and high-end programs. Unless you choose live events, your goal should be to set your offers up in an evergreen format so that people can enroll any time to begin solving their problem with your help. As you build out your evergreen program, you get to choose whether you want to set it up as a progression or front-end/back-end model.

A progression means you don't progress to the next level until you finish the previous level. As you progress, typically, so does the support and outcomes. With a front-end/back-end model, you have a shorter starting point, followed by a longer immersion program. The front-end program is your prerequisite to going deeper into the transformation and results. For years in our business, we had a front-end/back-end model. Clients would start with our Leverage + Scale Accelerator, where they spent three months working with our team on their first three assets. Then, they could progress into our Move to Millions Mastermind, where they would develop the remaining four assets and scale to the million-dollar mark over one to three years. Progression type offer suites typically have three offers and front-end/back-end suites typically have two. This is going to sound counterproductive, but you only need *one* signature offer to make the move to millions. Let me show you what I mean.

Say you create a signature offer that solves a SPICE problem (a specific, pervasive, insurmountable, clear, and expensive problem) that your ideal client has been searching for a SPICE solution to (a specific, positive, intentional, clear, and evident solution). This solution could be easily packaged and positioned and sold at $25,000 for a program that has a group delivery container. Well, with this one signature offer, you'd only need to enroll forty clients who pay you in the calendar year to hit one million dollars in gross revenue. With one program that enrolls forty clients a year, or three to four clients a month, you can have a million-dollar company. This is the power of a signature offer.

If you realized that one signature offer doesn't denote an offer suite, you're correct. To turn your signature offer into an offer suite, you can choose to include up to two additional offers. We consider these a *superb* offer and a *select* offer. I like the idea of having both a superb and a select to round out your offer suite. If you are a coach, consultant, or trainer who is working primarily business-to-consumer, your offer suite will likely contain three offers: a superb, a signature, and a select. Now, your focus is always on your signature offer because one offer is all it takes to make millions. The superb, or downsell offer, is offered to prospective clients when the signature offer is not the most logical next step for them. Typically, if you present the superb, you feel that there is work they need to do before they can maximize the results and benefits of working with you in your signature offer. The select, or upsell offer, is offered to prospective clients who require or desire more support than your signature offer. Typically, a select offer is an offer that gives more private access to your clients. You have to be careful though, because private access isn't scalable. For coaches, consultants, and trainers, your offer suite might look like this:

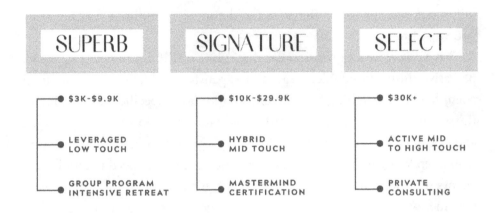

Similarly, as a coach, consultant, or trainer, if your ideal client is a small business owner, you may find you only need two offers in your offer suite, typically a signature and a select. It might look like this:

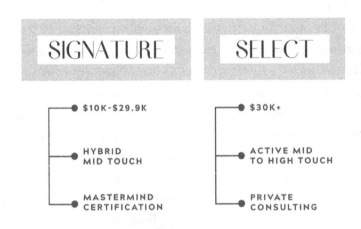

Now when you work with larger small businesses, nonprofits, or corporations your offer suite will be a little different. However, this gives you the gist of how to start the process of creating your offer suite.

To determine which is best for you, you'll have to once again think about your pinnacle client. If you work business-to-business, typically a front-end/back-end model will work best. If you work business-to-consumer, typically a progression model is best. Your offer suite is Move to Millions Continuum agnostic. It doesn't matter where you are and where you are looking to move. You need to go through the process of creating your offer suite in order to leverage the continuum to move to the next level. But there are no specifics based on where you start the journey and where you desire to finish.

The programs you design need to have SPICE: the solution must be specific, positive, intentional, clear, and evident. When it is, people will happily invest to access it. A SPICE solution delivers on one of the motivators. It will make, save, improve, reduce, protect, or increase something for your pinnacle client. Regardless of which you choose, you'll want to make sure that the program works the same for ten, one hundred, or one thousand enrollees. This is why private access is challenging—because it prevents scale. If you fail to think at scale, it can impact your ability to scale. You always want to look at ways of multiplying your income without increasing the amount of time you spend in service to your clients. You'll also want to make sure that you create a curriculum, roadmap, or defined path so that each client is working toward the solution you offer to the problem they've been unsuccessful at solving on their own. Lastly, avoid overcompensating, inflating, or overloading your programs in an attempt to cover for your lack of confidence or relationship with money.

When you determine your offer suite based on your ideal client and focus on getting your signature offer in front of them, you will start driving your business on the fastest path to the million-dollar milestone. I always recommend that your offer suite be simple because simplicity scales.

One of the things I love about having an offer suite that focuses on your signature offer is that you can serve your audience in a deeper, more transformational way. Your signature offer is the key to your business experiencing leverage and scale. The best part is that your signature offer is based on your signature business move, the exact framework you use that causes predictable results for your pinnacle client. Once you determine your offer suite, the next step is to figure out how to price it.

Million-Dollar Pricing

How to price your services is the number one question I answer as a business consultant—times three. I don't usually enjoy pulling prices out of the air. I have created a pricing calculator so that instead of choosing a number that "feels or sounds" good, you choose the number that leads to profitability. Listen to me. Having a company requires an understanding of your pricing. What you charge is not just for them to work with you. It's for you to be able to sustainably build a team and your company at the same time. Please keep in mind that we are talking about moving your business to millions. As such, there are three possible pricing models to choose from.

The first pricing model is low pricing. When you have access to a large volume of people for your offers, low pricing can work really well. That means your services are priced lower and will be more accessible to your customers. The second pricing model is high-end pricing. When you choose to price your services high, you're deciding that not everyone will be able to afford to have access to your services and solutions. There is nothing wrong with that. Just know that a higher pricing model, which I endorse and advocate for, means that you will serve less people more deeply. I love high-end pricing because it doesn't require you to have thousands of clients to hit the million-dollar mark. The final pricing model is parity pricing. Parity pricing is what we see in online businesses that attract clients through online marketing and advertising. In a parity pricing model, you start low and eventually you go high. Parity is actually my least favorite model because you work way too hard to get the clients you truly desire to serve. I also want you to know that all three pricing models work, just not at the same time. That is why I recommend that you pick the one that best brings your pinnacle client to you and master it. I also want to remind you that you're expending the same energy regardless of which pricing model you're using.

Yes, pricing trips so many people up. I get it. So many of us were not raised to understand money. We are trying to run businesses with our financial illiteracy unchecked.

It's sad, but so true.

That is all about to change.

This next part is going to feel a little weird, but stick with me. I am about to shift the way you look at your business and the money that comes into it. What comes out of your mouth comes into your life. So, we have to change what you speak over yourself and your business. By shifting what you say to yourself about money, you can watch your money change. Remember, money is an energy that has to move. It's constantly moving. It will move in your direction when you shift the energy you speak about it. Let's get started. Now, I need you to commit here. So unless you're listening in your car to the audio version, stand up and put your right hand in the air. Yes, you can hold the book in your left hand while you raise your right.

Repeat the following aloud:

I have a fiscal responsibility to myself, my family, and my business to operate as a business.

Don't put that hand down yet.

I do not offer insight or strategy as a complimentary service.

Okay, hand back in the air!

Undervaluing my products and services makes it impossible for me to deliver legendary service.

One more time for the people in the back!

I do not charge for my time; I charge based on the value and results I offer to those I serve.

While I believe that each of these statements are self-explanatory, I am unwilling to leave anything to chance. I created each of these statements for a coaching experience that builds the foundation of a million-dollar company, the Leverage & Scale Weekend. It was designed to teach new six-figure entrepreneurs how to lay the foundation for their first seven-figure year. It is a three-day virtual implementation retreat, where we work on three of the seven Million Dollar Assets: the offer suite covered in this chapter, the messaging suite, and the marketing suite. You might think that business owners at six figures know better when it comes to pricing, but they often don't. They likely chose prices that were someone else's in comparison or pulled a number that sounded like a lot. Your pricing is really a mirror of how you see yourself and the value you provide to the marketplace. If you feel inadequate, question your value, or wonder if you can actually help prospects get the results you claim, or think that what you earn means more hard work, that typically accompanies a lower price point. Therefore, most entrepreneurs are significantly underpriced, and it is why they are sitting in a seven-figure business making low six figures, if that.

You might be amazed to learn that every person who has come through our accelerator has struggled massively with associating their worth with the value of their offerings. Even though they are unrelated, because your client is not buying you, countless entrepreneurs associate their pricing with their own worth and worthiness. So, we use each of these four statements to shift what they are thinking by speaking what they must remember. Studies prove that the more you speak life-affirming statements over yourself, the more you shift the contrary behavior, which in this case, will help you to stop underpricing your services.[16]

Another misbelief that impacts pricing is the time versus results conundrum. You see, the average entrepreneur who was an employee first, enters entrepreneurship with the mindset of an employee who is used to getting paid by the hour. I certainly wasn't the last newly coined entrepreneur to think that charging $100 per session (which was an hour) was a lot of money *at first*. Take my client Bridgett Battles, for example. When we started working together more than ten years ago, she was charging $25 an hour to personally shop and style her clients. Bridgett started her business while working a full-time job. She admits that $25 an hour sounded like a lot because she was making the same amount she made at work but doing something she loved. Except, her clients weren't paying her for her time. They were paying her for the results she created for them by putting together a look that would match their brand and subject matter expertise when they took the stage at the conference they were sent to speak at on behalf of their company. They were hiring her to help them become more confident, exude executive presence, and leverage that image styling all the way to the C-suite. I bet if we asked one of her clients from even ten years ago, they'd say that working with her was priceless. Yet she had associated a price for it, and it was $25 an hour. At $25 an hour, she was working hard and barely making extra money.

That was until she met and hired me to be her business coach. The first thing I did for Bridgett was get her out of a by-the-hour pricing strategy. Instead, we created her offer suite, filled with three options that ranged from $2,500 to $10,000. The question I asked Bridgett that I am now asking you is: Why belittle your expertise by trying to drill it down into an increment of time? Charging by the hour is an employee-minded strategy, not an entrepreneur-minded one. If crossing the million-dollar mark is the goal, it's a mindset shift that you must make. And *quickly*. The truth is that more time doesn't make it better. People pay more for solutions to their biggest problems that are solved as quickly as possible. Bridgett got the lesson, and today, some ten years later, she is now enrolling clients into $25,000 packages while still working full-time with a thriving $250,000 business on the side. She's getting closer to moving into her business full time. The exciting thing is that she's got a million-dollar foundation upon which to build her company because she's learned how to package and price her services.

When people hire you, they are actually getting every book you've read, every hour you've studied, every expert or mentor you've learned from, every program or coach you've invested in to hone your skill, your years of life experience and practical application. They get all the mistakes you've made on the way to perfecting your solution, dollars spent on advanced degrees, certifications, or courses to perfect your expertise, and the work you put in to create a safe space for their transformation.

I am going to go against my better judgment as I say this. If you want to offer high-end pricing and you're not sure where to start the investment for your signature program and you have documented results from clients just like the ones you desire to attract, start at $10,000. Yes, it's worth $10,000. You're not just starting your business, and you have proof that your process works to get your clients results. Because you've been serving clients for years, you know that what you offer gives them a transferrable result. And $10,000 is the *floor* for your signature offer, not the *ceiling*. If you are as brilliant as I believe you to be, and you have helped others transform their lives, your work is more valuable to your clients than your pricing reflects. The transformation you will provide will make a return for them over the next five years. Ask yourself, "If someone handed me $10,000 or more, what would I offer them?" Before you add everything and the kitchen sink, remember that your package need only solve their problem. It doesn't have to include as much as you think. Think value and transferrable result, not "stuff."

Remember that benefits sell; features tell (your goal is to sell). So, focus on the benefits you can provide to solve their problem. Now, I recognize that suggesting that you charge $10,000 without coaching you might be a problem for you. If so, I understand. If you were a client, we would likely institute the Confidence Curve™ if you couldn't confidently see yourself charging $10,000 or more yet. I will share more about the curve a little later in this book. For now, just know that we have thought of how to best support you so we can get those prices to the level that will bring your million-dollar company into view based on the value you are already providing to your clients.

Once you raise your rates, you never lower them. You should always charge more when a client gets private access to you. If you focus on thinking about the value your solution will provide over the next five to ten years for helping your pinnacle client solve the problem, I think it will get easier to raise your rates! If this presents a challenge to you, to conquer the pricing challenge keep in mind that small minds don't close big deals. You will have to work on your money mindset every day (as often as you shower).

When it comes to setting your prices, you should now be clear on the value you provide for the transformation you offer. Start by understanding what your lifestyle goals are. If you personally want to earn six figures, your business needs should produce at least double. If you want six-figure cash flow, it needs to be four to five times your salary. Once you have thought through your lifestyle goals, you're ready to use my pricing for profitability formula. To help you determine the amount of money you'll need to live your ideal lifestyle, opt in and download our money MAP. It's waiting for you along with our other resources at https://www.movetomillionsbooks.com/resources.

Pricing for Profitability

As I have already stated, I believe in charging more than it costs to perform the service with excellence. I don't believe in discounting your services either. I actually learned about the value of price from my dad's mother, Nanny. Nanny was very clear that the cost was the cost, and your costs didn't go down when you gave the product away for less. To this day, I don't discount my services; the cost is the cost. Part of the reason that I devised these amazing pricing formulas for our clients was so that we could take the guesswork and emotion out of setting their prices. The calculator illuminates the price, considering all the variables in black and white.

The pricing for profitability formula for your signature program is:

Direct Costs + General & Administrative Costs + Overhead + [(Base Earnings Target[17] x the # of active hours) / # of clients] + Profit % = Price

I learned about Base Earnings Target from Dan Kennedy. In his book *No B.S. Time Management for Entrepreneurs*, Dan shares why entrepreneurs have a base target for earning versus an hourly rate. He further shares the formula to use to calculate your base earnings target:

Annual Personal Salary / 1,760 Hours x 3

I should warn you. The first time you use one of these formulas, you might swallow your tongue. The ending number may alarm you. However, the ending number is also what your program should be priced at to ensure that you get to experience profit at the transaction level and not at the end of the fiscal year, if you are lucky. We often have clients who can't wrap their mind around the rate the formula indicates they should charge. In those instances, we institute the Confidence Curve. The Confidence Curve is the pricing grace established between the suggested price and the price the client can confidently articulate in a sales conversation. My rule if we institute the curve is simple. You raise your rates after you enroll three clients at your Confidence Rate™. Your Confidence Rate is the rate you feel confident articulating when you meet with a prospective client. Experience has shown us that by the time the client has worked with three clients at their lower rate, they realize the error of their ways and are ready to raise their rates to where they should be based on the value they provide to the problem they solve! In case you are wondering, yes, I also had to institute a Confidence Curve in the early stages of my business. I was so afraid to charge what I deserved because I told myself that some income was better than none, more times that I can count. And I, too, found that after just a few clients who said yes too quickly, I was not going to keep underpricing my gifts. I raised those rates. In fact, the year we crossed the million-dollar mark for the first time was just because I started to charge what I deserved based on the value and transformation we provide.

As you round out this chapter, I just have one final thought for you. Make sure that your brand's investment matches your audience and what they expect to pay to experience the transformation you can provide.

Selah.

Chapter Action Plan

1. Create your Leverage & Scale Offer Suite.
2. Price your Leverage & Scale Offer Suite using the formula in this chapter.
3. Think of ten people who have expressed interest in working with you that you can call to share your new offer suite with.

Remember: Information without action is just a waste of time. So, make a plan to implement now so you are one move closer to your first million-dollar year.

Meet Crystal Perkins, CEO, God and Goals

While I was on stage speaking at an event, Crystal was applying for the Move to Millions Mastermind. It turns out that someone in that audience reached out to Crystal to tell her that she had just found her next coach. Crystal Perkins is a phenom. In and of her own brilliance, she is a bright beam of light and it brings me so much joy to work with her. When Crystal joined the mastermind in October 2021, her business was on track to finish the year at $500,000. By her one-year anniversary of joining the mastermind, Crystal crossed the million-dollar mark.

There were a few ways we supported Crystal to this milestone. First, we looked at her offers and messaging and helped her to up-level and tighten them. She's now got two powerful offers; one we'd consider signature and one we'd consider select. This, as I have already shared throughout this book, is pivotal. Second, we helped her develop some clear systems to start building a stronger team. She's now bringing on full-time employees to support her business versus running her contractors ragged with all she needs to fully operationalize her company. And lastly, we helped Crystal host her first ever three-day live event. With our help, she was able to fill a room with fifty ideal clients and generate more than $500,000 in just three days. Between these tactical strategies in our first year, Crystal joined our Moved to Millions Revenue Club and will be celebrated and speaking at Move to Millions Live 2023.

> *"Before working with Darnyelle and the IFU coaching team I was doing well in my business. Within this community, now I am doing amazing things. I love it here. The community, the coaching, and the support is top-notch. In one year in the mastermind, I made the Move to Millions and this community is the reason. The content is unparalleled. And access to the Leverage & Scale Enrollment Events course is a true game changer."*
> **—CRYSTAL PERKINS**

Her Continuum MOVE:
From Mastery to Millions in year one in the Move to Millions Mastermind.

CHAPTER SIX

Leverage + Scale Messaging Suite

"If you have millions on your mind, you'll need a compelling
message on your lip."
—DARNYELLE JERVEY HARMON

When I was ten years old, I realized my superpower. I actually have Mrs. Dixon, my fifth and sixth grade teacher, to thank for uncovering it at such a young age. By the time I got to Mrs. Dixon's class, she was exactly what God had ordained. She saw my potential and honed in on it by starting me on a path to write my thoughts down. Those thoughts turned into a love of reading. By the time I hit high school, I was in a full-blown love affair with words. Those words, which I devoured like peanut butter candy cakes after school, were my safe place. My haven. I started writing stories almost immediately, and I learned how to hone my words through public speaking as well. Many considered me a natural. I learned early that with the right words you could get someone to do whatever you wanted.

Whatever you wanted.

Now, more than thirty years later, I am still leveraging the power of words and my ability to use them to create an opportunity for people to get out of their own way and get into the transformation they are seeking at their next level. That is why the second Million Dollar Asset is the Leverage & Scale Messaging Suite. Remember when I said in the last chapter that people will pay more than you think for the right program that has been packaged and positioned well? In the last chapter, we covered the packaged part. In this chapter, we will cover the positioned part.

Positioning is a fancy way of stating using words in a way that induces immediate action. Your message is how you get known in the marketplace. Your message must be clear, succinct, confident, and not watered down. The more courageous you are to emphatically state who you serve and who is right for your offers, the more you'll be able to validate your positioning and confirm that your message is connecting with your pinnacle client. Your pinnacle client, when they consume your message, if your message is compelling, will connect with it deeply as it will touch each part of their brain and overcome their three biggest beliefs, all at the same time. I call this the message-to-market connection. You'll know you've connected when you use the words that evoke emotion and drive tactical change. This means that people are enrolling in your programs. If we were in one of my workshops or coaching programs, I would likely start by having you take an audit on your brand messaging. In fact, when you visit https://www.movetomillionsbook. com/resources, I will share that audit with you. It's very eye-opening, and it will give you an indication of where you need the most work from a brand messaging and market connection perspective. Your move to millions will be accelerated or delayed based on your messaging.

Yes, messaging is that important. After all, it's how a prospective client will know that they can look to you for help solving their problem. The truth is there is a lot of noise in the marketplace. Do you realize that in a twenty-four-hour period:

- 294 billion emails are sent,
- 2 million blog posts are written,
- 864,000 hours of video are uploaded . . . to YouTube alone,
- 48 million Google searches are conducted,
- 2.4 million tweets are posted,
- 16.4 million pieces of content are shared on Facebook, and
- 95 million posts are made on Instagram.

You'll notice that TikTok is not on that list. That should tell you there is even more noise in the marketplace today than is shown in this 2019 report.[18] Now, unlike most "marketers" who are contributing to this noise, you'll be different. You're about to learn my secret, which will help you shift from what most messaging includes into a little something I like to call SPICE messaging. To position your business on the Move to Millions, you'll need to make sure that your messaging connects deeply with your pinnacle client. I remember when I first introduced SPICE messaging to my clients. They were blown away. Never had they seen, as they shared with me, a way to isolate the power of the problem and pain points their clients were facing in messaging in a way that clearly and confidently articulates the problem they solve and the solution they provide. As I shared, it's my gift. I am able to literally inhabit my client and give them a marketing message that not only resonates with their clients and audience, but actually makes them money! I am notorious for creating the templates and cheat sheets they need to plug and play their messaging so that it gets the traction they need to accelerate their sales.

To reach your pinnacle clients, your message must be clear, concise, consistent, confident, compelling, contrarian, and most importantly, it must answer two questions: Will it work for me? And what's in it for me? The fastest way to hit all of these filters is by crafting a contrarian message. Contrarian, by definition, means that you are saying something that goes against what other "experts" are saying. It is very similar to former First Lady Michelle Obama saying, "When they go low, we go high." A contrarian message is one that your pinnacle client won't see coming. For example, I had the foresight to create this contrarian message:

A low six-figure business is small business poverty!

Let's examine the phrase to break down its contrarian nature. First and foremost, anyone who had visions of six figures will scoff at the thought of hearing anyone talk this way about that "much" money. Simultaneously, any entrepreneur who's actually made low six figures, let's call it $120,000 a year, knows that I am right! Let's just do the math. By the time you take out the self-employment tax, which is currently 15.3 percent[19], you're already down to $101,640. You haven't paid your income taxes yet, which will fall between 18–25 percent, depending on a few other variables. Let's take the median of 21.5 percent and subtract that from the remaining $101,640. Now we are down to $79,787.40. Surely, that is a good income. Right? Wrong. We haven't taken care of other business expenses. Let's say you spend $10,000 for marketing for the year, $2,500 for software and support tools, you have a part-time virtual assistant that is $18,000 a year, and already that $79,787.40 is down to $49,287.40. That is assuming that you handle almost everything else yourself to keep costs low. You probably made more at your job. And I don't know about you, but you probably didn't quit your "good job" to make less out on your own in the land of entrepreneurship.

I certainly didn't.

I ended up going back to work at the onset of Incredible One Enterprises because I couldn't keep up with the expenses. I also didn't have a book like this.

Now, while that side bar has nothing to do with the contrarian statement, it backs it up. Your contrarian statement must also be a true one. When your messaging is contrarian, it will incite an emotional response from your pinnacle client. Your message should be 93 percent emotional and 7 percent logical. Those same prospective clients, after they get over how you upset them, will come face-to-face with the reality and seek you out, especially when your message focuses on a problem that they are clear they have, elicits an emotion, shares an educational viewpoint, and offers an experience. When your message does each of these things, it will increase your reach above the noise.

We are not in the business that we think we are in. We are instead in the business of marketing and sales. To that end, every single one of us has an ideal market. Within that market, we will typically see it break down this way:

- 3%   Love Your Products/Services
- 7%   Consider Hiring You
- 30%   Know Where You Are If They Need You
- 30%   Have No Idea Who You Are
- 30%   Are Not Interested In Your Products/Services

Sadly, most marketers (that's you) spend all of their time on the 3 percent they already have investing in everything they bring to market and the 30 percent that are not interested in their products or services. When they do this, they actually leave a juicy 67 percent of their market unserved by their messaging. It will look like this:

- ~~3%~~ ~~Love Your Products/Services~~
- 7% Consider Hiring You
- 30% Know Where You Are If They Need You
- 30% Have No Idea Who You Are
- ~~30%~~ ~~Are Not Interested In Your Products/Services~~

Here is what I know: If you can learn how to create messaging that will speak to the 67 percent your current message isn't reaching, you will expand your reach and have more than enough people to share your programs with so you can cross the million-dollar mark without having to spend all of your time working.

SPICE messaging, which is the backbone of your Leverage & Scale Messaging Suite, is based on the universal law of business. It tells you to get found by a group of people (your pinnacle client) who have the *exact* SPICE problem you solve and are ready right now to invest in a SPICE solution to that problem. Before you can craft a marketing message that cuts through the noise in the overly crowded marketplace, you have to dig deep into getting clarity about the SPICE problem you solve and how that problem is wreaking havoc in the lives of your pinnacle clients. If that's not enough to get straight, your message has to demonstrate the problem, pain points, and the solution if you want to get and keep traction all the way to the million-dollar mark. If you intend to attract a higher end, more sophisticated affluent clientele, your content will have to address what is currently challenging them, making them uncomfortable, and forcing them to stretch. The only way to do that is to speak to their mindset. When your messaging causes a massive identity shift, whatever you're positioning to sell will become irresistible. If you do not leverage your messaging to dismantle their current limiting beliefs, they'll throw you out with the bathwater.

This is where most entrepreneurs and small business owners go wrong. They create surface-level marketing messages instead of messages that cut their prospects so deeply that hiring them is their only choice. Not mastering your message will stunt your business growth and keep you muddling in mediocre performance and traction for your business, regardless of what is going on in the economy. But when you craft a marketing message that is not about you—which means you don't have to like it—you can get the attention of your pinnacle client and start their journey toward transformation.

When your pinnacle client is a client who will pay premium or high-end prices for service, your message becomes even more important. For them, your message must be all about what's in it for them. Typically, the high-end buyer values inclusion, status, and exclusivity. Translation: You can't (and won't) be for everyone. Niching becomes more essential as you desire to charge more. It's important to keep in mind that having access to you comes at a premium. Your anointing, your gift, your expertise, and your results, cost you a lot. That is why your message must be elevated to speak to the client who is at the level to understand and appreciate your solution to their problem.

Before you begin creating the messaging in your marketing suite, you need to be clear on each of the following: (1) your pinnacle client; (2) your unique value and selling propositions; (3) your offers and value; (4) your call to action; (5) sales psychology; and (6) how you want consumers of your messaging to feel. There are two that I want to go deeper on for you: sales psychology and your pinnacle client, whom I will refer to as your "audience of one."

Let's focus on sales psychology first. Sales psychology is about how your client thinks. You have to know how they think in order to craft messaging that's going to get their attention, cut them deeply and emotionally, and position them to make the logical decision to take the next step with you. From a sales psychology standpoint, there are a few things to keep in mind:

- When selling high-end, you have to be clear on the dream outcome of your client and why they would do *anything* to experience that dream outcome.
- Price is never an issue when value is clear and present.
- People want access to the best there is (exclusivity).

- When it costs more, people believe that less can have it. That makes it more desirable.
- People buy for emotional reasons, but they justify their action with logic. Your goal is to give them the justification they need, the *why* they bought.
- People act for self-serving reasons only. Your messaging must relate to their needs, wants, and desires for solving *their* problem.
- You cannot motivate anyone into action without intensely stimulating emotion.
- You cannot instill or create a desire or a problem in people. You can only awaken or agitate one that already exists in their minds.
- Less options make it easier for people to see themselves shifting because of your solution.
- When you tap into their emotion concerning their challenge, your price ceases to matter. That is why no matter what you charge, you should charge more *if* you can deliver a SPICE outcome (you also don't have to alert them to your price).

The reason sales psychology is so important is because it taps into all three parts of the brain of your pinnacle client so that you can leverage your messaging to get their attention and position your solution to their problem. Once you understand these important components of sales psychology, which will aid your desire for clients to convert, you are ready to go deeper on your pinnacle client, or audience of one.

I refer to your pinnacle client as your audience of one because messaging is a conversation that you have with one type of person, who has one clear problem that you provide one robust solution to quickly and efficiently. To solidify the audience that your message will be for, ask yourself the following questions (some of these questions likely look familiar as I mentioned then during the chapter about the Move to Millions Method):

- **Who would they say they are?** Use the words they would use to describe themselves so that they self-select into your ecosystem. This typically starts by identifying the strongly held label that they'd use to describe themselves. Labels like mom, entrepreneur, diva, disruptor, and leader are all examples of strongly held labels.

- **What would they say they are struggling with the most, and what's causing them pain?** Again, you want to use the words that they would use because it makes it easier to get their attention. A person who is in pain is actively looking for a painkiller. If Excedrin didn't make it obvious that it was for headaches, people wouldn't grab it when they had one. You have to be bold about what they are struggling with because this is a signal that you must have a solution.

- **Why is your audience willing to do almost anything in order to experience a different reality, eliminate their full problem, or amplify their next level?** When you understand how your pinnacle client thinks, it's a game changer. You literally have to get into their minds so you can craft messaging that brings to the forefront their beliefs, insecurities, and greatest desires. Your solution will have to be formulated in a way that it answers this question. You have to take the time to figure out what they'd do to experience in their life, eliminate from their life, or amplify and enjoy more of in their life.

- **What stories are they telling themselves?** Your pinnacle client is stuck in their head. They have bought into a belief that never served them, but they don't know how to let it go. They need you to show them how to radically dismantle those limiting beliefs and stories that are holding them back from the level they desire.

- **What beliefs are they protecting with everything they hold to be true?** This is an important question because what is *really* stopping your pinnacle client from achieving their big goals is their ego. They have fully convinced themselves that what they're experiencing is part of their journey. Except, it's not.

- **What do they most need to shift out of their limiting beliefs and stop the pain and struggle?** This will be your SPICE solution. Because you have been studying them, you should know what they most need. This information is likely gained through both primary and secondary research. Primary research is when you are talking directly to your audience. Secondary research is based on what someone else has learned about your audience.

- **What, if they heard you say it, would stop them in their tracks to learn more because it goes against everything they know and believe about their biggest, SPICE-iest challenge?** Contrarian is the new conversion. If you want to get out of the sea of sameness, you have to say the things that your "competitors" aren't saying. In messaging, the best thing you could do is go left when everyone else is going right because your pinnacle clients are programmed to notice what is different.

- **What is waiting for them on the other side of the struggle or fear?** When you know what they desire instead of what they're experiencing, you can paint them a picture with your message that shows what is possible. The possibility is what opens them up to looking at the problem from a different vantage point and ultimately seeing you as the solution.

- **Where do they gather in large enough numbers?** When you know where to find them, you and your message can show up there as often as you need to achieve your goals. You'll always find traction because your message will resonate and cause them to connect emotionally. Remember, the sale is 93 percent emotion and 7 percent logic.

Once you are clear about your audience of one, you are ready to dig deep into their SPICE problem. SPICE™ is an acronym that stands for:

Specific & Substantive

A specific, substantive message is specially targeted to an area that will be easily identified and recognized by the person with the problem. A specific message is clearly identified so that there is no question as to what you might be referring to. Messages that exude these qualities go beneath the surface. They are meaningful and impact filled. They actually force the consumer of the message to confront their problem head on. Starting your messaging with a hook or headline that is specific is a great way to get and keep attention.

Pervasive & Persistent

When you think about the problem your audience has, it should be affecting them like a rash. If you've ever had a rash, you know how pervasive and persistent it can be! When you speak to your audience in your messaging, you want to remind them of how their problem will only get worse and more aggressive until they access your solution.

Immediate & Insurmountable

You'll know it's a SPICE problem when it needed to be solved yesterday, but despite their best efforts, your audience has been unsuccessful at solving it on their own.

Clear, Conscious & Contrarian

This art of the SPICE problem filter is really about the audience. Your pinnacle client should be clear and conscious that their problem exists; otherwise, you're operating outside of the universal law of business. This will increase the amount of time they spend in your sales cycle. Equally, you should be clear in describing who they are and what their challenges tend to be. To display this, you'll refer to them by their strongly held label. This label starts the emotional connection very early in the messaging process. Your message should confidently articulate how you have become aware of this and, more importantly, how you can solve the problem.

Expensive & Expansive

The longer the problem goes unsolved, the bigger it gets and the more it costs them. Let's be clear. Money talks. This applies to your audience as well. The expense typically starts like a whisper. First, it's barely noticeable. They just keep feeding the problem. But eventually, it starts to scream. The scream is the equivalent to a major purchase all because they didn't seek the help they needed at the moment the problem started.

Each of these have to be present in your message in order to paint the picture they need to see to realize that you are their *only* and *obvious* choice. Once you have validated that the problem you solve is a SPICE problem, you're ready to make sure that the problem hits all of the categories that impact the lives of your pinnacle clients, including (1) identity/purpose/legacy; (2) health/wellness/mental health; (3) love/relationships/communication; (4) money/career/business; (5) time/life balance; and (6) happiness/fulfillment. You should be able to draw a parallel to each category if you truly solve a SPICE problem.

Your motivators are what truly validate that the problem you solve has SPICE. A SPICE problem also hits all of the categories of motivation, making it a no-brainer for a prospective client to make an investment in themselves to access your solution: make, save, improve, reduce, protect, and increase. As you review your message, make sure you can speak to how your solution provides a result that includes all six of the motivators.

When I first started helping my Move to Millions Mastermind client Dr. Pamela Ellis with her messaging, she could immediately see the difference as to why she wasn't able to get traction consistently. In her own words, her message was "hit or miss." But once we drilled down her audience of one and she spoke to them every time she sat down to write marketing copy, it got easier and easier to connect with them in writing. The more confident her message became, the more ideal clients she attracted to her ecosystem. Tightening her messaging definitely aided her on the move to millions. This year, she was able to double her business again and come just shy of the half-million-dollar mark.

There's just one last important component of SPICE messaging: to be truly effective, you have to deepen the SPICE. This is a true game changer for your messaging. Remember those life categories I mentioned earlier? This phase of your messaging plan is all about diving deeper into how each area of your audience's life is impacted by their SPICE problem. Deepening the SPICE makes sure that the message-to-market connection is strong. Deepening the SPICE ensures that your message resonates at the highest of levels, breaking through the barriers your prospect has built up to continue to say no to themselves. Taking the time to think of the symptoms and scenarios your pinnacle client finds themselves in translates into powerful copy that converts.

For example, say that your audience's real problem is that they haven't been successful in raising their rates and having anyone pay them. More than likely, if this is their problem, they are constantly questioning their value and worth. They feel like a failure or imposter. They secretly look for a job because they can't figure out their business. As a result, they are under undue amounts of stress and find themselves spending more time alone, isolated from their loved ones, in fear that they will ask about their business, and they will be embarrassed to share the truth of how their business is doing. Because they are working all the time, they are missing out on important family moments. They are stuck, unhappy, and unfulfilled. See what I did there? That is a brief, albeit powerful, example of deepening the SPICE.

Once you have thoroughly run the problem you solve through the filter and deepened the SPICE, you're ready to start working on your full-blown Leverage & Scale Messaging Suite. This suite houses all things messaging. Taking the time to break messaging down into its own category, first and foremost, is a disruption. Most entrepreneurs and small business owners lump it all together as "marketing." But here's the thing: Messaging will determine *if* your message ever gets seen through marketing. So, you need a message that hinges on a strong, powerful, SPICE problem and one that offers a SPICE solution and outcome, in order to demonstrate that you have a compelling message that makes it clear to prospects that you can help them. When you base your message on the SPICE problem and the solution you offer to said problem, you'll start to rise above the noise.

Your messaging suite will include:

- **Your Pinnacle Client Profile.** Have a copy of everything you know about your pinnacle client as a part of your messaging suite so that, before you sit down to create copy (or send the task to a copywriter), you are in the mind frame of the client. You have validated that the solution will solve their problem. Your message will get traction in the marketplace, and it won't fall into the Sea of Sameness many have become accustomed to hearing and seeing. Your pinnacle client is your aspirational client, the client you know that, if you served them, would experience the result you are known for.
- **Key Messages Document.** This is a living, breathing document that holds all of your messages. It is best kept as a Google Doc if you have other team members who will need it.

- **Must-Have Marketing Messages.** These are the ten messages that you will use most often as you share your business in general and specific programs with qualified contacts.
- **Calls to Action.** These are the action-oriented statements that will accompany every piece of copy you share. Never share a message without a call to action.
- **Brand Messaging Cheat Sheet.** This is your digest document to be shared with your team so that everyone is on the same page with your message and messaging. This creates consistency amongst your team so that the same message is being conveyed by everyone in your company.
- **Compelling & Contrarian Sound Bites.** I recommend that you have at least twenty-five compelling sound bites that you can leverage in your marketing for short videos, tweets, memes, and headlines. These are designed to quickly gain attention and promote a need to learn more.
- **Email Sequences.** There will always be emails to send to your marketing list (more on this in the next chapter). These emails will be housed in your messaging suite.
- **Sales Page Copy.** Your web pages that are positioned to promote a product or service will need a sales page. All of your sales page copy will be housed in your messaging suite.
- **Video Scripts.** Scripts for your long- and short-form video will be housed here. Yes, you should start scripting your video! It ensures that you keep your message succinct. We now live in the time when short-form video trumps all other content.
- **Signature Stories.** Your suite should also house your story vault. It will share all of the stories that you can and should share when speaking or training, when on social media, or when engaging in sales conversations. Always remember that nothing converts better than a well told story.

As you round out this chapter, I just have one final thought for you. Your messaging is the key to building authority so that you'll be seen as a thought leader in the marketplace. That authority will lead to more opportunities to attract and retain more clients. Take your time developing this suite. Revisit and add to it often. As you up-level your audience of one, you'll need to tweak and tighten your message.

Selah.

Chapter Action Plan

1. Confirm that you solve a SPICE problem by running that problem through the SPICE filter.
2. Write your scenarios that deepen the SPICE problem.
3. Start your messaging suite.
4. Post a message from your suite on the social media platform where your pinnacle client spends the most time to see if you get traction.

Remember: Information without action is a waste of time. Make a plan to implement now so you are one move closer to your first million-dollar year.

Meet Dr. Erica Jordan Thomas, EJT Education Group

I was introduced to Dr. Erica via another client in our Move to Millions Mastermind. Dr. Erica immediately impressed me as a former principal and consultant for educators of color. She enrolled in the program in October 2021. Now in her second year in the mastermind, Dr. Erica has truly embodied becoming a CEO. I have watched her shift from $30,000 months to $100,000 months, and from a solopreneur to CEO with full-time team members. I have watched her push her own limits and kick her limiting beliefs to the curb. She's increased her leadership skills and made decisions as a multimillion-dollar CEO.

Our work together has included raising her rates, helping her to streamline and tighten her service delivery, plan her first live event (which when I met her wasn't even on her radar), and work on her business operational systems.

Within her first sixty days in the mastermind, she had her first multi-six-figure launch, and in her first year in our mastermind, she held her first live event, Six Figure Educator Live. Between the two, she crossed the million-dollar mark. Through our work, her systems and strategies are evolving. I truly love watching her shine.

"I've made the move to millions with the help of Darnyelle and the IFU Team. Before working with Darnyelle I had a solid multiple six figure business, and I knew that millions were on the horizon for me. Crossing the million-dollar mark wouldn't have been possible without Darnyelle and the IFU Coaching team. From the moment I've stepped into this powerful community, I've been up leveled in so many ways. With the IFU team's help we experienced a $300,000 launch right away and went on to host my first event and generate $620,000 in three days! I've hired full time employees and am consistently stepping up my CEO leadership game. Their input has been both invaluable and immeasurable. The coaching, community, and safe space Darnyelle creates is unmatched. I'm so grateful."

DR. ERICA JORDAN THOMAS

Her Continuum MOVE:

From Mastery to Millions in year one in the Move to Millions Mastermind.

CHAPTER SEVEN

Leverage + Scale Marketing Suite

"Marketing is the oxygen of any business. If you don't master it,
your business won't live very long."

—DARNYELLE JERVEY HARMON

When I was fourteen years old, I had my first experience with marketing. In my geography class, our teacher gave us an assignment. We had to research a state and present a report to the class. We had to build a case that demonstrated why our assigned state was the best state in the union. I was assigned to Nebraska. *Nebraska*. I didn't even know if there were black people in Nebraska. But I did my research and due diligence, and I created my presentation. I had so much fun researching the people, places, and things that made the state great.

As I put my presentation together, I appealed to our classmates from different angles. For our cheerleaders and football team, my focus was on entertainment. For our studious bunch, my focus was on history and state facts. I found that by segmenting the class by their interests, it was easy to demonstrate what would be in it for them to move to Nebraska. My approach was spot on. Not only did I get a standing ovation upon finishing my presentation, but I also won because 88 percent of the class wanted to move to Nebraska thanks to my presentation. When Mr. Remsburg asked key members of the class why they chose Nebraska, resoundingly, the class stated that my presentation spoke directly to their needs and desires. It was then that I knew that I could use my words to get people to take the actions I wanted them to take.

That's marketing.

I love marketing. The way I saw it, it was really about leveraging my words to get people to do what I wanted, needed, or felt was best for them. As I recount that tenth grade Geography class, I realize that, even back then, I had the makings of a marketer.

Right off the bat, I want to make sure that you understand that you are not in the business you think you are in. Your title is not really what you do or who you are. You, me, and every other small business owner on the planet is a marketer. We are in the business of marketing our products and services. To experience mastery in this area as you move to millions, that has to be your first realization.

For real.

It's going to be important because there are so many moving parts of marketing. With the number of new strategies and tools that pop up seemingly every day, it will be even more important that you get clear about which are vital to your ability to attract and retain ideal clients. So many business owners are so afraid of marketing; or they don't like it or understand it. The truth is we are all marketing every day, all day. When I ran the women's business center years back, I developed a series of marketing workshops that later became a part of my core curriculum. I developed a knack for explaining marketing in a way that made sense and, more importantly, wasn't daunting.

I share my marketing formula in my book *Market Like a ROCK Star*. Marketing is often misunderstood, which is why people struggle with leveraging it. But there is no way your business can grow to the heights you desire if you are reading this book without it. Marketing is one of the hottest topics in the business world. But it's also one of the most misunderstood topics in business.

Because you are really in the business of marketing your products and services, you'll need to make a poignant shift to learn how to leverage marketing as a strength for deepening your impact in the marketplace. While you have experienced some success in your business at this point, I don't want to assume that you understand marketing enough to skip breaking this suite down in an elementary fashion. When we onboard a new client into our Move to Millions Mastermind, we ask them to complete a series of assessments for their business. We do one assessment on each of the seven areas of their company. Even when we have clients who have made $500,000 in the year prior to working with us, we go through this process and always find gaps and holes that, once plugged, will accelerate them achieving seven figures in their business.

Without a focus on marketing, or deploying your message, you'll remain a best-kept secret and, more importantly, a low six-figure broke secret. Whenever I have an opportunity to speak to audiences, I remind them of this fact: It's seldom about what you're selling. It's always about how you package and position it! And that, Incredible One, is what marketing is all about—deploying a well-positioned message.

Marketing is simply a conversation you have with people who have the problem that you solve. Your marketing copy simply lets them know you're the one who can help. When I am working with my clients who have struggled with marketing in the past, I help them to make the shift in the way they look at marketing by simply considering marketing to be a conversation. When they look at it in this way, it removes the anxiety and positions them to get traction from their ideal clients.

Let me share my personal definition of marketing with you. Marketing is the act of creating a SPICE message, then deploying that message through the appropriate delivery system to a defined target market of your pinnacle client in a way that will have them willingly make an emotional investment in it.[20]

There are at least fifty ways you could be marketing at any time in your business. The key is to identify the five to seven ways that will bring your audience of one, or pinnacle client, into view. You likely won't use all five to seven at once. You'll test the five to seven to arrive at your Incredible One, the one tried-and-true marketing strategy that delivers qualified leads that become paying clients as they work through your marketing system.

To leverage the power of all the marketing at your disposal, it's important that you understand your pinnacle client. It is easy to get distracted. New trends will pop up daily. Set your marketing intentions on your pinnacle client and take actions that only bring your pinnacle client into view. For instance, at the time of writing this book, five-day challenges are a big deal. They work. But you have to make sure that your pinnacle client is a challenge person. Not everyone will participate in challenges. If they aren't going to show up every day for five days to learn your framework and make an investment decision after multiple days, it might be better to hold introduction events. Over five hours, you teach everything you'd present over five days. You can also host webinars that are sixty minutes. Taking the time to clarify what your pinnacle client responds to best will save you time and money.

Marketing will only be as good as your due diligence about your pinnacle client. In our coaching programs, we walk our clients through a fifteen-page questionnaire about their pinnacle client. It's vital to know everything—except for maybe the client's underwear color—to create messaging and use the right strategies to get their attention.

The Leverage + Scale Incredible One, also referred to internally as the Business Success Formula™, is what we teach our clients to master when it comes to marketing that makes millions. We like to refer to this set of strategies as a formula rather than a funnel. It allows you to continue to circulate prospective clients versus a traditional funnel where the lead goes in the top and comes out the bottom if you aren't able to quickly shift them from cold to hot. The beauty of this formula is that it works business-to-business and business-to-consumer as well as in online marketing and offline marketing. Let's walk through each component of the Business Success Formula:

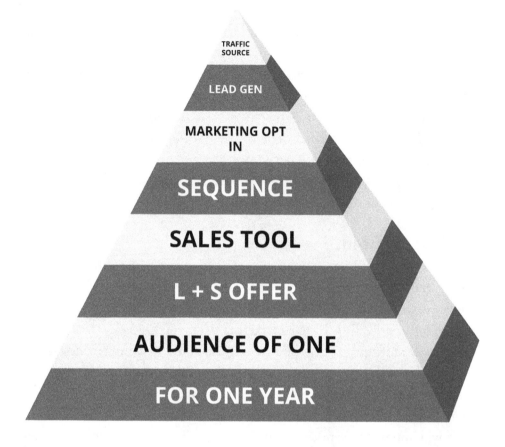

Traffic source

In order to get pinnacle clients into your programs, you first have to get them to know that you exist through driving volumes of them into your business's ecosystem, funnel, or sales cycle. When it comes to traffic, you really have three options. Organic traffic is traffic that you build through your own efforts. Paid traffic is traffic that you buy through advertising or sponsorship. Partnership traffic is traffic that you borrow through established relationships with colleagues, communities, and your network. It also means gathering your ideal clients and serving them in ways that are different, but complementary, from the way you intend to serve them.

Lead generator

Once you have traffic flowing your way, you'll need a way to get it to stop long enough to learn more about you. Your lead generator does that. There are at least fifty ways to generate leads. These ways are broken down into online generators, offline generators, and generators that work both online and offline. The good news is that new ways to generate leads are being developed every day. The bad news is that knowing which will bring your pinnacle clients closer may take some time and testing. This is why we advocate for first identifying the five to seven tactics that could become the one that you focus on.

Marketing opt-in

Once the traffic and lead generators are defined and proven to yield leads, you'll need a marketing opt-in tool to collect their marketing data (name, social media handle, phone, and email) so you can continue to market to them consistently. To get their marketing data, you'll develop a marketing opt-in or lead magnet. The e-book, checklist, audio download, video series, webinar, white paper, etc. must be juicy enough for them to be willing to give you their information before they disengage. This is why you have to study your pinnacle client and get into their minds. You have to figure out what will appeal to them so much that they'd be willing to give you their email address, full name, social media handles, and cellular phone number. When they do give you all four, you have everything you need to market to them via traditional emails, text messages, direct messages on social media, and good old-fashioned telephone calls. Your campaign sequences should include all of these to move them through your Business Success Formula.

Nurture and conversion sequence

Once you have their email and cell phone number, you're going to send them an automated sequence that includes both email and text messages, and maybe even phone calls. Making welcome calls has been one of our best demonstrated practices for years. Prospects love to hear from us. We make this part of our nurture and conversion sequence. This sequence typically covers the first fourteen to thirty days that they are in your community. This helps build the know, like, and trust factor and gets them to self-select into your sales tool so you can help them. I highly recommend that you tighten your sequence so that you strike while the lead is hot to qualify them. If you have the capacity to offer phone calls to welcome them to your community, please do. This has truly been a game changer for us.

Sales tool

While we will go deep into sales tools as a part of the next chapter on the Leverage + Scale Sales Suite, for now, I will say that you want to identify the one way you will focus on bringing new clients into your business. There are six different sales tools to choose from I will tell you all about in the next chapter.

Audience of One

You've already read about your ideal audience, or pinnacle client. The important thing to note is that your whole success formula starts with being clear about who can most benefit from your solution to their problem. And if you desire to up-level your programs, you also need to up-level your audience. Trying to get previous prospects to enroll in higher-end services is like trying to sell bottled water to someone currently drinking water. It's not likely to work. I typically recommend that when a client is performing their year-end company review, they evaluate their pinnacle client to see if adjustments are needed. This greatly impacts your marketing efforts.

Focus on each of these for one year. I have found that, by doing so, you can cross the million-dollar mark like thirty-eight of our clients have, including Dr. Madeline Lewis and TerDawn Deboe. It actually only took Dr. Madeline nine months to make the move. Dr. Madeline is an executive coach and consultant who works primarily with corporations. Dr. Madeline worked with me in our Strategic Business Retreat where over three days, I spent time helping her to refine her first four Million Dollar Assets. By the end of our retreat, her offers were updated, her messaging was tight, and she had a new plan for her marketing and sales suites, too. She went home and got to work. Nine months of focusing later, she was elated to call me with the news. She crossed the million-dollar mark in her executive coaching firm, and she also won the Enterprising Woman of the Year award for new million-dollar companies. What I love about the Business Success Formula™ is that it works no matter who you serve. Focusing in this way gets you to your next milestone in record time, if you're consistent.

TerDawn, who runs a marketing and branding agency and a coaching program, started ascending the continuum within thirty days of working with me in our Leverage + Scale Accelerator (the updated version of the Strategic Biz Retreat Dr. Madeline attended). Just by helping TerDawn to shift her signature offer to one she could easily charge $25,000 for, she brought in $125,000 in her first thirty days in our program. She went on to double that in the ninety days through completing the program. By the end of that year, TerDawn's focus on up-leveling her client and shifting her offer suite and business model presented her with her first million-dollar year when she held her first live event and got a major corporate contract.

When I started my business, I tried *everything* to market, and you already know how successful that was. I filed bankruptcy and ended up back in the workforce within a year of starting Incredible One Enterprises. As the saying goes, I didn't know what I didn't know. What I thought I knew kept me from being open to learn what I needed to know. I realize now that it is because I was doing too much, chasing every bandwagon, trying every strategy, and not giving them time to work, that I couldn't get enough traction to avoid both the bankruptcy and returning to work. I didn't even take the time to do market research. I just got right into "grind mode" and it cost me so much.

Today, I like to make sure that, no matter how far you've already gotten in your business, I take the time to make sure that a marketing suite is designed to do the heavy lifting for you. Making millions will not happen without a marketing suite. With a clear marketing suite, focus can happen almost naturally. Had I realized this at the onset of building this company, I likely wouldn't have had to go back to work and moonlight to learn the lesson! The truth is I am easily distracted and live for a new bright, shiny object to take my attention away from where it is supposed to be. My early marketing style was the same. I had no idea that the answer was to set my sights on one thing. Once I honed in on my marketing reins, I found *the* strategy that worked for me. It brought my pinnacle clients into my ecosystem and set me on a trajectory to change their lives. It wasn't until I got sick and tired of throwing strategies at the wall to see if they would stick that I did the one thing that must be done as soon as possible if you have millions on your mind: FOCUS.

Follow One Course Until Success results!

Focusing changed the game for me and the business. Focus, in full transparency, is why I am here today to write the story of how we, and our clients, are moving to millions. If I would have kept doing what I had been doing, it would've been a hot mess. I would be somewhere working for someone else because trying to do all the things is the fastest way *not* to grow your business. Your marketing suite is the key to consistent traffic, leads, and eventually, sales. Your marketing suite will include strategies to generate awareness and strategies to generate revenue when used in conjunction with your sales suite.

Most entrepreneurs "take a stab" at marketing instead of identifying a systematic way to share their products and services with their pinnacle clients. Or worse, they follow what worked for someone else blindly, hoping and praying that it will work for them. But hope and prayer are not business growth strategies. This is where most people go wrong. You've already heard me say that you can "oops" your way to six figures. But it will take strategy, sales, systems, support, and a success mindset to make it to seven figures, without losing yourself in the process. While marketing is not a science, it is strategic.

Well, let me say it *should* be strategic if you want to make an impact with it. Millions-minded CEOs are not "willy-nilly" marketers. They are clear, concise, strategic, and consistent. In order to become strategic, it will require research—primary and secondary—to get into the minds of your pinnacle client so that you can show up in the places they gather in large numbers and get their attention. When I first started my business, I made so many mistakes. That's why it took me three years to finally cross the threshold. If you are stuck at six figures, you might be making one of those mistakes, too.

Mistake 1: You're unclear on your pinnacle client.

As already expressed, this is business building 101. Even knowing that doesn't stop people from making this mistake and impacting the success of their marketing. To cross the million-dollar mark, you will have to up-level your pinnacle client. It's a priority to get crystal-clear about who they are.

Mistake 2: You're inconsistent with your marketing.

Writing an article, posting to social media, or sending an electronic newsletter or email occasionally does not make a marketing strategy. If you want to be seen as an expert, you must consistently appear in various forms where your pinnacle client can find you. It's actually easier than you think to repurpose content into various formats. For instance, once a week you create a ten-minute video answering a question that your pinnacle client currently has. From that video, you create a blog post, ten mini one-minute video clips, an educational carousel for Instagram, a personal note in your weekly newsletter and feature the article, a signature talk title and pitch to get booked to speak. In this way, this one topic is expanded into five different formats for delivering the same content. That way whichever modality of consumption your pinnacle clients like, it is available to them. To change this problem, you must create a marketing and content calendar, so you know what you're talking about each week for your pinnacle clients. Then, you can have someone deploy it throughout the week. You should be marketing every day you would like to make money in your business. Statistics show that it can take fifteen to twenty impressions, on average, before a pinnacle client is aware that you exist.[21] They have to perceive you as a credible, consistent resource who might be able to help them. If it takes that long to create a level of trust, then by *not consistently* speaking to your market, you are lengthening the prospect cycle.

Mistake 3: You're not using the 3 *E*'s of Millions-Minded Marketing: Education, Experience and Emotion.

The 3 *E*'s of marketing method means that your marketing materials and copy will focus on ensuring three things:

1. **You create an experience.** Experiential marketing is an often-missed marketing opportunity for companies wishing to rise above the noise and stand out from their competitors. Experiential marketing is about evoking the senses of your pinnacle client. Not only do you remember that there are different ways to engage with a prospect, but you leverage all of them inside of one marketing piece. By being experiential, you get engagement and engagement leads to building a connection. Experiential marketing also means that, from the very beginning, you create an environment where they feel inspired and ready to solve the problem once and for all. Your customer service, your communications, and your website, all are designed to create a favorable experience among your audience.

2. **You educate your audience while demonstrating your expert status.** We still live in the information age and marketplace. You will get paid more for what you know than what you do. Because you know something that your pinnacle client doesn't, which is why they are saddled with the problem, you can leverage your knowledge to get their attention. When marketing includes education, it talks to the logical part of your audience. Seven percent of their decision to move forward will be based on how confident they feel about your expertise in the area they need help. Educational marketing also means you provide tons of value and content that illustrates your expert status, including social proof in the form of case studies and success stories of others you have helped experience the same result your pinnacle client is now seeking.

3. **You evoke an emotional response from them.** Ninety-three percent of any decision to invest is an emotional one. *Ninety-three percent*. That means, if you desire to get traction in today's marketplace, your marketing must pull on their pain points in such a way that their response is one of emotion—the need to get out of pain *now*. You help them to feel that in working with you, they will increase their happiness and fulfillment. As a result of your assistance, your audience will reduce stress and anxiety, and stop the pain. You help them to connect to the vision of what their lives will be like when

the problem has been solved and how they will feel. One's feelings create their beliefs. Those beliefs either create action or excuses, but it all starts based on how they feel. If your marketing can tap into these feelings, you are positioning your products and services for purchase! It is proven that when your marketing does all three, you increase the likelihood of a purchase from your audience.

Mistake 4: You're not highlighting the problem you can solve and the pain points they're experiencing.

When I was working on my MBA in grad school, I chose to write my thesis on the differences between pleasure-based and pain-based marketing. There have always been two schools of thought on marketing. And honestly, the school you attend may be determined by your ideal client as there is a time and place for pleasure-based marketing. Maybe you've taken the pleasure-based marketing approach to reaching your pinnacle client. My experience and research tell me that if you focus on a pleasure-based approach, your marketing and sales cycle will be longer. Maybe you're good with that.

Pleasure is delightful and it creates a harmonious, leisurely feeling in the minds of your audiences. But it seldom creates a sense of urgency. Pain, on the other hand, moves the one in pain to scour to find a painkiller. They will do anything. They will pay anything to stop the pain. Pain-based marketing is much more attractive and leads prospects to a solution much faster. When you position your solution strategically using your marketing, they will buy, and buy quickly.

When I first started, even though I was well aware of the benefits of pain-based marketing, I chose a pleasure-based approach. I was reminded the hard way that pleasure-based marketing really only works well when you are marketing to affluent people making decisions based on desires, not needs. Most of the marketplace, however, makes buying decisions based, at least in part, on solving a problem. Pleasure-based marketing is ideal if you sell cars, appliances, homes, vacations, and other items considered luxurious. However, if you are selling services like accounting, legal, consulting, speaking, or coaching, you should look into the pain your clients are experiencing. Lucky for you, I shared my secret about your messaging suite. When you deepen the SPICE, you'll have enough pain-based marketing ammunition to get the attention and traction you need to convert more clients into your signature program.

Mistake 5: You don't have an effective call to action that includes a logical progression.

While it's been said that you can lead them to the water, but you can't make them drink, I tend to believe that if you tell them *how* to drink, they will. What better way to do this than through your marketing? You don't want to build them up, then let them down. That is exactly what you are doing if your marketing doesn't clearly tell them what they should do next. When I first started marketing, I would literally lay out the problem without giving an indication that because I knew their problem, I also knew their ideal solution. And as a result, I got a lot of feedback expressing how educational the post was. If I had to guess, after consuming my content, they would go hire someone else because I never told them to hire me. You have to assume that common sense isn't that common. Tell your audience how to engage in your products and services. Furthermore, you may have to tell them more than once, in more than one way. Be sure that your call to action includes all pertinent information that will help them get to the exact place (your website sales page) to purchase your solution.

As important as not making each of those mistakes listed above is, none of them are my biggest marketing mistake. As I have already shared, we started a rebrand in early 2021. By the end of 2021, everything was ready to go. We set a plan to launch our new brand in January 2022. It was going to be great! We mapped the strategy, created the marketing assets we'd need to pull it off, and planned for the launch event. Our launch event was going to be a free webinar where I would unveil our new brand, tell the story behind the shift, and announce that we had decided that we'd be going all in on transforming six-figure service-based entrepreneurs into seven-figure CEOs. I was excited. The team was excited. The early buzz of our rebrand had our community excited.

We knew that going all in on an audience that was already at six figures meant that the majority of our existing community could no longer qualify for our programs. We were alright with that because the mandate had been clear. When God said "Move to Millions," He meant for us to equip those ready to understand and prepare for millions. This meant that the average brand-new entrepreneur who wasn't making any money in their business was no longer going to be ideal. So with that clarity, we proceeded.

We relaunched the podcast first. Upon changing the name from the *Leverage Your Incredible Factor Podcast* to the *Move to Millions Podcast*, we immediately saw that our new brand identity was resonating. In a matter of weeks, we had grown to 50,000 downloads when the two previous seasons and one hundred episodes didn't even crack 25,000 combined. The podcast continues to grow, and at the time of writing this book, we now have more than 500,000 downloads. We are clear that this message is what is needed right now. The success of the podcast told us that we hit big. The rebrand launch event was next. During the rebrand launch, we were going to announce our Move to Millions Tour.

I should sidebar here to share that we had done a tour where we visited three to five cities every year since 2011. Our tours always performed well. We'd get fifty to one hundred people in each city, and we'd enroll them to join us for our annual live event. This event was held in May, and over the last ten years, the event had a few different names and focuses. The names and focus would change every time God spoke that it was time to move on. We started with Unleash Your Incredible Factor, which we held for five years. Then God said, "Breakthrough in Business," which we held for three years. Then, as you have already read, in 2020, God said, "Move to Millions." We took 2021 off so that we could manage the rebrand properly and set a date to relaunch our annual event in May 2022.

With date changes over the years, we settled on the Wednesday through Friday preceding Memorial Day for our event. With us choosing this corridor of time, we also knew that every year we'd have a percentage of possible attendees who wouldn't be able to join us because they had children attending prom or graduating high school. We were okay with that, too.

As planned, we held our relaunch event on January 13 and had a great turn out. During the event, we launched our Move to Millions Tour going to our best represented cities: Washington DC, Atlanta, Georgia, and of course, we'd hold a stop in Newark, Delaware. During the tour, we'd also show an exclusive preview to our forthcoming docuseries, also called *Move to Millions*. The docuseries features me and four of our clients who all had their first or next million-dollar year with help from me and my team. It is so powerful, and I can't wait for you to see it. Every other year when we held a tour and announced it, within days, we'd have thirty people registered. This time, as the team and I were heading to each city, we didn't have thirty people registered *anywhere*.

What went wrong? We ran the same strategy we always run when we are doing a tour that introduces the live event.

Did you catch that?! *We ran the same strategy we always ran.*

Therein lies the problem and the biggest marketing mistake I have ever made. We ran the same strategy without remembering that we up-leveled our pinnacle client. Please write this down so that you don't find yourself making this mistake on your own move to millions. When you up-level your pinnacle client, you will also have to shift the marketing strategy you use to reach them. Likely, the strategy that used to work like a charm will not work on the new client. We totally missed this point. That is why it was an epic failure. For the first time ever, our tour cost us money. I'm shaking my head as I write this because, every time I think about it, I can't believe that we didn't realize what we needed to do. Essentially, we tried to pour new wine into old wineskins. Just as Jesus explained to the disciples with this parable in Mark 2, I knew better. Yet I didn't do better. I honestly think I was so excited that I didn't question if the strategy would work because it had worked *every* time before. But within weeks, I knew we had an epic failure on our hands. Being the woman that I am, I had to move forward, knowing that we weren't going to hit our goal. We would typically do our tour and fill our live event in thirty days. That wasn't going to happen this year.

Mark 2:22 says, "Likewise, no one pours new wine into old wineskins. Otherwise, the wine will burst the skins, and both the wine and the wineskins are ruined. Rather, new wine is poured into fresh wineskins."

In this instance, our old, outdated marketing strategy to fill our tour and live event that we leveraged successfully with a different ideal client represents the old wineskins. Our new pinnacle client, fresh rebrand, and up-leveled live event experience represents the new wineskins. We thought we could run the same strategy when all the variables were different. I wanted to share this with you because, invariably, as you up-level on your own move to millions, you will choose to shift parts of your business model. You may shift your ideal client, your signature offer, and absolutely your messaging. When you do, make sure that you also shift your marketing strategy.

This story doesn't end as bad as it might seem. We course corrected it when we realized the tour was an epic failure. When we shifted into a new strategy, it produced much fruit. So, we were still able to hit our revised attendee goal for the annual event. We went on to generate more than $1,000,000 from that three-day live event, enrolling new pinnacle clients into our programs. We were able to identify that the strategy wasn't working quickly, so we could save face.

It can take up to ninety days to determine the effectiveness of a marketing strategy. But you, or whoever oversees your marketing, must pay attention and look for the small wins and cues. Make sure you don't miss your opportunity to shift. This is a big part of the reason that your marketing suite needs to have a manager who is on top of your key performance indicators (KPIs).

Earlier in this chapter, I alluded to the fact that there are many moving parts of marketing. So, getting to the point where you have an appointed marketing manager or head of marketing is key. You might opt for a growth manager that oversees both marketing and sales since these two functions work in tandem inside of your company. The moving parts of marketing are vast and could be a book all by itself. Here, I will list the main areas of your Leverage + Scale Marketing Suite. To download the complete list, including The Moving Parts of Marketing, visit https://www.movetomillionsbook.com/resources.

- **Business Success Formula:** Your success formula includes your pinnacle client, traffic source, lead generator, marketing opt-in, nurture, and conversion sequences on the marketing side of the formula.
- **Marketing/Content Calendar:** You'll need a calendar to make sure that you are being consistent with deploying your message to the

marketplace. Your calendar should link all content topics and marketing activities being completed by your full team.

- **Social Media Management:** Social media marketing is important for your business. At minimum, using social media to generate awareness is an important part of your marketing suite.

- **Marketing Software:** You'll have to identify which software is most essential for your company based on your other marketing assets and variables. You'll definitely want to have a customer relationship management (CRM) software that manages the marketing and sales functions of your business. There are a lot of software options available, so I won't take us down a rabbit hole here.

- **Marketing KPIs:** When I was in corporate America, I learned the importance of key performance indicators. What gets attended to gets done and what gets done gets tracked. Your metrics will help you identify marketing success and failures quickly so you can avoid pitfalls.

- **Product or Service Launch Calendar and Strategy:** When you create your new offer suite, do yourself a favor and launch it. A launch is just an event to let your pinnacle client know that you have something new to solve their problem. Launching—a process that typically we recommend allotting six to twelve weeks to accomplish, depending on some other variables—is the best way to introduce a new offering to the market. Everyone launches. We all sit on the edge of our seats each year, waiting for Apple to launch the new whatever. You want to create the same kind of fear of missing out (FOMO) in your own products and services.

- **Automated Marketing Sequences:** One thing you definitely don't want to have to do is go back to the drawing board every time you want to communicate with your marketing list. By writing and automating your marketing sequences in your CRM, you'll be able to save time. Now, as you load them up, be sure to test their effectiveness and to make sure all the pieces work. Keep in mind that a sequence typically includes the solo messages, the click but no action messages, the follow-up messages, and the reminder messages. You may also want to integrate a text message as one of every three messages in the sequence to vary attempts and to increase open- and click-through rates.

- **Marketing Materials:** You'll need lots of marketing assets to promote your campaign. These include, but are not limited to, post cards, social media graphics, rack cards, video, short-form content, audio clips and soundbites, banners, and headers.

By now, I hope you see the relevance of having each of the assets we've discussed so far. Your offer suite will create packaged and priced offers that will achieve your revenue goal. Your messaging suite will position those offers and start the conversation. Your messaging connects deeply with your pinnacle client so that they see you as their only and obvious choice. Your marketing suite will keep the conversation going so that they make the decision to take advantage of your call to action. This is what we call the Leverage + Scale Pathway.

Package & Price Your Solution → Create Messaging That Highlights Your Solution → Create Marketing That Brings Your Pinnacle Client to Your Solution

You can ride this pathway all the way up the Move to Millions Continuum!

As we round out this chapter, keep in mind that while some of the ways to market will change and new ways will be developed, the fundamentals of marketing will never change. With the creation of your Business Success Formula, you will always be able to develop the right formula to turn your contacts into contracts. Finding your best way to market is your ultimate goal so you can create a marketing suite that bears much fruit. Personally, I have chosen speaking as my primary traffic source and lead generator, and it has worked extremely well for us.

Chapter Action Plan

1. Clarify your pinnacle client.
2. Determine your Business Success Formula (identify each element in the formula).
3. Narrow your five to seven marketing streams.
4. Craft the assets in your marketing suite.
5. Start testing your sequences.

Remember: Information without action is just a waste of time. So, make a plan to implement now so you are one move closer to your first million-dollar year.

Client Case Study

Meet Althea Hearst, Hearst Home Team

I met Althea on Clubhouse. Althea was clear and confident that she was going to become a million-dollar CEO. In one year in the mastermind, she became just that. When we started working together, she had already built a $250,000 business. To make the Move to Millions as a real estate agent, she could either have more financial transactions or look for other ways to diversify her income. We did both. With our help, Althea built her real estate team, getting to ten agents at one point. She also let her love of teaching start the process of building a coaching business to supplement her agency sales results. In one year, she grew her team and quadrupled her business. Althea is also featured in our *Move to Millions* docu-series, and during filming, she lost her father. Her business afforded her the opportunity to be absent for more than a month and still have her best quarter and cross the million-dollar mark! This is the power of the Move to Millions Method. With a clear strategy, sales infra-structure, systems, and support, making millions doesn't have to be hard, sacrifice the time you need for family matters, or take ten years!

"Being part of the Move to Millions Mastermind has been amazing! I'm building my team, stepping fully into being the CEO, and we just had our first million-dollar year! In fact, we celebrated our best quarter ever and hit this milestone while I was away from the business and my team didn't miss a beat! I highly recommend this mastermind if you want to truly build a company that impacts and generates millions and shows you how to have time for yourself and what matters most."
—ALTHEA HEARST

Her Continuum MOVE:
From Momentum to Millions in year one in the Move to Millions Mastermind.

CHAPTER EIGHT

Leverage + Scale Sales Suite

"It's as honorable to sell as it is to buy."
—DARNYELLE JERVEY HARMON

t had been three months since I called my engagement off, the first time. My first ex-fiancé had admitted three months before our September wedding that he had gotten an older woman, his fellow trustee, in our church pregnant. I was beside myself because, just eighteen months earlier, he had begged me to abort our pregnancy.

I slapped him so hard that his head hit the passenger door window and made a loud thump.

I can see you digging in for what is sure to be a *"Real Housewives of [insert your city]"* kind of story.

Sorry to disappoint; but it won't be. I only shared what happened because it is the reason that I learned how to sell, for real. If you want to read all about it, grab my first book, *If You Understood My Past, You Would Understand My Praise*. A good friend, to cheer me up following the most embarrassing season in my life at that time, introduced me to selling when she invited me to a Mary Kay Cosmetics skincare class. I think she got tired of hearing me mope and complain. (Can you blame her?!) As I sat in that skincare class and washed half of my face to see the difference the product made, I literally plotted my big comeback. Sure, I might not have had a man on my arm, but I was going to keep it moving and work on my career instead.

When I started selling Mary Kay, I was a vice president in a financial services company. I found Mary Kay at a time when I was beginning to ponder the meaning of life. I wondered if all I was supposed to be was a vice president. I was over the office politics and tired of the "black tax" of working twice as hard for half of the recognition and pay. Don't get me wrong. I wasn't ungrateful. By the time I was twenty-eight, I was making six figures in my job. That was a lot of money. But money isn't everything, especially when you don't understand how to leverage it.

Mary Kay changed my life. *Literally.*

Out of the ashes of my first failed engagement, I found something that played to my strengths. And I was good at it. I could sell water to a water cooler. There was something about this company and their philosophy of God first, family second, and career third that spoke to my heart. Following my breakup, I was fresh off of an intensive of going deeper into God. I decided to study all religions because I realized that my relationship with God had been based on that of my father, Aunt Ida, and my step-grandfather, Mr. Henry. I didn't know God for myself. So when ex-fiancé number one did his dirt in the church, I realized that I didn't want to be religious. Instead, I wanted to develop a *relationship* with God for myself. Through my intensive studies, I learned that the principles of each religion are the same. Today in my work, I focus on teaching the principles. I truly believe that understanding the principles are a big part of the reason that I make, move, and will leave millions.

One of my favorite parts of Mary Kay was the leveraged sales approach. While you could hold individual facials with customers, they advocated for you to book skincare classes. That meant that instead of working with one woman, you would be working with her and three to five of her friends. She'd be your hostess, who was eligible for extra products and prizes. This leveraged sales approach helped me to grow my Mary Kay business and team quickly. Because of leveraged sales, I left my "good job" in early 2005, and within five months, I was picking up my first of two pink Cadillacs. I was on the path to becoming a national sales director. In one year, I grew my unit to five hundred women, off sprang five sales directors, and grabbed the coveted number one position in my national area. The secret to my success was understanding the importance of a leveraged sales approach.

To this day, I teach my clients about leveraged sales. The primary tools our service-based clients use to achieve leveraged sales are webinars, speaking engagements, and live or virtual events. Not that I have anything against one-on-one sales calls, as I cut my teeth on them when I started and began to grow my company. I realized that you can't sell in a leveraged way if you can't first sell one-on-one. But the fact of the matter is it will take too long to scale your sales if you are selling one yes at a time. I'm also really big into helping our clients land bigger deals. Deals that take one yes and multiply the impact to tens or hundreds of people. This is how you move millions while you are making them.

This premise is what led to the development of the Leverage + Scale Sales Suite. Inside this suite, you have your sales tool options (most of which offer a leveraged sales approach), and you also have the systems, support, and software required to optimize your chosen sales suite. Before you build your sales suite, you need to understand the sales process and have a level of mastery over the sales conversation. Mary Kay Ash said, "Nothing happens until somebody sells something." The only way to sell is to have a clear understanding of your prospective client's problem, pain points, limiting beliefs, and promised possibilities. When it comes to the sales conversation itself, there are seven phases of the conversation, with only a small variance if you work business-to-business versus business-to-consumer/entrepreneur. Taking the time to nail down the sales conversation components, which I learned in Mary Kay and from watching infomercials, is how I've been able to experience a 43–50 percent conversion rate in leveraged sales over the last twelve years. Let's start by understanding the phases of the sales conversation.

- **Part One: Set Expectations/Introductions.** In this first part of the conversation, you are establishing rapport. After exchanging pleasantries, you'll set the expectations of the conversation and make it clear that if you both feel that you are a good fit, you will offer them the opportunity to hire you.

- **Part Two: Discover the Cost of the Problem.** This is the most important phase of the conversation. If you are not able to help them understand what holding on to their problem is going to cost them, you will not close a new client. When you find the monetary value associated with their problem, you will get and keep their attention. In this phase, keep in mind that you have to show them how much it will cost them to say no to your solution before you tell them how much it will cost to say yes.

- **Part Three: Transition the Problem into Possibility/Difference It Will Make.** Once you have a clear understanding of their problem, shift the conversation into what is possible if the problem gets solved and the difference having help while solving the problem will make. This will open them up emotionally. Once they are emotional, that will create a sense of urgency to get help solving the problem.

- **Part Four: Recap/Introduce a Solution.** This phase is about recapping what you've discovered so far so that your prospective client feels seen and heard. Highlight this: If your prospective client doesn't feel seen and heard, the call will not end well. This increases the likelihood that they will make an investment decision to work with you to get access to the solution they are most desiring. After your recap, you'll share how you can help them by introducing them to the benefits of your solution. Remember: Benefits sell; features tell. You're looking to sell.

- **Part Five: Ask for Permission to Help Them.** I believe that you have to earn the right to make a prospective client an offer to solve their problem. This phase is just about you asking for their permission to help. It's as simple as saying, "Would you like my help?"

- **Part Six: Advance the Sale/Overcome Objections**. In this phase, you will share about the investment to have you help them solve the problem and overcome any objections that spring forth once they know the investment. Now, I'm from the old school. So, I believe that once you state the investment, you close your mouth. History tells me that the one who speaks first after the amount has been released is the one that leaves with the offer.

- **Part Seven: Close the Deal (Get the Payment).** As you finish overcoming the objections, if there were any, the last phase is to close the deal. In this phase, your confidence is key. Your prospect is likely to have to borrow your confidence to make an investment in themselves. You'll need to be ready to take their payment, show a QR code, or give them a URL so that they can complete the transaction. To maintain the sale, you will want your congratulations and onboarding process to start as soon as the payment is completed.

I have worked with a lot of people to help them with sales. Sales is one of those skills that you have to master because you will always be selling. Now, please keep in mind that selling is not convincing; it's about the power of persuasion. In fact, I encourage you to never convince anyone to let you change their life. That is what will happen when they hire you. You will change an area of their life. Instead, I invite you to use your power of persuasion to help them decide to solve a problem they have already been actively seeking a solution to without your help thus far. The persuasion helps them come to the realization that now is the time to get the help they need.

With a firm understanding of the sales conversation, you're ready to take a leveraged approach to sales by building your sales suite. To build your sales suite, you first need to determine the sales tool that will work best for your pinnacle client. There are several tools to choose from, but you need to understand how your ideal client wants to learn about how you can help them before you choose. That way, you ensure that getting enough traffic into your chosen tool will achieve your goals.

At the time of writing this book, your sales tool options include:

- **Enrollment webinars**—The webinar is becoming an increasingly popular way to enroll new clients in a leveraged format. The webinars that convert the best and lead to high-end program sales are designed to be anywhere from forty-five to ninety minutes in length. Your pinnacle client will determine how long your webinar should be. As long as you cover the important phases as outlined above, you're good. There's an old school paradigm that doesn't believe that you can sell higher end programs without a sales call. We do it all the time.
- **Sales pages**—This is a page on your website that highlights the sales conversation in the form of marketing copy. The copy follows the natural progression above so that as your pinnacle client reads it,

they come to the conclusion that this is the solution they've been seeking. Since it's not a live conversation, the tone of your copy will need to infer what their problem must be for your offer to be the solution they most need. If you're using this sales tool, it will be imperative that you have a way to track who actually went to your sales page so you can follow up with them.

- **Requests for Proposal (RFP)**—Typically only used in government, non-profits, or corporations, this sales tool offers the least amount of flexibility. In general, organizations who request a proposal have a defined process that you can't circumvent, and they are often price shopping. This is the one tool that isn't a leveraged sales tool. It is what it is. If you work with organizations, you'll have to play by their rules. It won't be all bad though. The pay days are much more lucrative if you can make it through the proposal process. Here, where possible, we advocate for an engagement letter over a typical proposal. Engagement letters shorten the sales process and pretty much guarantee that the proposed scope of work will be accepted. The only way to submit an engagement letter is to first have a needs discovery meeting (sales call) with the prospective organization.

- **Live events (including hybrid or virtual events) and speaking**— My personal favorite, speaking/live events, which include all virtual event types (challenges, summits, virtual conferences, multi-day workshops, webinars, video series), are one of the most lucrative forms of a leveraged sales tool. This is largely because people have an innate need to gather and belong in community. It takes work to fill the room. But when your Run of Show follows the format that we highlight in our Leverage + Scale Enrollment Events framework, you will convert many clients at once. At our most recent Move to Millions live event, we were able to enroll nearly fifty new clients at one time as a result of this sales tool. Now, of course, your systems will have to be tight to pull an enrollment of this size off. I will share more with you on systems in a future chapter.

- **Sales calls**—Considered the OG of selling, a sales call is typically a one-on-one conversation between a solution provider and a prospective client. In a traditional sales conversation, you will typically spend twenty to sixty minutes on the phone with a prospect walking through the phases of the sales conversation to get them to make an investment decision at the end of the call. Some salespeople are skilled in what is referred to as the "one-call close," while others take two or more calls to close a deal, especially when the investment is higher and requires creativity to access the funds to invest. If you leverage sales calls as your chosen sales tool, you'll usually book the call in advance, and request some information about the prospect to review prior to the conversation. I do not recommend holding sales calls on the fly, as they typically require more convincing to close.

- **Direct message selling**—Definitely one of the newer ways to sell, sliding into the DMs is fast becoming a go-to method of selling for many service-based entrepreneurs. Instead of building traditional sales teams, many are opting to build social sales teams and maximize time spent on the various social media platforms to generate new clients and customers. Basically, you'll leverage the direct messages on your favorite social media platform to engage in a sales conversation and close the sale.

- **Open/closed cart launching**—Based on a sales event, open/closed cart launching is when you make your offer available for a short period of time, typically three to seven days. Anyone who wants to work with you must make a decision during that time. If they don't, they run the risk of having to wait until you open up your cart again. Most people do one or two launches a year, if this is their sales tool. Launches start with an awareness campaign and launch event that culminates into a sales pitch. Once the cart closes, any stragglers are left living with their problem until you open your cart again.

There is no right or wrong sales tool. It's about identifying the one that your pinnacle client is willing to enter in order to consider enrolling in your signature offer to solve their problem. At some point in time on my own move to millions, I have used all of the sales tools. They all work. They may even all work for you. You'll have to determine which is the sales tool that can position you to generate millions in sales and revenue each year. Doing so will create consistency instead of your sales being all over the place because you're trying too many things. Too many options will split your focus. We've settled on leveraging the power of live events as our primary sales tool. Each year, hundreds of service-based entrepreneurs spend three days with us at our annual live event, Move to Millions Live. It's like a homecoming of sorts for millions-minded entrepreneurs. Over three days, we educate, empower, entertain, and equip them to plan, prepare, and position their companies for the million-dollar mark. And at every event, we invite attendees to enroll in one of our programs to get support as they work the plans that we help them to create during the event. Just because you are reading this book, I want to invite you to join us at Move to Millions Live.

Visit https://movetomillionsbook.com/event now to learn how you can come experience this book's content live with me and my team.

The key to any of these sales tools working for you is the infrastructure you put in place to allow for you to sell one to many. The sales infrastructure is pivotal to your sales success. A typical sales process includes identifying the length of your sales cycle and which levers help to shorten and speed up the time it takes a prospect to become your paying client. Your infrastructure will also need the right tools added to the sales cycle journey so that your prospects don't get lost or sidetracked, but instead, stay the course until they have access to the solution they have been seeking. Your sales infrastructure might look like this:

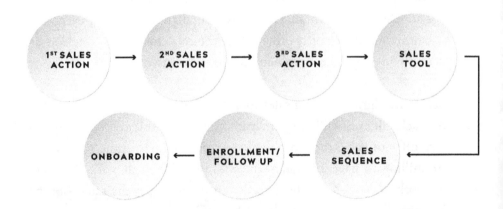

Each action is going to be determined by what works best for your pinnacle client and gets the most traction between stages. It's also possible that you could go from the first action to the sales tool to enrollment without any of the other steps.

Every suite is all-inclusive. So, in addition to choosing your sales tool, you'll need:

- Software
- Key Performance Indicators (KPIs)
- Sales Scripts
- Sales Team/Assistance

To be successful in sales, you'll need:

- Offer Development
- Key Message Development
- Lead Generation
- Sales Pre-Qualification
- KPI Tracking/Development
- Sales Conversation Mastery
- Sales Conversation Consistency
- Follow-up System to Keep Track of Leads/Prospects (typically housed within your sales software)

As we round out this chapter, keep in mind that sales is a natural evolution of connecting with your pinnacle client. When they understand that you can solve their problem, and you have proven success doing it for others, they will naturally gravitate toward your chosen sales tool. With the creation of your sales suite, you will be able to always be one step closer to turning your contacts into contracts.

Chapter Action Plan

1. Determine your chosen sales tool.
2. Develop your sales process in that tool.
3. Craft your sales scripts for the various scenarios that are possible for your clients to get themselves into and to need your help.
4. Craft the assets in your sales suite.
5. Hold sales conversations.

Remember: Information without action is just a waste of time. So, make a plan to implement now so you are one move closer to your first million-dollar year.

Client Case Study

Meet Marquel Russell,
Client Attraction University

They call Marquel the King of Client Attraction. His business was already doing well when we were introduced by a mutual colleague. He was closing in on the million-dollar mark, but he hadn't gotten there just yet. I introduced Marquel to the power of live events as a way to accelerate scaling his company. Once we added live events to his business model, he was making multimillions within our first year of working together.

I also helped Marquel think like the CEO of a company, not an online business. So, he began to build his team and infrastructure to support growing his company to eight figures. Together, we developed key infrastructure and systems that helped him to build a dynamic team while tightening his operational systems.

Over the last three years that Marquel and I have been working together, I have watched him grow his company to more than $5,000,000 in sales and revenue! And it's not just about the money. It's helping him to build wealth for his young family. He's a bona fide millionaire and his children will be too!

"When I met Darnyelle, I was already a very successful marketing coach (my business was doing more than three quarters of a million dollars a year), but I knew that this business should be doing millions . . . and I wasn't quite sure what I was missing. After attending Darnyelle's Profit from Live Events, I invested in a VIP day with Darnyelle and the pieces came together. With Darnyelle's help we've put the right business model, systems, and team in place, and now just finished our first multimillion-dollar year. If you need help fine tuning your systems so you can explode the impact and income of your business, I highly recommend Darnyelle. Working with her has contributed directly to $2 million of my business's growth in 2020 and even more when you count 2021 and 2022. What I have learned from Darnyelle will continue to make me money for thirty to fifty years from now."
—MARQUEL RUSSELL

His Continuum MOVE:
From Mastery to Majesty over three years as a private client.

CHAPTER NINE

Leverage + Scale Systems Suite

"Systems make millions predictable."
—DARNYELLE JERVEY HARMON

'm truly grateful that I started my career working in a Fortune 500 company. When I graduated college after deciding that I wasn't going to attend Georgetown Law, I did the lazy thing. I went full-time at my then part-time job. Yeah, it was lazy of me to just take a full-time position, making $19,038 a year. That's not a lot today, and I promise you, it was even less back in 1997 when I accepted it. In full transparency, I thought I knew better than my mentor at the time who just happened to be a vice chairman at the bank. He wanted to put me into the management development program, which would have made me a VP upon graduation. But I had heard stories that they never left the bank because they basically worked 24/7. No thanks. So, I turned down his offer and became an entry-level representative in TACS (telephone access customer service).

What was I thinking? *I wasn't.*

Today, I know that success is accelerated when you have insight and connections that decrease your waiting time. I worked in TACS for twenty-four months. Then, I applied and got a job in the credit department. I was a credit analyst for nine months before an opportunity presented itself for me to go work in the Corporate Compliance department. It was in Compliance where I became a personal banking officer, then a senior personal banking officer, and finally an assistant vice president! I've said all that to say, when I started this company and started operating it like a true company, I had the systems on lock. If I didn't learn anything else from my days at MBNA, I learned that what got attended to got done, and there was a system for getting it done.

Even in those first nine months when we were pre-revenue, I was documenting and systematizing everything. *Everything.* That's part of the reason we were pre-revenue! Seriously, I knew from day one that, if I intended to build a company (and I did), I was going to have to begin the process of documenting everything that we would need as we built a team. I was already thinking like the CEO of a company. As I was documenting everything, I was also giving energy and voice to the culture before there was anyone to share it with.

I will never regret having the foresight to think like a compliance officer from day one. As we have built our team, we have eight full-time employees as I write this book. All of that documentation paid off. I still remember when I brought on my first assistant. I've never been one for my primary support to be virtual. So once I got a *real* assistant, they had to come work in the office with me. Notice I said *real* assistant. My first assistant was fake. It was me masquerading as "Regina," named after my mother! I guess you could say that I was faking it until I made it. It was important to me from the beginning that I be perceived as a true business. When I did finally bring my first assistant on with me live, within weeks, she was able to be productive and add value to the business. That is truly a testament to our systems.

Now, as you set your sights on becoming a million-dollar CEO, it's important to know that you will need systems, both kinds. Some systems are software and tools that aid in the development or fulfillment of the services you offer to clients. Others are standard operating procedures, or SOPs, that often govern what the software does for you. You will need both to operationalize your company. Systems create duplication and allow for automation so you can reduce the amount of time you are actively working to receive a specific result. Once you create the systems that govern your company's operations, you will increase your company's valuation (how much it's worth and could be sold for).

In full transparency, it may take time to develop both. Start where you are and build as you go. I often recommend to clients and students to record everything they do today that they want someone else to do tomorrow. Highlight this: Your business will only run as well as your systems have been documented for duplication. Your systems make your millions possible and predictable.

There are seven systems that ensure that the core areas of your business run succinctly. Work on each of them individually and keep them in a place that you can get to them. Make changes, as they need to be living and breathing systems. As you develop the systems, you become duplicatable as they shorten onboarding significantly. As you are starting, get in the habit of documenting everything that you do. If it's hard to write them down, record yourself doing everything. There are video and audio recording tools that are easy to use on your smartphone. As you start the process to create the seven systems that will take your business to seven figures, think about duplicating yourself. Your ultimate goal is to create an environment to build a team and move into a true million-dollar CEO role within your company, regardless of how big your team is. Trust me. It need not be eight team members like mine is today. We got to the million-dollar mark with an executive assistant and technical virtual assistant. The most important thing to keep in mind is that the point of erecting systems in your business is to position you to spend 80 percent of your time on the business and 20 percent or less of your time *in* the business.

Let's start talking about the seven systems that make up your systems suite. First, I will list them all out: operational, financial, legal, client management, marketing management, sales management, and finally, talent management. Each system's role is defined by the title of the system. Let's walk through each, one by one. And let me just say this is not the fun, exciting stuff; however, this is the stuff that gets your business to the next level.

LEADERSHIP + LEGACY
How you create a life you love

MINDSET
How you win the inner game of business

TALENT OPTIMIZATION
How you get the competitive edge

THE SEVEN PILLARS
Of Business Optimization

BRAND MESSAGING
How you get known

OPERATIONS
How you build your business

MARKETING
How you get found

SALES
How you get paid

Operational Management

Your operational management system will govern the day-to-day operations of your company. Initially, this system will be managed by you. Eventually, your operations manager, director of operations, and/or COO will oversee your day-to-day operations so you can just "show up and shake it." When it comes to working on your systems suite, I always recommend that you start with your general operations. This is typically the heftiest system, so it will take a lot of time to get all of the items documented, although you will find yourself doing or looking at most of these items at least once per week.

When your company is operationally sound, you will be able to rest easy, knowing that what must get done is getting documented, which will aid in it actually getting done. I am the queen of a good checklist. I think I love checklists so much because I am easily distracted, but the checklists keep me focused. I'm not sure if you are familiar with the Kolbe A assessment. It's an instinct-based assessment that tells you your natural strengths and how you will show up if you are free to be yourself. Well, when I am free to be myself, I am caught by almost every bright, shiny object. I am a big picture visionary, so having these systems, complete with all the checklists for all the moving parts, helps to keep me on track. I'm grateful for my job in compliance because it helped me to learn how to document to duplicate. This will be your secret weapon as you scale your company toward the million-dollar mark. You're welcome.

Inside of your operational management system, list everything that pertains to the company, from the highest of levels to the intricacies and little details that make your company uniquely yours. Some of the items inside your operational management system will also appear in the other systems. I recommend keeping them in both places as a cross-check. Included in this system is everything you'll need to operate your business. When you visit https://www.movetomillionsbook.com/resources, there is a checklist for the operational management system for you to download.

As you develop this system, be sure to access some tools that will make your life easiest in the process of getting everything document, such as Google Drive, Vimeo to house your videos, Loom for screen recording, and a project management software tool like Notion.

Financial Management

I'm sure this goes without saying, but your financial management system is systematizing how you manage the financials in your company. I love all things finances for a multitude of reasons. Mostly because I want you to get comfortable with the numbers, even though I'm an advocate for having a financial management team that includes your CPA and bookkeeper, and eventually a CFO (but you don't start with a CFO). I would be wrong if I didn't tell you that, even though you have these people on your team, you still need to know and understand how to read every financial statement they send you so you can discover discrepancies. Listen to me. Don't ever take anything they send to you as law until you review it and validate that it makes sense. I have this uncanny sense of my business that I can look at our profit and loss statement (P & L) and notice that something is off and doesn't look right. I truly believe it's God beside me when I review them so that we can get the discrepancies fixed. If I didn't know how to read financial statements, I might have missed a data entry error on our P & L statement one year in the business. Hear me again when I say, review every P & L statement, balance sheet, break even analysis, and cash flow projection as they are provided to you. Make time to review them ASAP so that you can leverage what you learn to help your business in the current month! I recommend that you have your financial reports no later than the tenth of the month, ideally by the fifth. That way, the statements actually mean something so that you can leverage the data to make strategic decisions to move your company forward, make more revenue, review expenses, and get rid of those things you no longer need to pay for.

Experience tells me that this is the one system that gets the most neglect, especially amongst those who are struggling with money mindset issues. If you want to be the CEO of your own company, you're going to have to get comfortable with the money. I remember years ago when Oprah told me that I should never let anyone sign the checks but me. Actually, she was telling Beyonce when she was a guest on her show, but I was listening, and I was taking notes (as if she was telling me directly). Even when it was painful to write checks, I did it. Even when I first started Profit First, and it was like pulling out a tooth twice a month, I did it. As a result, now I am comfortable with and around money. Access to money and my finances has normalized it for me. To this day, I have a financial management team that reviews and reports on what we are doing financially, offers strategy and oversight, and even starts the process to pay our bills. But I have the final say. Even for my team, some of whom hold management level positions, we instituted a purchase request process. As items that they need to do their jobs need to be purchased, they can submit a request to me so I can approve it. Then, they receive permission to make the purchase. Procedures like this along with the chain of command are what you'll document in this system. To make sure that you know exactly what is housed in this system, there's a checklist waiting for you to download at www.movetomillionsbook.com/resources.

As you access that checklist, you'll want to combine your procedures for each financial item and matters into a Google doc entitled: Financial Management System. This system governs your financial management and accounting procedures to ensure you are effectively running your business.

As you build out this system, be sure to leverage software, such as Quick-Books along with a merchant account, Microsoft Excel, Payroll Software (QuickBooks has this feature available at a certain level), and you may even need a collections service. Even though I recommend that you get a book-keeper and CPA, make sure that you are the owner of your QuickBooks file in the event that you decide to make changes to your team in the future.

One last thing I want to say here, and it has served me well, is what you focus on expands. Every day, I focus on deposits. I keep this spreadsheet, which I call my daily money capture spreadsheet, and the purpose is to capture the money I earn daily. I am really big into declaring what I desire, and I desire for money to move to me easily and effortlessly every single day. I play this game with myself to make money every day. Most months, if I miss it, it's only by one to two days. Try it. That level of focus could be one more thing that brings your million-dollar company into view.

Legal Management

Your legal management system will keep you honest! Seriously, this system governs all of the legality of your company. You may be tempted to see an agreement online, change a few things, and claim it as your own. But I actually don't advocate for you to do that. While I am not an attorney, nor do I play one on TV, I want to make sure that you understand the importance of being protected at the state level, and federally as well. When it comes to just claiming an agreement you found online as your own, this is a problem for several reasons. First, you have no idea if an attorney drafted that agreement, which also means you have no idea if it's legally binding and protecting you as the company CEO. You also have no idea if the stipulations in it would hold up in court in your state if you had to defend the agreement. Trust me. I get it. I was barely over the six-figure mark once, too. I was trying to do all the big girl CEO things on a shoestring budget. When I was there, I leveraged the power of LegalShield to make sure that my company was properly protected. I did eventually graduate to lawyers with retainers, but I'm an advocate for starting where you can. Today, not only do you have LegalShield, but many attorneys have created bundles of the basic agreements and templates small business owners and freelancers need to start their business with a legally sound foundation. Needless to say, there is no reason for you to be without what you need as you can access bundles like that for less than $500 in a lot of cases.

The biggest thing to remember here is that you are building a company. You want it to have longevity. Taking the time to develop this system will serve your business for years to come. Your legal management system must-haves are included in a checklist waiting for you to download it at https://www.movetomillionsbook.com/resources. Everything inside your legal system will make sure that you're not bootlegging your business. As you build out this system, be sure to have an electronic signing tool, like DocuSign, in addition to your legal support. The development of this system is key to protecting your business from potentially costly mistakes and lawsuits that could derail your move to millions.

Marketing Management

As you already know because we have a whole chapter on your marketing suite, this system is about managing how you get found by your pinnacle clients on a consistent basis. Messaging may determine how you get known, but marketing systems and strategies will get you found by them in large enough numbers to impact your business. Marketing is the oxygen of your business. If you don't develop the right systems to automate and create consistency in your marketing, your business won't live very long. Your marketing management system is going to include all of the moving parts of marketing. There are so many moving parts, but you'll have access to all of them when you go grab your checklist at https://www.movetomillionsbook.com/resources. You'll notice right away the importance of your marketing plan and your marketing calendars. There are three of them that you need. Every August, I buy a large, laminated calendar for the next year. As a team, we start plugging in every marketing piece, every content piece, and every launch date throughout the year. I highly recommend you do the same in the third quarter of each year. Waiting until the fourth quarter, or even the New Year, is too late, as marketing can take up to ninety days to be effective.

As you build out this system, be sure to have access to software, including a customer relationship management tool, a landing page software tool, and possibly a lead management tool, if your CRM doesn't offer that. But truthfully, if it doesn't, it shouldn't be your CRM.

Sales Management

Again, the sales suite chapter went deep into the sales management process. Developing this system will manage your sales process so that you bring consistent sales and revenue into your company to complete its objectives. I have to say this up front. You can't spend sales. Sales are important. They are essential. Yet, every sale doesn't turn into revenue. Sometimes people ask for a refund, return a product, or default on their payment agreement. You need to be prepared for and have policies that speak to each occurrence. All of those things will be managed inside of this system. You'll need to track both sales and revenue to make sure that your financial management system is accurate.

To tell the difference, let me give an example. Let's say Sally buys your $5,000 course, but she enters your twelve-month payment plan. Because she wants the twelve-month payment plan, her access to the course will be $6,000, an additional $1,000, because you like to reward those who can pay in full. When people pay in full, you track both the $5,000 as a sale and as revenue. However, when customers like Sally enter a payment plan, you can track a $6,000 sale, but you can only count the $500 payment as the revenue received on that sale. Each month as another payment comes in, you can count the revenue and you will continue to do so monthly until Sally has paid for her course in full. These are the types of subtle nuances you have to be able to account for in your systems.

Your sales management system is also pretty thorough. It covers the entire sales cycle from lead generation to cash collection. Don't worry. The checklist for your sales management system is waiting at https://www.movetomillionsbook.com/resources. Once you register and log in, you'll see all the goodies so you can get one step closer to making your own move. Sales can be tricky if your mind isn't right. So, make sure you read the Mindset for Millions chapter again before you start building out your sales process.

To manage this system, you'll also want to have the following software: a CRM tool, a sales pipeline management tool (if your CRM doesn't offer it), a launch pages tool, scripts, a phone, a text marketing tool, Zoom for webinars, and a calendar scheduling tool. And as great as all of these software tools are, all you really need to sell is a phone, a loose script, and someone to call.

Client Management

We are doing all of this to get clients. Right? So, you're going to need a system to manage all of them. At our height, we've had more than two hundred clients. I promise you that managing two hundred clients, especially when you're onboarding more than one hundred of them at one time, can be something without some client systems! This system will manage a new client from onboarding to renewal to offboarding if they choose not to continue working with you. It will also encompass client policies and procedures so you have some boundaries in place. One of the biggest mistakes I made in the early years of my business was not having a business cell in addition to my personal cell. So often, clients would text me at the point of their despair because I didn't have that boundary in place. Once you bring on someone else to oversee your client management, the time spent developing this system will have been well spent because it will make their jobs so much easier, and it will keep your clients happier longer. We have an 85 percent client retention rate from year to year, and I know that is due in part to our client management system. Grab your checklist at https://www.movetomillionsbook.com/resources. For your client management system, you're going to need a good back-end system that can house your content and client records as well as a tool for community engagement. You'll also be relying heavily on your CRM software. It will do a lot of the heavy lifting in this system.

Talent Management

While your clients will start out hiring you, God willing, they will begin to hire your company, because you'll have a talented team of people to support them, and you are not left to do all the service delivery. Sure, at this point, it's very likely just you and an assistant—more than likely, a virtual assistant. There's nothing wrong with that, except it means that you are marketing, sales, and service delivery for your company. This also likely means that you have created a job for yourself that requires more than the job you left to become a million-dollar CEO. I'm not judging you; we all started there. Developing this system is important for when you're ready to truly be the CEO when the *E* doesn't stand for everything.

Your talent management system will encompass how you manage the team that you employ (as employees or contractors) to help you expand your brand. It's likely that you will start with contractors, but you'll need to quickly move to employees. What I tell my clients is this: Having contractors instead of employees will be okay, until the IRS finds out. For us, that came in 2014. We were starting to make a lot of money. Often this presents a red flag to the IRS and my accountant at the time strongly suggested that I bite the bullet and make all of my team members employees. The rules are vague. There's a lot of misinterpretation out there. Look at it this way: if you tell them what to do and when to do it, they are an employee. You'll likely want to make them your employee before the IRS, back fees, and penalties for payroll make you.

Inside of your talent system, there will be some fun things, like hiring and creating culture. There will be some not so fun things, like performance reviews and corrective action. Either way, I am proud of you. You are inching closer to being the CEO with a team of people supporting you as you leverage and scale your company. Your talent management system will make it easy for you to focus on building out the team that will support you to and beyond the million-dollar mark. One of the things that changed the game for us inside this system was the institution of an accountability agreement. We actually have our team recertify and agree to it every ninety days. Can you say game changer?! When you head over to https://www.movetomillionsbook.

com/resources, you'll have access to the checklist so that you'll know what a talent system that will build your million-dollar dream team entails.

In the next chapter, I am going to go deeper into talent. It has a lot of moving parts, too. From a software perspective, you'll need an HR solution, a tool to create your organizational chart, a training backend to house your training plans, modules, SOPs, and a project management tool.

I always recommend that you start with your general operations system. That is the one that you will add to the most once you decide to develop your systems and SOPs. Start documenting everything you do as you work in each area of your company. You can sort them later into a cool directory by system. If you already have a team, have them start documenting and reviewing SOPs immediately. Going forward, make sure that they are reviewed on at least a quarterly basis—all of them. Keep your systems in a living, breathing format so that you can update it consistently. We moved ours into Google Drive when we hired our operations manager last year. This made them more accessible to our growing team. Now all of the systems are cataloged and easily found from our project management and company operation tool Notion. Each system is included in the larger directory, and each has the SOP, a process flow, and a video. No matter how our team members learn, they can view the procedure to help them perform their role with ease.

Let's move into the chapter on the talent management system so that I can dive deeper. I totally geek out on all this systems stuff. I promise you that, although it sounds and feels like a lot, your company's valuation will thank you. By developing these systems, you will be able to add value and increase the likelihood that someone might want to buy your company. It becomes a sellable asset because of the development of your seven systems—well, all of your Million Dollar Assets, really.

You're welcome.

Chapter Action Plan

1. Map out each of your systems.
2. Capture the processes and procedures you use to complete key tasks in your company.
3. Organize them, as indicated in this chapter, by making them living, breathing documents that you can continue to update and add to as needed.

Remember: Information without action is just a waste of time. So, make a plan to implement now so you are one move closer to your first million-dollar year.

Client Case Study

Meet Keira Ingram, K I & Associates

I actually first met Keira because she downloaded our Bible Scriptures for Business Owners. She then booked a discovery session with a member of our sales team and then canceled it. I immediately picked up the phone and called her. Some might say that the rest is history. Keira, at that time, was a real estate broker and owner of a real estate school. Oh, and she was also coaching agents to grow their real estate businesses for *free*. By all accounts her businesses should have been doing millions, but they weren't.

In working together, we were able to help Keira start building her Million Dollar Assets, which included solidifying her coaching division and raising her rates substantially. Within months, she was closing clients and increasing her revenue for that division of the company. With real estate, the broker can't control what they earn per transaction. So, it was important to help Keira diversify her income streams in a way that was in alignment so that she didn't have to work hard to earn more.

By taking something that she was already doing and putting a formal program in place, we saw an immediate increase in her income. We also added retreats and intimate events to Keira's business model. Keira has also built a full team to support her in her business. In 2021, Keira closed her first $100,000 coaching client, and through leveraging the power of live events, she was able to grow the coaching side of her business substantially. At Move to Millions Live 2022, Keira was recognized as an inductee in the Moved to Millions Revenue Club.

> *"As a real estate agent, I wasn't sure if I could make money outside of my industry until Darnyelle helped me create my coaching offer suite. I just closed my first $100,000 coaching client! You need to get into this mastermind. I am renewing for my second year—it's been too good to walk away!"*
>
> **—KEIRA INGRAM**

Her Continuum Move:
From Momentum to Mastery in year one. From Mastery to Millions in year two in the Move to Millions Mastermind.

CHAPTER TEN

Leverage + Scale Talent Suite

"If you have millions on your mind, you need to focus on building
your team because support equals scale."
—DARNYELLE JERVEY HARMON

A
ll that systems talk got me so excited. Systems make it possible for you
to hire your million-dollar dream team. Now, as we jump into this
Million Dollar Asset, I have a confession to make.

I graduated summa cum laude from the If You Want Something Done
Right, Do It Yourself University (IYWSDRDIY). I used to be a proud diploma-wielding aficionado. Notice I said I used to be. Today, it's a different
story. But before we talk about today, let's journey back to what sent me to
IYWSDRDIY University. When I was in corporate, I was very clear that I
never wanted to be a people manager. Projects or processes, sure. But people?
Absolutely not. Remember how I told you that I progressed from entry-level
representative to vice president in three years? It happened so fast, promotion after promotion, that I was accused of sleeping my way to the top. I
never really paid the rumors any mind because at the top there were mostly
bald, white men. They just don't do it for me. But I digress.

As I made the climb, I kept moving in the direction of my dreams, managing projects and processes. I loved unearthing a good strategy to move my
division and department forward. I distinctly remember one meeting with

one of my mentors at the company. My mentor told me that my best bet was to avoid any people-facing positions because I wasn't good with people. I actually wasn't offended. People, at the bank especially, could be a pain in the butt. But I wanted to be a boss, even though being a boss meant that you had to be available *all the time*. Once I had the pager and was on call 24/7, I realized that being a boss for someone else wasn't for me. For months, I stifled the feeling of settling in the name of success. I mean, I couldn't exactly complain about my career to my friends. They would call me crazy. I was under thirty making over six figures. What in the world was there to complain about?

It was then that I realized that my journey couldn't be all about money. Was money important and did I want lots of it? Yes. But I couldn't make decisions or take jobs just to be well paid. The truth was the money wasn't enough. The truth was that I actually hated being the boss. I was responsible for an *entire* department. It was too much, and I was too young to give up my freedom and flexibility. When I should've been traveling the world, I was on duty for the weekend. It's no wonder I couldn't keep a man! I reached my breaking point one weekend when I was onsite for an install and things went awry. But my big boss was nowhere to be found. It dawned on me that I was there so he could travel. That was the beginning of the end of my executive career. I still remember the day like it was yesterday. I call that day my first Keith Sweat Moment. I woke up and something just wasn't right. I tried to ignore the knot in the pit of my stomach. But by the time I got to work, it was a lump in my throat. In an instant, I knew what I had to do. So, I put my big girl panties on and went into my immediate boss's office. I took a deep breath and spoke my peace. I mumbled something incoherent that alluded to the fact that I wasn't ready for my next level. I waited for what felt like twenty minutes for her to express her disappointment, but she said nothing. I could tell she was disappointed. But I couldn't continue to be disappointed in me not speaking up about what was best for *me*. As a result, I asked to step down from my role.

The company obliged, but they also punished me. My punishment? Managing the efforts of others on a frontline team in the fraud department. As I have already expressed, I never wanted to manage people. I mean *never*.

Taking care of myself was hard enough! There I was, thrown head-first into the throws of managing the efforts of twenty adults in a nearly entry-level position. To top it off, they gave me the department's *Bad News Bears*. My team had so many people on a "Plan for Success" it was funny. I told myself that I wasn't cut out for it. While I ended up turning the team around, and our team became the department's top performers, I kept telling myself as I finally left the company a few years later that I didn't want to have a big team ever again.

Like for real. Never again.

And if I had my way, that would still be my story.

Remember I said that what holds us back are the stories we tell ourselves? I told myself that story so many times that when I started to grow my own company, it was still lingering. Highlight this: Your actions will always follow your beliefs. Yes, I realize the irony as I tell you that my team today consists of eight full-time employees and another ten contractors. Oh, trust me. The first time I built a team that story lingered and dismantled my team and company so fast.

Today, however, I have stopped telling that story. Today, having the right team gives me life and freedom. I have learned to love working with others and I am especially grateful, as they are pivotal in the success our company is enjoying. The key, which I didn't realize back then, was having a team who was sold on the vision. The fact remains that there really is no such thing as a self-made million-dollar company. Companies that make millions do so with the help of others. While there are ways to do this with contractors, especially if you are okay with labor from other countries to avoid IRS issues, do your thing. I, instead, am going to share how to build a talent suite filled with full-time team members who will support and sustain your business to and beyond the million-dollar mark in the way that has worked for me and will likely work for you as well.

Once you have tightened your strategy, built a leveraged sales infrastructure, and created some powerful systems and automations in your company, you're ready to build your team. I get that the thought of having a team of employees that you are responsible for feels overwhelming and daunting. But the fact of the matter is that you're looking at it all wrong. With the right team, you will expand your reach without compromising your values. You will also deepen your impact. Your team can be a source of consistent extreme gratitude. Your team is the key to you scaling your company. While you can grow to six figures with one team member, whether a contractor or an employee, crossing the million-dollar mark is about scale. Scale requires more than one team member if you want sustainability.

Scalability is a mindset, too. Sure, you need to have the right systems and processes, people, and plans. But you also need to think big to become big. Having a scalable business means that you are free to deepen the impact you create, build a life you crave, make a lot of money, and have fun doing it. Once you get your mind right, scalability becomes easier.

In order to get to the point where I am today where I love teams, it took work. And to be able to champion the importance of building a team, it's taken systems. To become a million-dollar CEO, you will have to build a team. You'll also have to build a leadership team.

Typically when we first connect with our clients, they have one to two team members, usually including them. Their executive assistant is a "catch all" role, doing all the things that must be done that the CEO doesn't want to do or doesn't have the capacity to do. The CEO, on the other hand, is doing everything else, including service delivery, marketing, and sales. This will only get you so far. I am one of those business coaches who advocate for building your team from your vision point, not your vantage point. Your vantage point will always question if you can afford to hire. Your vision point is looking ahead and will do whatever it takes to experience the next level in your business. Hiring is simple. Pay someone to do $20 to $200 tasks so you are free to do $2,000 to $20,000 tasks. Simple.

A question I get often is: How will I know that it's time to hire to scale my company to and beyond the million-dollar mark? There are five indications that you are ready to hire to scale your company. First, your existing team isn't opening up space for you to work *on* and not *in* your business. If you find yourself with more days than you have time to set strategy, you can't find the time to get in the rooms that elevate your business and spend more than 20 percent of your time performing the key functions of your company, you're ready to hire to scale. If, even with a team, you're spending too much time outside of your zone of genius (as mentioned in one of my favorite books, *The Big Leap*[22]), that is another indication that it's time to think about hiring to scale. Next, once you know that your signature system has been "perfected" to the point where you can get the result you claim for your clients consistently and you've determined how to offer that system at scale, you're one step closer to hiring for scale. And lastly, if you find time each day to think about what is next for you beyond the walls of your business—thinking of philanthropic interests, other business ventures, or partnerships that expand the reach of your vision—then hiring to scale is for you!

Now, just to solidify that this is your next best move, there are a handful of questions to ask yourself:

- **Is there enough demand for your services?** If you were to focus on serving more clients, would there be enough demand for you and your growing team to stay focused on delivering a quality experience to these clients? Do you currently have a waitlist of people who want to work with you? Do you have a community or group where these people are already gathering to begin an indoctrination sequence with you?

- **Is your financial management system tight?** Yes, it's going to take cash to build a team. So, you want to make sure that you have a financial management team supporting your efforts as you hire. At minimum, you'll want a CPA and bookkeeper (no, they are not the same). You'll likely want a tax strategist, too, if your CPA is not an expert in tax management and mitigation.

- **Do you have the right technology?** This becomes increasingly important if your team is going to be virtual. If you'll have team members in different locations, you'll have to make sure that you have the right technology to support them all so that your business doesn't suffer due to lulls or lags.

- **Do you have an HR consultant who can guide you as you start hiring?** This is important because laws around hiring team members change frequently and vary from state to state. If your team will not be located where your headquarters is, you'll have to know how to manage the process. Don't try to do this by yourself.

- **Do you know your customer expectations?** As you grow your client count, you'll have to be clear on your client and customer management processes and policies. If you are not, this could create a bottleneck that could impact your ability to grow and scale this part of the company.

- **Do you have the right processes/systems in place?** If you can't say yes, just refer back to the last chapter. Systems not only make millions predictable, but they also make hiring so much simpler. Every time I think of the difference that bringing on another team member with ease has made because we took the time to create standard operating procedures, I thank God.

- **Who do you need on your team and in what order should you hire them?** I will shed some light on this question below.

Once you know that you're ready, your first stop is your talent suite. Your talent suite includes the systems and procedures you use to manage the team of your company. I'm sure you've already snagged your checklist that breaks down everything that is included in this suite. Let me say this: Be sure to work with an HR professional to build your team. While you won't be required by law to have in-house HR support until your team size grows beyond your state's limits, you definitely don't want to break any laws of violating anything that could put your million-dollar company in jeopardy. New laws are being instituted each year, so make sure someone is thinking about those things for your company. Trust me. The right solution will be an investment in your business's sustainability.

When it comes to building the team that will take you to and beyond the million-dollar mark, I already shared that the high-level that you want to think in terms of is three ultimate teams—your operations team, your talent team, and your marketing and sales team. To determine what each of these roles will do, I highly recommend my Change the Way You Work exercise. This activity can be found in our Move to Millions 90-Day Planner. To complete this exercise, you'll take a sheet of paper and make three columns: hate to do, tolerate doing, love to do. Filter everything that has to be done in your company into one of the three columns. The things you hate and tolerate will become the jobs of others who will join your team. What you love to do will be what you focus on. To be clear, it could be a few years before you're only doing what you love, but that is absolutely the goal. To start, let's look at where you are more than likely as you read this book. Here's a graphic representation of how your team should be when you're ready to scale beyond low six figures on the Move to Millions.

But here is what your team probably actually looks like right now if you're just over the six-figure mark:

Our goal is to get you thinking about your team based on the first image, with three clear teams (even if, right now, you are the only team member on all of them). Doing this is the beginning of thinking like a CEO of a major company.

At this point, your team includes you as the CEO. If you're lucky, you have some administrative support. You're wearing all the hats as you celebrate hitting the six-figure mark in your business. This happens for several reasons. But mostly, at this point, you have to set the pace for your company by doing the most. Even though you start here, this is just a steppingstone, not a stopping point. Because it's likely just you, you are also likely the talent team, as the only person performing the service. Your executive assistant, if you have one, is the operations team, which includes client care, customer service, and administrative functions. He or she assists you in running the marketing and sales team by helping with scheduling, marketing related tasks, and sales follow-up. More than likely you're not calling your assistant an EA because they are a virtual assistant who you share with other entrepreneurs who are also trying to build and grow their companies. Right now, you are *in* the business. Wait, right now, you *are* the business. That's right. Your clients are hiring you.

If you have had the foresight to hire a business coach or consultant to guide you, they are helping you with strategy because you can't do a lot of that on your own. You're doing most of the things in your business yourself, and your assistant is doing the rest. Between the two of you, you're tired and overworked. This team got you to six figures, $100,000 a year, and to the momentum tier of the continuum. But if this continues to be all who is on your team, it will create massive bottlenecks as you move up the continuum toward seven figures. And in full transparency, my team at this stage consisted of me and my phantom assistant, Regina. Well, at least for the first year or so. Then I brought on a part-time physical assistant for twenty hours a week. Because I needed more support, she became a full-time assistant. Eventually, we needed some technical support. So, I hired a technical marketing VA, who worked with us twenty hours a month. This team took me to the million-dollar mark, but we did it the hard way. I really should have hired a few more people to support us. But because I was working *in* and not *on* the business, I didn't realize that we needed more people to support us. Between the two of them, all administrative and technical support was covered. I did all the rest. I want you to learn from my mistakes. That is why I am suggesting that you do what I was too afraid to do during that time in my business.

As soon as you decide that you want to move to multiple six figures and are heading toward $100,000 quarters, what we consider the mastery tier on the continuum, here are some of the adjustments I recommend making on your team:

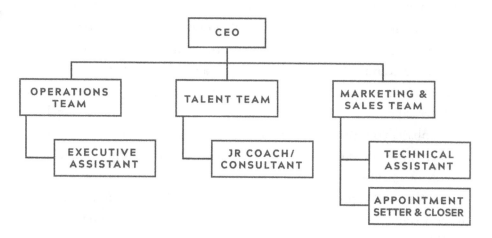

At this level, your EA is also being trained to manage the day-to-day of the business as your operations lead. They will start, update, and continue creating your SOPs, manage your calendar, and protect your time so you can work on the business at least 20 percent of your time. They will also start to coordinate with your other team members, giving you a bit of separation in preparation for when you shift out of the day-to-day altogether. You'll want to have someone else who can assist with the client service delivery, even if it's only part-time.

Depending on your current client count, you should consider one team member for every thirty to forty clients, based on the amount of support they receive in working with you. You can use this as a good gauge to determine when to hire next. Bringing a person on at least part-time should free up eight to ten hours of your time each week so you can start working *on* the business. It is mandatory that you have 20 percent of your time to work *on* the business at this point. If you can bring on a full-time talent team member, that can free up twenty hours of your week, giving you 50 percent of your time to work on the business. That is even better. We eventually need to get you to 80 percent working *on* the business and only 20 percent *in* the business.

Lastly, you'll want to add a technical assistant to your marketing and sales team because your marketing will start to intensify. To hit six figures, we are talking ten clients paying you $10,000. To hit $500,000, we are talking about fifty if you have a $10,000 program. Depending on your conversion rates, that means a little more intricacy in your business sales cycle. You'll need technical support for that. It's also now time to get some help with sales, one person who can set appointments for you. They will qualify prospects so you can meet with them and close them. I do recommend that, in this phase, you still be part of the sales process. But I also recommend that you begin the documentation process to start to move away from having to be present to close the sales.

As your team approaches the millions tier of the continuum, experiencing consistent $100,000 cash months, here is an example of how your team should grow:

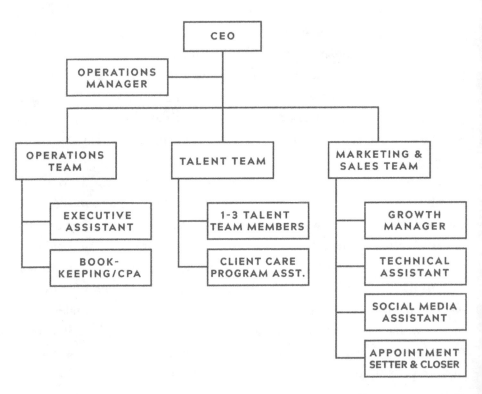

At this level, you now have an operations manager, which reduces how much of *you* has to show up in the day-to-day once they are up to speed. Your ops lead is focused on the day-to-day management of the company and all of your core teams. As you can imagine, you're now free to create and be in the rooms where deals and decisions are made. On your operations team, you still have your EA and financial management support. Your EA is working more closely with you on helping you preside strategically over the company. They are managing your time and your calendar and booking your travel. They are also doing some light prospecting for speaking engagements to help you determine where you should be so you can make the right connections to continue to open up opportunities. They will still handle your general customer service as well. If you're now approaching one hundred clients, it's time to consider a full-time person just for your company's client care needs.

On your talent team, you should now have at least one full-time talent team member and potentially a second full-time, or at least a part-time, team member. The full-time person should be a support team member and the part-time person should be a complimentary team member. That additional coach/speaker/trainer/consultant/attorney/accountant/designer is making a difference, and you can see it! Your client care/program assistant is making sure that your clients are having an experience that continues to wow them. This helps with your renewal rates, so you don't have to go find more clients. (This role could still be managed by your EA at this point.) As your client count accelerates, your client care or program assistant becomes more important. They are managing the communities of your clients online, as well as getting feedback and making sure that your testimonials are captured and featured appropriately by your marketing and sales team.

Speaking of marketing and sales, did you notice that you now have a growth manager? Your growth manager's job is to oversee marketing and sales, which means you don't have to. They personally will also be focused on finding and creating opportunities for you to expand your reach through speaking and getting on podcasts as well as identifying joint venture opportunities. Reporting to them will be your technology assistant, social media manager (which could be a part-time VA), and members of the sales team.

You now have someone else closing sales both through sales calls and in the DMs. Because each member of the marketing and sales team reports to your growth manager, they are maintaining your KPIs and reporting that up through your operations manager.

You are successfully reducing the amount of time you spend in the business. You're still participating at a high-level in service delivery, perhaps leading some group experiences and/or delivering the core strategy, and then handing it off to your capable team members to run the ball all the way to the desired outcome for your client. The number of meetings you facilitate has also changed. You've begun to oversee just two meetings: your all-hands meeting and your management team meeting. Each management team member is responsible for meeting with their teams. Can you smell that? It's *freedom*. You're free to keynote, start a podcast, book some media interviews, write the book that will expand your reach, and look at how you'll continue growing this company to the majesty and monumental levels on the continuum.

One last note here: As you hire, I always recommend that you start hiring at the assistant or manager level and promote team members into director level roles. This will save you money. The first year or so when they join your company, they are learning more than they are adding value, and you don't want to overpay for that.

Focusing on your talent suite is an act of vision. When we get into the vision section of this book, I will share so much more. I am so proud of you because, at this point, you have walked through each of the Million Dollar Assets that are required to firmly position you on the Move to Millions.

Chapter Action Plan

1. Create your current organizational chart. (Yes, fill your name in for every job you're currently doing. We all start where you are now.)
2. Create your *ideal* organizational chart using the examples we share with you in this chapter. We need to know what we are working toward.
3. Create key job descriptions by completing the Change the Way You Work activity.
4. Meet with your financial management team to verify that you can begin the hiring process.
5. Design your hiring process and start hiring for your future million-dollar team.

Remember: Information without action is just a waste of time. So, make a plan to implement now so you are one move closer to your first million-dollar year.

Client Case Study

———

Meet Jasmine Womack, the EMPACT Group

I met Jasmine in a coaching program we were in together. I was immediately impressed with her heart, spirit, and commitment to excellence. Our work together began in my Leverage & Scale Weekend program, but she quickly upgraded into our Move to Millions Mastermind. Just before joining the mastermind, I helped her tweak her slides and sales approach for an already planned launch. That resulted in $39,500 in sales. Once she joined the mastermind officially, within her first month or so, she had a $249,000 launch and went on to end the year with her first live event that produced nearly $500,000 in sales, which meant that in one year we tripled her business. (She was around the $250,000 mark when we started working together). In our second year, she grew her business again by 85 percent and moved to millions! She'll join our Moved to Millions Revenue Club at the event in May 2023.

As I share with all of my clients, growth is not just financial. For Jasmine, there's also been a lot of growth in her team and her stepping into being the CEO of her company. Watching her own this space has been a joy. I have really seen her strengthen her leadership skills and right fit her company in our second year working together in the mastermind. She's changed her contractors into employees and is actively hiring and building out the team that will support her beyond the million-dollar mark with more ease. The Move to Millions requires a lot of support and leadership, which is typically an entirely different skill set than most start with. Jasmine has grown so much, and I am excited about the sustainable multimillion-dollar company she is building.

> *"Before working with Darnyelle, I already had a business that I was proud of. Darnyelle is the GOAT! She's helped me grow my business, hold profitable events and step into the role of CEO for my company. In working with her, I've more than quadrupled my revenue and over two years, her coaching and insights have assisted me in making the move to millions. I'm forever grateful for Darnyelle in my life and business."*
> **—JASMINE WOMACK**

Her Continuum MOVE:
From Momentum to Mastery in year one and from Mastery to Millions in year two in the Move to Millions Mastermind.

Part 2:

Operational Obedience

CHAPTER ELEVEN

Move to Millions Confidence

*"Having confidence is like telling God that
He was right to create you."*
—DARNYELLE JERVEY HARMON

When I was in high school, I spent as much time as I could with my friend Nina. Nina's whole family had the kind of home I think most wish they lived in. There was an unspoken confidence that they each had in themselves and in each other. That confidence was as a result of a clear love and appreciation for one another. Man, I wished I lived in a home like that. My home, on the other hand, was chaotic at best. We were five people, living in the same house, with the same last name. Dassit. We didn't eat meals together. We didn't vacation together. There were most certainly none of those "How was your day today?" moments that I think other families may exchange. I could never relate to being from a family like that, but man did I dream. And I decided that one day I would have my own family. It would be everything mine wasn't.

By high school, my dad was traveling most weeks. That meant we were left home with my stepmother, who made it painstakingly clear that she wished we weren't there. I already told you how I used to hear her on the phone talking to her mother saying, "I wish Jeannie would come get her kids."

As you can imagine, this kind of energy can eat away at your confidence. That is why time with Nina was so important. With her help, I started to believe that I did matter. That gave me the confidence to set goals and aspirations for the future versus sitting in the disappointment of not feeling loved. Nina's mom, English, was my personal cheerleader. I used to love to have her take me in her arms and just love on me.

Confidence.

It's that thing that everybody wants, yet few know how to get. Now, if your upbringing was anything like mine, you were probably told more than once that children should be seen and not heard.

Can you relate?

That will definitely mess with your confidence. I have clients who are more than forty years old who still struggle with being seen and heard. Every time they think about shining the light on their brilliance, they hear mom or dad (or an auntie or a nana) in their head. So, they shrink back. While I don't think your parents meant to stifle your creativity, your connection, and yes, your confidence, they likely did if that was what you were told.

We had family over to the house once. I was dancing and my dad didn't like it very much. He screamed my whole government name and told me to sit down. Then, he said the words that made me start to question myself: "I have to see you, but I don't want to hear you."

You see, I was told often that I wasn't supposed to be here. My presence was something others regretted. And as a result, it stuck with me. It made me angry. Well, pissed is a better expression of how I felt. But I was also confused. How could this be my life? How could someone wish that I wasn't here? I took this anger with me everywhere I went. In spite of this, Mrs. Dixon sought to protect my potential and showed me how to be confident. First in words; then in action. As a result, I grew into a woman with confidence. Extreme confidence. Confidence so high that I am often mistaken for cocky. No matter how the person labeling me this way's insecurity bumped up against my confidence, I haven't wavered in my knowledge of who I am.

Listen. It doesn't matter where I go. People always ask me, "How did you get so confident?" They always expressed a desire to be the same. The truth of the matter is you can be this confident, but it is going to take work.

Now, part of the reason this principle, along with faith, is its own chapter is because your confidence is everything on your journey to making, moving, and leaving millions. I wanted to talk about confidence and specifically something that I've created for my clients: The Confidence Clause. I know how hard it can be to undo the boatloads of damage that may have been offered to you over the course of your childhood.

We talked previously about the Model of Abundance. In my opinion, your confidence is what allows you to be. *Being* is about identity, and there is confidence in identity.

When we are born, although we are born as vessels of light, in full abundance, seldom does that abundance make it into adulthood. This is not because the desire for abundance goes away. In fact, abundance is an inherent birthright. We always crave it. It dissipates often because of how we are raised. From birth to the age of seven, our confidence, or lack thereof, is fortified in what we experience, what we are taught, and what is caught from those who are raising us. If your upbringing was anything like mine, then you may not have been exposed to confident women. Instead, you likely were exposed to fear, lack, doubt, disbelief, and even religious bondage. If you weren't exposed to confident, bold women who spoke their mind, walked in boldness, and didn't downplay or dismiss their greatness, you likely weren't taught that it is okay to be confident and that your confidence is your way of thanking God for creating you. People told me all the time that anytime I wanted to exude confidence, I was being cocky. That really made me stifle and downplay all that I am because I didn't want to be perceived that way. Although *I* didn't believe I was being cocky, I would shrink, because as people always say perception is reality.

I bought into those fallacies, and they stifled the way I showed up for myself for a lot of years. It wasn't until I began to get older, as a result of the seeds planted by Mrs. Dixon, that I began to see that confidence is actually a virtue. Everyone should aspire to be confident.

[sidebar] If you are a parent of a child who is bold and audacious, can you do me a favor? Please stop stifling their genius. You will do more damage than good. When they are forty years old, they will still be trying to unpack the fact that there is nothing wrong with them. They are okay the way they

are. In my forthcoming docuseries of the same name, *Move to Millions*, there is a scene where one of my featured clients, Marissa, describes what happened with her niece and sister. In the clip, Marissa recounts a time when her niece, Blake, was told to "do it right" when asked to sing the ABCs. *Right* meant that she would do it in a boring, traditional way. Marissa recounts for us how it immediately stifled Blake's creativity. She reminded us that there is no right way to express yourself. Confidence is about being true to who you are. As you endeavor to move your business to the million-dollar mark, you may find moments when your confidence wanes. Let Marissa's words be a reminder that you are right for your next level.

Once I realized that my confidence was a gift, I finally understood what Marianne Williamson said in her poem "Our Deepest Fear."[23] Me shining my light [in confidence] was me giving others permission to do the same. Listen to me. Confidence negates fear. So, I guess really, you can thank God, Mrs. Dixon, and Marianne Williamson for me being the confident woman you are getting to know through this book. I am, unapologetically, extremely confident, oozing with confidence, loving living every minute of a confident experience. And I want the same for you. If you recall, confidence is from God. Displaying it is saying thank you for your creation.

Can we talk about what confidence can look like for you? It's kind of sad that I even have to ask you, but the fact of the matter is that it's extremely unfortunate that tons of women, entrepreneurs, and small business owners don't have confidence to see themselves as million-dollar CEOs. It is a proven fact that women undercharge, act inferior, and they're noncompetitive in the marketplace. They often allow fear to keep them from positioning themselves to build bigger businesses.[24]

In fact, did you know that studies show that over 85 percent of all women entrepreneurs struggle with confidence, mindset, and fear when it comes to setting their prices, closing the sale, and attracting new ideal paying clients?[25] This is bothersome to me. I totally get it because I work primarily with women entrepreneurs. I see it all the time. What I've come to realize is that even though you may not display the confidence that says you've got it going on, more often than not, you do have it going on.

I see you out there. You are brilliant. Sure, you have moments when you question or rethink. But you know that you know that you know your ish! You just don't know how to exude it and how to share it in a way that is completely and authentically in alignment with who you are and who you are becoming. That is really what I'm hoping to share with you in this chapter. You do have the necessary skills to exceed your clients' and customers' expectations and stand boldly, flat-footed in the belief that you are confidence personified.

I know you. More than likely, you think that being humble means that you shouldn't brag about your skills. While I would agree that bragging in and of itself may not be a good look, highlighting your successes builds trust and credibility among those looking to invest in themselves through you. So, if you are amongst the 85 percent, you should be really excited that you're reading this book right now. I'm literally going to share five ways that you can instantly up your confidence so you can start to accelerate your business as a result.

"Your confidence will close more sales than your skills ever will."
–Darnyelle Jervey Harmon

This statement right here is the reason I created the model of financial and spiritual abundance.

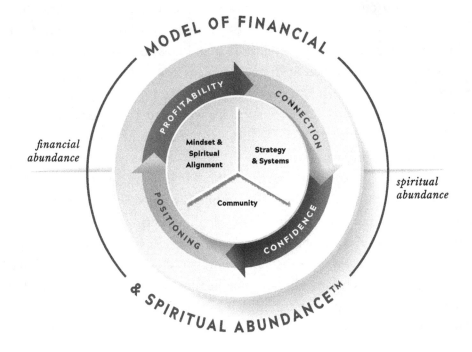

Basically, your connection to God determines your confidence, which impacts your positioning and ultimately your profitability. Helping our clients understand and shift their confidence based on this model is one of many game changers they experience in our programs.

When you don't see yourself as an expert, one who adds tremendous value to others, you'll struggle with sales. There will be no millions if there are no sales. You'll struggle with whether you should, and can, charge what you know you need to charge in order to position your business to experience profitability. Conversely, when you see yourself as a gift to the world, and the value that you add as priceless and transformative, you won't struggle to set rates that position you and your business to grow and experience profit. This model exists so you can build the team required to make you a million-dollar CEO. Your confidence will make room for you to move your business forward. In fact, your prospects will often have to borrow your confidence to make an investment decision in themselves because they see you as a catalyst in their next level.

I always recommend that entrepreneurs learn how to think like a major corporation CEO. At that level, you don't hear about CEOs allowing their fears and emotions to impact the business building process. They know that business is quite simply a numbers game. They know that the one who has the best command of their numbers is usually the one who experiences big growth and wins.

Several years ago, I did an episode of *Incredible Factor TV* where someone asked a question about the role that confidence plays in the leveraging and scaling of a business. I believe they were wondering if they could be successful in their own business if their confidence was low. This could get me into trouble, but I'm going to go so far as to say that if you aren't confident, you should have a job.

No matter where I go to speak, I do what I call a confidence check with the audience. I started doing it to get some firsthand market research for a program I was working on. Once I am introduced to the audience and start my talk, I always take a survey.

"By show of hands, how many of you would say that you have a relationship with God? And you'd say your relationship is at least seven to ten?" Ninety percent, if not 100 percent, of the hands would go up. Then I would ask my follow up question: "Now, on that same scale of one to ten, how many of you would say your confidence is a seven to ten?" Eighty percent of the hands would go down. How can that be? How can you be in a relationship with God but not be confident?

If you ask me, you can't.

Yet, it happens every day.

It has to stop. Women, especially, need to be restored to an understanding that they are confidence personified. That is a big part of my mission. In 2019, I was invited to speak at my largest speaking engagement to date. There were twelve thousand people in the audience. If that excites you, wait until I tell you how I ended up being invited to speak. Unbeknownst to me, while in the bathroom, I had a conversation with a powerful woman. We never exchanged names or anything. We were just being pleasant while washing our hands together. It turns out that she was a decision maker who had the ability to change my life in a minute. As we were washing our hands,

I happened to say something that stuck with her. She asked for my info, and I returned to my seat. Approximately a month later, I received a call from the woman who was a C-suite executive for a company that was producing their annual event, where they anticipated ten thousand attendees. They wanted *me* to be the opening keynote speaker. The executive shared that they only had a budget of $25,000, and she hoped that my fee would allow for my participation. I never told the woman that my keynote fee was $10,000 at the time. I happily and confidently accepted the gig for $15,000 *more* than I had ever been paid to keynote an event.

Others have always admired my confidence. My confidence has never been in question. But I know that not everyone can say that. So, it is for them that I developed the Confidence Curve. As you might recall, I introduced you to the Confidence Curve earlier when we were talking about pricing your offer suite. The curve takes two things into account: first, that you understand that you should be operating at a higher level; and second, that you need time to make the shift. Whether we are talking pricing, clientele, your relationship, whatever—you should be operating at a higher level. The challenge is that although you know that deep down, you're not there yet. So, it's not easy to act as if. As a result, you still self-sabotage and let your fear run the show in the various areas of your life. We understand that getting to the point of confidence to take the next step will require work, so we instituted The Confidence Curve to bridge the gap. The curve allows us to make a deal with our clients. They agree to trust our guidance, and we agree to create a pathway for them to walk to close the gap confidently.

Here's the thing: I can tell you to raise your rates until I turn purple. But if you don't believe that you can charge that amount, you won't raise them no matter how many times I tell you. Take Lindsey, for example, a brilliant consultant. Her work really is amazing, and she gets amazing results. But she has spent a lot of time confronting her beliefs based on what others have told her. In their words, "She's not a pretty girl. She should be happy with what she has instead of trying to get more." Well, I know firsthand that if you hear something enough, you start to believe it. Lindsey was no different. She believed what she had been told for years. As a result, she found herself constantly questioning her business skills and lowered her rates because she couldn't imagine coming face-to-face with another example of what others had been telling her for years.

To help Lindsey shift, I got her to document all of the success she had helped her clients achieve. The list was full. After having her write out the list, she immediately saw the fruits of her labor. I noticed her countenance change slightly. After she finished compiling the list, I had her go back and write down what each client had paid her and what they had made as a result of their work. When Lindsey added up the list, there were fifty-nine clients on it and they had made a combined $3.35 million dollars *because* of her, although they had all only paid her a combined $120,000! Sometimes confidence needs receipts. When your confidence is in question always look at your competence. Your competence can fill the gap until your confidence can catch up. We are often so busy moving on to the next thing that we forget to stop and reflect on the last thing. By showing Lindsey hers, we were able to institute her Confidence Curve™.

When she came to me, Lindsey was charging $5,000 for a six-month consulting agreement. After running her program through our pricing calculator, we realized that her $5,000 program really should have been priced at $18,000. Lindsey admitted that she was struggling to get to the $18,000 number, even though she saw what her clients had achieved. She agreed that she should at least double her price to $10,000. I agreed with this, with one stipulation. For the next three clients who enrolled, the fee would be $10,000. After that, she had to raise it by $2,500, so that the next three would pay $12,500. Then, she would raise it again by $2,500 to allow the next three clients to enroll at $15,000. Her final price bump, after serving nine new clients and getting them results, would be to $18,000. I'm proud to report that Lindsey completed her curve, and she did it in a record three months. I will happily give clients the curve if it helps them to confidently arrive at the price that they should be charging their clients in record time like it did for Lindsey. She told me that if she weren't working with me and my team, it might have taken her three or four years to get to that price point!

This is the value of having a coach that sees you, supports you, and also holds up a mirror of who you are and what you can actually accomplish. One of the joys of the work that my team and I do in our Move to Millions Mastermind is giving our clients permission to blow their own minds because their confidence inspires them! Confidence will hold space and close gaps. Confidence will shift paradigms and defy odds. Confidence says, "I got this, and I am the best thing since pockets!" (I mean really is there anything better than pockets, especially in a cute dress?!) That is the benefit of having confidence on this journey to the million-dollar mark. I am going to go so far as to say that you won't make millions if you aren't confident. That is also a big part of the reason that those statistics are what they are. I truly believe that if we could increase the confidence of black women in business, we would also increase their company revenue, value, and positioning. Standing boldly and flat-footed in the obedience of living life like you know who created you is essential to operating a company that serves you both financially and spiritually.

Chapter Action Plan

1. Write down every client you've ever helped to get results.
2. Write down the results you helped them to achieve and what they paid you to achieve those results.
3. Knowing what you know and realize now, are you confidently articulating your value in the marketplace? If not, start showing up more confidently.
4. Write down a minimum of five ways you can show up more confidently in the marketplace to boost traction and sales.

Remember: Information without action is just a waste of time. So, make a plan to implement now so you are one move closer to your first million-dollar year.

CHAPTER TWELVE
Move to Millions Forgiveness

"Unforgiveness is the reason you experience flex
instead of flow in your business."
—DARNYELLE JERVEY HARMON

A few years ago, I realized something very profound: You can't have a booming business when you have a busted life. When you hear the word busted, what comes to mind? For me, a busted life includes anything that keeps you from alignment and peace. Anything that you settle for that is less than your abundant birthright contributes to a busted life. I still remember that fall day in September 2019 when I was driving down the road, minding my business, when out of nowhere, God spoke these words to me:

"I will let them live on whatever level they settle for."

I had to pull my car over to process what I'd just heard God practically yell at me. Once I got the car safely over to the side of the road, I put the car in park and asked God to repeat Himself to make sure that I hadn't misheard Him.

He repeated, "I will let them live on whatever level they settle for."

"Who is them, God?" I asked.

"Entrepreneurs. You are called to entrepreneurs, so I am talking about entrepreneurs."

I paused and really let that set in. If I heard God correctly, He was saying that as entrepreneurs, we have decided to have lives and businesses that don't serve us fully.

Wow.

I know firsthand that so many entrepreneurs settle for a busted life when God created them to live a booming one. This realization got me wondering. Was it because entrepreneurs undercharge? Don't understand marketing? Aren't clear how to position themselves with their messaging? Can't sell water in the desert? Are they afraid to hire the right team members? In my mind, regardless of the reason why entrepreneurs are settling, it needs to stop. The truth is if we can live on whatever level we settle for, we should settle for our Next Level Everything. To me, settling means that you aren't experiencing the desires of your heart.

Just before God gave me Move to Millions, He gave me Next Level Everything. And a Next Level Everything life is a life where every area of your life is booming. Because we live in a fake-it-until-you-make-it society, it might be hard for you to realize or admit that there is a "bust" in your life.

Here's a list of some of the ways you might be living a busted life:

- You know that you're not charging enough to have a business that serves you.
- You find yourself comparing yourself to others all. the. time.
- You constantly question why you aren't where you know you should be.
- Fear is the true CEO of your business.
- You're hiding behind someone else's brand or worse, desk.
- You call yourself a CEO but are secretly looking for a job; or secretly driving Uber and Lyft to make ends meet.
- You spend a lot of time stressed or in overwhelm.
- Your marketing strategy feels like you're throwing spaghetti against a wall to see what, if anything, sticks.
- You believe that money and success are hard to have (and currently don't have enough of either).
- You think that by succeeding you'll leave loved ones behind.
- You secretly envy others who are experiencing what you pray for.

- You set big goals but don't hold yourself accountable, even though achieving them would change your life.
- You're not convinced that you are an expert and that you are able to solve problems for your prospects.
- You suffer from imposter syndrome and question your worth when no one is looking or listening.
- You are stuck in perfection, instead of being focused on progress and being productive.
- You find yourself justifying why you are still harboring ill will and feelings toward someone else instead of forgiving them.

That last one though. Of all the examples of how you're living a busted life, likely without even knowing it, that last one—unforgiveness—will upset your money cart. It will wreak havoc on your life. We will talk more about forgiveness in a minute. Seriously, the sad thing about a busted life is that it may not be obvious to anyone else, except you. Every day, I see entrepreneurs with the most busted lives, looking like (or at least acting as if they look like) a million bucks—although making that in their business is far from their reality. What's even more sad is the fact that there is an unbelievable cost to living a busted life. You're spending an *incredible* amount of energy, inspiration, intelligence, time, and money, allowing fear, and limiting beliefs to stop you from living up to your God-ordained potential. When you're in struggle, you have no access to ideas, inspiration, creativity, vitality, God, or intelligence. You are literally *stuck*. I mean, seriously, are you stuck? Have you been spending time each day feeling stuck?

Let's say you struggle two hours a day with stress, unforgiveness, overwhelm, fear, self-criticism, comparison, or worry, which shows up as you feeling stuck. That's 732 hours a year. If you earn $300 per hour, that's $219,600 in lost income per year and $2.19 million lost over ten years. But it's more than the money. How about not reaching your full potential? Or questioning the purpose God gave you day in and day out? Let's not forget not being fully present for yourself and loved ones, plus the physical toll on your body. I must wonder if you feel it's worth it to meander in the mediocrity of being stuck when you could be strutting in the significance of your

Next Level Everything. Here's what I know: If you want to stop settling for life at your last level because God has already ordained your next, you need to forgive.

I only know about living a busted life while looking like I'm living a booming life because that used to be my story. I used to be the queen of faking it until you make it. I haven't told you the complete truth about myself yet. I am a Scorpio. If you know anything about Scorpios and believe the horoscopes are true, you might understand where I am going with this unforgiveness thing. The whole truth is that I can hold a grudge better than anyone you know. I can create a reason as to why you're "black history" and nothing you can do will remove my grudge and get you back into my good graces once you piss me off. For more years that I care to admit, I struggled with unforgiveness. That was the source of my busted life.

My therapist used to call me a volcano. She said it was all good until I was triggered because I felt violated. That violation would produce Mt. Vesuvius (if you recall, that's the volcano that erupted and killed all the people). I struggled to forgive myself, my parents, my siblings, that girl that cut me off when I first got my license—basically, anyone who wronged me. I felt justified to hold on to the offense for dear life. I was deep into my thirties before I realized that holding on to these offenses was literally choking the life out of me. Most of the people who "wronged" me had no idea I was still lamenting over the issue. They were off living their best lives, and I was stuck, stagnant, and struggling to let ish go.

To look at me, you wouldn't be able to tell—just like you can't tell that your favorite celebrity, business owner, or influencer might be struggling with it, too. The thing about harboring unforgiveness is that no one has to know. It can be your little secret. Except unforgiveness will eventually mess with your money, alignment, and flow. Unforgiveness will cause you to flex because you can't bring flow into your life. You'll be thinking that "it's just not your turn or season" and placating your next level, when in reality forgiveness will be the only thing that can break the cycle you're in.

That will make things hard, like pushing a boulder up a hill, hard. It will be disguised in being unable to close new clients, getting rejected for speaking engagements, and clients suddenly being disgruntled and wanting to leave your program, or get a refund, or even not paying their bill. You'll likely shake it off as "part of the cost of doing business," when in reality it's the cost of your unforgiveness. If you desire to have a million-dollar company, forget about it (in my best Italian voice). Holding on to unforgiveness will inhibit you from accessing your million-dollar company slowly but surely. Unforgiveness is like a slow leak. In the moment you can't see any effects on your life or business. But eventually, everything goes flat. Most often, unforgiveness shows up in your ability to make money move.

What I have come to learn is that my unforgiveness was a big part of the reason that I didn't make it to the million-dollar mark once I initially set the goal to do so. If you recall, I set the goal for three years before it became my reality, almost by accident. I told you the story of how, in 2014, in preparation for our live event, the order form that I tried to change back to our lower rates was "magically" corrupted upon being sent to the printer. As a result, we couldn't get it fixed unless I confessed to my team that I really didn't believe in myself and, therefore, them. There was no way I was going to do that. What I didn't realize until I recently started reflecting on the story in preparation to sit down to write this chapter was that the *real* reason we crossed the million-dollar mark that year was because I had forgiven the one person who I held in contempt for ruining my life up until that point.

As I started to recount what was happening at the time that we were preparing for the live event, I was finally able to release the person of the wrong they had done. That forgiveness, coupled with the increased rates, sound strategy, and our ability to fill the room with more than 250 attendees combined, is what created the flow right into $1,300,000 in three short days. While unforgiveness may appear to be a slow leak, taking it's time to suck the life out of you, forgiveness is an accelerant for your next level and your millions.

One of the catalysts for that forgiveness is now something I consider to be a secret weapon. In 2013, I stumbled upon a book called *Forgiving Forward* by Bruce and Toni Hebel. I admit that the book sat on my desk for months. Every time I went to start reading it, I got distracted. One Saturday morning, I woke up with a strong need to read that book. I read the whole thing in five hours, only stopping to use the bathroom. When I say that the book changed my life, it feels like an understatement. But it did. I realized that forgiveness was for me, and that I could heal and move on with my life. Were it not for the fact that very soon after I ran that person through the Forgiveness Protocol, which I now do on a weekly basis, I wouldn't have been able to see the correlation to forgiveness and the uninhibited flow of my money.

It was important to include forgiveness in this section of the book because understanding the significance of the role forgiveness plays on your Move to Millions will help to make sure nothing stops you from moving. You may have thought that, to make millions, you just need to do $83,333.33 a month for a year. While that is true, when you look just at math, opening up the flow for the $83,333.33 to even come into your life and business won't happen if you don't do your forgiveness work. Strategy won't unblock the flow of your funds, nor will closing more sales, writing better copy, tightening your systems, or building a team—alone. Sure, you'll need each of them to make millions happen. But you'll also need to do what one of my favorite Scriptures says you should do.

Let me paint you a picture of what is happening in Mark 11:12-26, so that you can understand why forgiveness is centrifugal on your move to millions. Oh, and this is the Darnyelle version of the Bible. I do recommend that you read what the actual Scripture says. Here's my version:

So, Jesus and His boys, the disciples, are walking from one town to another. On the way to the town, Jesus gets hungry. So when He sees a fig tree, He goes over for a fig newton (this is my version, remember). The fig tree is not producing figs. He gets a little heated. He curses the fig tree and tells it to die. The disciples are looking at Jesus and they are kind of shocked. I imagine that they may have even said something like, "Yo, Jesus is straight tripping." But they keep walking. The next day, they're coming back past the same tree Jesus cursed the day before. All of a sudden it dawns on them that this is *the* tree Jesus cursed. The disciples are like, "Yo! That's that fig tree that Jesus cursed yesterday. Look at it. It's dead! Dang!" Jesus then turns around, and He explains to them that you can tell any mountain to move, and it will under three circumstances. One, you have to believe. Two, you cannot doubt. And three—this is the one that gets most of us in trouble because we don't want to do this—you have to *forgive*.

Wait! What?

Yes, I am telling you that the reason your business isn't already making millions is tied, at least in part, to the unforgiveness that still sits in your heart. I see it all the time. In fact, I will go so far as to say that 75–80 percent of my clients have a million-dollar business when they come to me. It's just not packaged, positioned, and priced right. They also haven't pardoned those who have wronged them on the journey. Who they need to pardon could be their parents, spouses, loved ones, or clients who have wronged them, run out on the program, dodged them for payments. Anyone who you need to forgive but don't, can block the flow of the funds coming to you. Money is meant to move; it's an energy. If it's not moving for you, then the first place you should check is your unforgiveness. For money to move, you need to be free to flow in alignment with the money you desire.

According to the universal law—the law of abundance—abundance (money) is expanding around us at an ever-increasing rate.[26] That means that money never stops moving. *Never.* It's like a river. It's supposed to flow and move. If it has stopped moving for you, there is some unforgiveness somewhere. According to the law, there are several things we can do that will stop the flow of money. High on the list is unforgiveness (like number one). Unforgiveness could be harbored for yourself and for others.

Jesus gives us the success formula for life:

Speak + Believe + Don't Doubt + Forgiveness = *Any* Mountain Moved

This is universal. When God first gave me operational obedience as a part of the MOVE, admittedly, I was like *What does that have to do with making millions of dollars?* But then it dawned on me. It has everything to do with it. My own journey to the million-dollar mark the first time, and the most recent and sustaining time, was as much about forgiving myself and others for any and everything as it was having the right strategy, sales infrastructure, systems, and support.

Part of the reason I run the Forgiveness Protocol every Sunday is because I don't want anything keeping me from the abundance which I am due, the abundance God already earmarked and reserved for me. You shouldn't either. Forgiveness unlocks the breakthrough in your business that takes you to the million-dollar mark and beyond. Sure, you will see *some* success without forgiveness. But it will be limited, and you will be playing small. The right opportunities will not present themselves or, if they do, you will self-sabotage. You will think you've won, only to discover as you awaken and begin to forgive that you were actually losing.

Prior to holding the Move to Millions live event experience that we hold now, we used to have an event called Breakthrough in Business. Breakthrough, for short, was a mindset shift and spiritual alignment incubator for entrepreneurs who were ready for their Next Level Everything. During the event, I facilitated experiential activities and sessions on alignment, surrender, and clarity for what they truly desired and taught them how to see themselves the way God sees them. We talked about loving themselves first and foremost. Everyone was on board with all of that. They loved it, and you could see the breakthroughs happening right in the room. It was so beautiful. The moment we started talking about the most important part, *forgiveness*, all of a sudden, people couldn't hear. They were distracted, or they needed to take a break. They became instantly belligerent.

A good portion of the attendees were unwilling to consider forgiving the people they felt wronged them. It was not the thing that they wanted to do, no matter how I shared the release and open door they'd experience once they did. They didn't care. They'd rather hold on than let go. If you feel the same, you're missing my point. If you maintain that breaking through in your business is all good, until it requires you to let someone off the hook for what they did to you, write this down: *Forgiveness is for you.*

Forgiveness is not for those who have "wronged" you. Forgiveness is so that nothing separates you from what has already been earmarked and reserved for you by the Creator of the abundant universe that you reside in today. I can't speak for you, but I can tell you that I don't want to get to Heaven and get ushered into a room that holds all the gifts I didn't get to open while on earth because I was stubborn and held a grudge that didn't serve me and absolutely didn't hurt them. By in large, our families, who typically represent the people who wrong us that we need to forgive, don't wrong us on purpose. I think about my parents. I believe that they did the best that they could with what they had. Now, their best left me needing to spend time with my therapist, but I'm better for doing my work. So, it would actually be ill reproach of me not to forgive them, to continue to hold them accountable for the things that they did when they thought they were doing the right things. Did I ever starve? Absolutely not. Did I ever not have clothes on my back? Absolutely not. Was I introduced to fear, lack, and chaos? Absolutely. They didn't know what they didn't know. So, to come into that knowledge and still hold it against them is not serving me or them.

This is not just about forgiving others either. This is about forgiving *yourself*. In fact, most of the time, the reason you're not experiencing the abundance you're due is because you haven't given yourself grace. And trust me, I get it. I have struggled to forgive myself, too. I held on to my bankruptcy and the shame I felt for way longer than I should have. I used to let my three failed engagements talk me out of desiring to be happily married one day. Holding on to the abortion I had in my twenties and blaming myself for not being able to conceive now that I am happily married has kept me awake more nights than I care to admit. Every time a launch went awry in those early years, I lamented and cursed myself. I talked down to myself. I told myself that I was worthless. We are so hard on ourselves, and we have to learn to give ourselves grace and to forgive ourselves. We did the best we could at that time. Now that we know better, not only can we do better, but we can also let it go so that we can move on to our Next Level Everything.

By doing your forgiveness work, you can open up a source of abundance into your life experience. Now, you may be cursing me because I wasn't there. I don't know what they did and how they messed up your life. No, I wasn't. But if you are here to voice your frustration as you read this book, here is one thing that we know: They didn't kill you. They didn't take you out, and because of that, you have a distinct opportunity to get your life back. You've lost and missed so much already.

Whenever a client in one of our programs is struggling with money, I always spend time with them, helping them to clear the blocks. We look at those three things I shared in the Mindset for Millions chapter: hoarding, unforgiveness, and their gifts. We can always find the source of the leak and plug it so that the money starts flowing again. It's not magic; it's principle. God is principled. Those who follow the principles unlock the abundance. This is a big part of my gift as a prophet for profit. I can see what is causing the blockage and shift clients so that the money flows. This is one of the reasons we have *so many* client success stories. And no, our work is not just about money. We do, however, seek to normalize access to lots of it because, again, money is a "lesser" thing that we should have dominion over. We were created in God's image and likeness. I am clear that by helping our clients see themselves the way God has always seen them, we can remove anything that threatens to derail their God-given destinies. Please do not despise the significance of the spiritual principles with your strategy. They make the difference a million times over.

As a little brown girl born in the projects who was told that to have enough was the goal, I forgive my family. Enough isn't my ceiling; abundance is. The way I love, serve, coach, and CEO is different because I decided to forgive anyone for everything so that nothing would keep me from the millions I was born to make, move, and leave. If you are millions-minded, I highly recommend that you read *Forgiving Forward* by Bruce and Toni Hebel. As the Bruce and Toni share boldly, "No matter what has hurt you, there is a simple yet powerful answer to your healing: forgiveness."[27]

There are seven steps in the protocol, and I highly recommend getting the book so you can learn the whole process. You can also become a client in one of our Incredible Factor University programs and we will get you a copy. I love the protocol so much that it is now required reading for our clients. Upon enrolling in one of our programs, we send a copy of the book and a bookmark in the welcome box. What I know for sure is that, at some point in time, someone has hurt you. That hurt has caused a block that will delay your Move to Millions. I don't want unforgiveness to be your money block.

Forgiveness changed the game for me. It's made me a millionaire ten times over. It's allowed me to rebuild my team after being hurt by previous employees. It's even allowed me to redeem client relationships. It's made me a better leader, wife, daughter, sister, and friend. It's not only working for me. It's changed the game for countless clients, too. It has, more than once, been the biggest change a client made as they moved from one level on the continuum to the next. I think forgiveness could do the same for you.

Got next?

Chapter Action Plan

1. Order *Forgiving Forward.*
2. Read it.
3. Live the protocol.
4. Watch abundance come into your life.

Remember: Information without action is just a waste of time. So, make a plan to implement now so you are one move closer to your first million-dollar year.

CHAPTER THIRTEEN
Move to Millions Surrender

"Surrender is the most powerful action you can take
to shift the trajectory of your life and business."
—DARNYELLE JERVEY HARMON

Would you believe me if I told you that making and moving millions was less about strategy and more about surrender?

There was a time in my business when you'd hear me don my best Italian accent and muster up a "get outta here!" I didn't think there was any way that surrender would be a strategy I would be teaching as an important ingredient to my success in business.

Let alone actually living.

In the early days of my business, I was a control freak. Everything I did was based on what I thought would achieve the goals and deliver the results.

That's a big part of the reason I wasn't successful.

I know you might be scratching your head because you think that success is about being in control. But stick with me. I can literally still hear those ten two-letter words I learned in elementary school that have wreaked so much havoc: if it is to be, it is up to me.

Yeah, lies. Big fat ugly ones.

Now I get the impetus of the saying. We have to take action and responsibility to achieve what we desire. I'm all for that. After all, I'm the one who's been saying we have to give God something to bless since I started this business in 2007. But the premise that we alone control what occurs in our life experience . . . yeah, not so much.

That is ego-driven. And ego, which many define as Edging God Out, is the demise of success in every area of your life, if you ask me. Today, I'd change that mnemonic to "if it is to be, it is up to He."

Now, I didn't start this way. Ten years ago, I was still saying the first version and dancing a little jig at the same time. I really did believe that if it was to be, it was up to me.

Me.

But then I realized that is not enough to live for. And it's a breeding ground for hustle, grind, and overwhelm. Not to mention that it's a lot of pressure and stress to live up to the constant dynamic that I alone determine my destiny. Think about it. If you alone determine what you get, how could you not want to hustle harder? Or, as we all see all day on Instagram: Wake. Grind. Repeat. I know that entrepreneurship gurus all over Instagram have led you to believe that all you have to do is grind.

So let me ask you a question.

Why, then, are you not making and moving millions?

Exactly.

Perhaps it's because while getting clear about what you desire and taking action toward your goals is important, it's not the sole ingredient in the magic pill to your next level. The magic pill is to get clear, take inspired action, and detach from any outcome by surrendering. It's about actually realizing that every result is working for your good, regardless of the outcome. That failed launch was really an opportunity to tighten your messaging and streamline your core launch strategy.

Yeah, it tripped me out, too. You mean the way to get more is to release? Wait! What?

Admittedly, it was hard to stomach at first, which is why I now know why my early years in business weren't that spectacular. And it was not for lack of effort; it was because effort alone isn't the move.

I now realize that the fine line between surrender and control is often crossed consistently in the pursuit of living your best life as an entrepreneur.

Truth be told it wasn't until 2014 (kinda) that I started to get it. But by 2018, I had the principles of surrender and forgiveness on lock. They have each changed my life so much. Before I share the story that started my pursuit of this principle, I feel that knowing the definition of surrender, as I mean it, might be helpful.

The first definition I found by entering "surrender" into Google made me chuckle.

It read: "1. to cease resistance to an enemy or opponent and submit to their authority."[28]

I chuckled because isn't it normal to make everything about someone else being at fault? In my experience, seldom is there an enemy, unless we consider ourselves.

Once I stopped laughing, I realized that defining this for you can't really come from a traditional source. You see, surrender, as a principle on the Move to Millions, is about physical and spiritual alignment. For most business scholars, this goes against all they believe in.

Surrender is about faith. You already know that I am one of those who believe that you don't have to separate church and state to experience success. In fact, success accelerates when the two meet. Surrender, as a guiding principle for your entrepreneurship journey, is about a greater understanding that your company is a vessel used to fulfill the purpose for which you were sent into the earth realm. So, the truth is when it comes to what I have learned, and how I govern my own life and, therefore, business, I have come to define surrender this way:

sə-'ren-dər—the act of releasing the need to control the outcome based on an understanding that purpose is being fulfilled in the actions taken and the results will be for your ultimate good. Surrender is an act that is a blend of faith and execution. Surrender is an act. A complete action.

Sometimes, on this journey, all I do is surrender. And in doing so, the result I desired and prayed about manifests in a way that was far better than I could have imagined it. Surrender is a spiritual term that means you accept rather than reject what is presented to you with an understanding that, regardless of the outcome, you will experience an undeniable benefit. It's about living into a power and source that is greater than yourself. It means you remove the need to control every moment of every day in your life experience, and by doing so, you actually experience more.

Again, I am very aware that I am an entrepreneur talking to entrepreneurs about building million-dollar companies. The irony is not lost on me that I maintain that if you want to make and move millions, you need to follow the principles of operational obedience, confidence, forgiveness, and in this chapter, surrender.

In practical application, this would look like you are making a decision that the work you do isn't all about making money; it's about being the change you want to see in the world. For me, surrender looks like God being the true CEO of the company I run. I'm simply a steward. With God's help and direction, I make decisions that give Him the glory. That allows me to serve our clients deeply and focus on being of value. It allows me to serve from my overflow instead of having a spirit of lack, enacting desperation energy, or treating my clients like a Stripe notification. Trust me. I have hired those coaches before—the ones who feel that they can't tell you everything they know because you might do better than them. I'm the opposite. I love it when my clients exceed my results. by applying my strategies.

It wasn't that long ago that my work with Marquel was instrumental in growing his company to $5 million while mine was only at two. I couldn't have been happier for him. I know because of the abundant mindset in which I live that both of our lights can shine, and the world just gets brighter. I don't lose if he wins, and vice versa.

I heard this on a podcast once and it really changed the way I saw surrender. As I define this concept for you, I thought this example might help you to see what I see and understand why this is an important principle if you want to make and move millions.

Imagine being arrested. Depending on your backstory, you might not have to think too hard to see it. I personally have tons of convicts in my family, and I have seen a few of them getting arrested. Just for the visual, think about the arrest process, but change the arresting officer from the ugliest, meanest cop you can think of to God. Now, I know that based on how you were raised and whether or not you grew up in church, you might see God other than who He really is. Contrary to belief and lessons taught by religious doctrine, God is not anything like a police officer. He's not tyrannical and mean, nor does He get off when you experience failure, hurt, or pain. God is the sweetest gentleman you will ever meet. As Lashaon, a member of my team, says, "He's a master at capturing your heart and your attention because He desires only His best for you."

God says that there is no good thing He will withhold from you when you walk uprightly. Walking uprightly is about doing good, treating people well, and operating in integrity. While this digression is in fact a digression, it is important because I need your mind to visualize the possibility of seeing God the way He really is and also to seeing yourself the way He sees you. I want to invite you to see His loving nature, His grace, and His true love of all that you are, without condition. I want you to see Him as a loving Father who desires only the best for you. This next part might get me into trouble, but it must be said. Most religious people were taught a fear-based religion and view of God. To the contrary, God is about freedom and relationship. If you were one of those raised in a denominational religious situation that made you a sinner who couldn't do right and earn God's love, nothing could be further from the truth. You were born in His love. I will admit, in order for surrender to take place, you're likely going to have to do some major healing work.

Wait! What? Are you telling me that my ability to make and move millions has to do with healing my heart to see God differently than I was raised to?

That is what I am telling you. I have watched it happen in the life of client after client. Their struggle to get to the next level financially is held captive by their need to hold on to something that no longer serves them. As I invite them to surrender, the floodgates begin to open. Before they know it, they are sitting in the significance of their greatest desires becoming their reality.

The cool thing is that it's possible for you, too. And it starts by redefining what surrender looks like for you.

Now back to my analogy of being arrested, but by God. First, you'd be told to put your hands in the air. When you lift your hands, you are making it clear that you are not armed and dangerous, and that you are surrendering or relenting your power in the situation as a result of an acceptance and appreciation for His authority in your life. Next, your raised hands will be taken and placed behind your back in preparation for them to be "handcuffed." Through this act, God is searching your heart and person to validate that you are His beloved. He is seeing your heart and true intentions. From that place, He sees your readiness and willingness to relent. Lastly, as your hands are "handcuffed," the final piece of the surrender commences, and you are taken into His custody to be changed, transformed, and revived.

Is that not the most beautiful depiction of surrender you have ever experienced?!

Every time I think of this process of surrendering with God as my arresting officer, I get the most insatiable chills running down my spine. He loves me so much that He willingly, as often as needed, will search my heart and person and take me into His possession to love on me, change me, and transform the way I relate to Him.

When I decided to surrender my business and invite God to become the CEO as I took the seat of steward, I noticed that everything shifted. First, the pressure I felt that I had to perform at a certain level dissipated. I recently saw a quote on Instagram by Marshawn Evans Daniels, which said, "It's God's job to finance the mission. It's your job to follow His voice." When I saw it, I had to pause because it's the perfect reflection of what surrender looks like.

Once I started my own surrender journey, it opened up a space to co-lead and co-manage the company with the best partner. I was able to consult with God for everything. When things went wrong, I had someone to go back to for modifications (as well as someone to focus on for the solution). This has truly been the best decision I have ever made in my business career. Deciding to take God at His Word and yield to His leading in all things is absolutely the reason why the company is what it is. It's the reason the company experiences the growth and results for clients the way it does. Some call it favor; I call it surrender, and that surrender reveals an anointing.

What would it look like to enact this depiction in your business?

Yeah. Exactly. It's a game changer.

Now, the principle of surrender isn't for the faint at heart. It's not for control freaks who actually believe that *they* are the reason for all they have. If you think you're in control, you probably won't be able to live in surrender. On the contrary, if you desire to experience all you could ever desire, give up control; it will change your life and business. It certainly changed mine.

One other important note: Contrary to popular belief, surrender is all about action. To live surrendered doesn't mean you just wait and let life happen to you. Quite the opposite is true; surrender is about alignment and obedience. Remember, we shouldn't be waiting on God because He is waiting on us. He has already gifted us with all we need to live at the next level in every area of our lives. Surrender includes the following steps:

Contemplation and Clarity

I have come to realize that the easiest way to surrender is to get clear and determine the ultimate goal for you and your company. This process will likely include visualizing, journaling, prayer, and perhaps meditation, so you can set a vision for what you desire to bring into your life and business experience. This is about getting clear about why you started your business in the first place. When you know your why, your what (what you do, the products and services you offer) has more impact. Taking the time to sit in quiet contemplation is a gift to give yourself often, especially when you are the co-CEO of your own company. Taking those moments to sit and process, or just be, are essential to being able to move your business forward. I also believe that God speaks in quiet contemplation. Sometimes we get caught up in talking *at* God in prayer; yet the value happens when you sit and listen.

Surrender starts with clarity so that you can let go. Clarity takes time. This isn't about your microwave mentality. This is about giving yourself time and space to decide that what you desire is valid, validated, and valuable. You don't need anyone else's buy-in for it to become your reality. My understanding and need for quiet contemplation and clarity grounds my greatest desires and most profitable strategies. It's the time when I hear God speaking the loudest. Trust me. There is no better marketer than Jesus! I actually do my clients and my team a tremendous service by loving myself enough to take the time I need to get the clarity.

It has been my quest for quiet contemplation that has kept me sane in the various stages of my own company's development. When we were first ready to "play bigger" a few years ago, I decided to listen to the sage wisdom of my Nanny. She would often invite me to "get somewhere and sit down" when I was visiting her. She'd say that when she saw my passion stirring up. I had the potential to be distracted. So, she'd use these quiet interludes to bring me back to myself. It actually kind of ticked me off that I couldn't be out playing with the other kids in the South Bridge Projects. But today, Nanny, I got it and thank you.

Quiet contemplation is essential for surrender.

After gaining clarity, there is a distinct moment of release. Because you are clear about the what and the why, you can confidently release the how. That release is the surrender. The how isn't your job anyway; it's God's. The openness and willingness to release the how is the fastest way to have it come into your life. When you believe it, and have extreme clarity of purpose, it allows you the will to completely detach from any and all outcomes because you have faith and know that what you desire is already yours. In fact, it's on the way.

It's already yours.

Following the quiet contemplation leads you to alignment.

Alignment

I have always believed that the stillness of clarity is the best way to get "right." Alignment is the gift you give to yourself because you are clear about who you are and the purpose for your life. Coming into alignment is about seeing yourself the way God has always seen you. *Always.* His view of you has never changed. The way you see yourself fluctuates until that quiet contemplation becomes alignment. Alignment is a present state of being based on a past understanding and the future promise of who you will be.

Be.

Being.

It's a clear knowing and embodiment of purpose. Alignment is what allows for flow in your life experience. When you are tuned into your body, it will become clear when you're out of alignment. Alignment for me has always been the missing link. It's often the reason why you don't have a business that serves you both financially and spiritually. Alignment for me is a daily discovery, and I love leveraging several modalities to stay in alignment. One of my favorite ways to check my alignment is to check in with my body. God loves us so much that He made our bodies computers. Our central nervous system, much like a computer's CPU, makes it clear when something is off.

Have you ever been to the chiropractor? If your first visit was anything like mine, before you arrived, you didn't think anything was "off" or out of alignment. But once you got that adjustment, it was like the jingle from those old Folgers commercials.

That's alignment.

This is why "hitting the ground running" is the worst thing you could ever do for your life and business. Instead, you have to spend time feeling into your body so you can get clear about where things are off. I remember back in 2016 when I was feeling extremely overwhelmed by my company. As I shared earlier, it felt like I became the CEO of a million-dollar company overnight. Okay, well maybe over three days. But still, as I sat into that reality, my back hurt for literally eighteen months. No matter what I took, if I saw a chiropractor, if I stretched, if I got a new mattress, my back never stopped hurting. On the surface, you think you solve the alignment issue by solving the known problem. But it's the unknown problem that is wreaking havoc on your next level. It wasn't until I had literally tried every physical thing that I could and ran out of options that I turned inward. When I did, I opened an opportunity for the pain to dissipate.

The whole time I was out of alignment, making decisions out of desperation or unknown urgency instead of what felt right. I didn't even know that I was out of alignment. I was taking the next breath, hoping that it would free me from my personal prison. But it didn't. In fact, the cell seemed to get darker, smaller, and deeper. And I will be honest. The one thing I didn't want to do was look inward. If I did, I would have to admit that what I held to be my dream had become a nightmare that I couldn't wake up from.

I thought getting my business to the million-dollar mark would change my life and validate my existence. At that time in my life, I felt like I had been trying to justify my existence with every breath I took.

Want to know the fastest way to know if you're in alignment? Make an "I am" statement, then change "I" to "God." If the statement no longer makes sense, you're out of alignment. For example, often when we aren't where we want to be financially, we say things like "I am broke." Change that to "God is broke." That makes no sense. Because we were created in His image and likeness, we are literally gods of the earth with the power to dominate and subdue. We are like God, and when we tap into our God power, we are in alignment and flow. If you speak or think of yourself as anything other than that, you are out of alignment. That misalignment will impact your business as much as it impacts your life.

When your alignment is off, everything is off—how you see yourself, who you attract, what you believe to be true about yourself, what you charge, decisions you make, your spirituality, everything. Did you know that when you are out of alignment, you are literally cut off from inspiration, positive energy, and clear communication with God? Alignment is your lifeline, and it vacations with surrender. In fact, I will go so far as to say that you can't truly surrender if you aren't in alignment.

I once had a client who I worked with several years ago named Christine. She was brilliant. When we first started working together, we grew her business by $50,000 cash in our first forty-five days together. Then, all of a sudden, she hit a massive block and was completely stuck. She started missing our calls and making major excuses for why she wasn't "on." She had a personal situation occur that took her out, and rather than process it in clarity, she let it mess with her confidence and how she saw herself. It took her off her game. It took me a few months to get her back on the phone for a coaching session. When we finally got to meet, I could immediately sense that her mojo was gone. I suggested that, rather than give her another strategy, I could coach her in the traditional sense. She agreed and about fifteen minutes into the session, she had a major breakthrough. That was the opening she needed to get back on track. Within a few weeks, her business was moving again, and we developed some modalities that she still uses to this day to make sure that she stays in alignment.

Another important part of surrender is obedience. In order for you to let go, you have to yield the power to someone else's authority. Obedience takes faith. As humans, we are taught to believe that we control our life steps. Yielding those steps to a higher call and authority will require faith that rivals the faith it takes to believe a chair will hold you, or that when you go to start your car it will start. Now, as I say the word faith, I am not speaking religiously per se. This is not about religion. This is about your relationship with your God, the Creator of the abundant Universe and the Source of all that is good because of His Holy Spirit. One of my favorite movies, *Not Easily Broken*, has a line spoken by the character played by Morris Chestnut as the film is ending that I always remind myself of. It goes something like: If you want to know the purpose of a thing, consult the maker of the thing.[29]

Surrender is about consulting your maker in all situations, even your business. I mean if I can keep it real with you, the Move to Millions is about surrendering your CEO title to God. I can tell you honestly that when I surrendered this company to God, it started to flourish; and the ideas, strategies, and goals I had actually came into being. Prior to me surrendering, I had the same ideas, strategies, and goals, yet they weren't being realized because of the very thing I thought made me the CEO: my ego. Trying to operate in your own strength usually produces the opposite result—spinning your wheels.

At my 2013 live event, Unleash Your Incredible Factor, we had about seventy people registered. We had an amazing experience. I was teaching and giving them access to the tools they needed to market their brands and businesses more effectively. It was, as I look back now, almost all surface content. You know, identify your ideal client, determine the problem they have that you can solve, tell them you can solve it with a strong message, kind of surface.

But on the morning of day three, I woke up with an unction in my spirit to draw nearer to God for the attendees. So, really early, I headed down to the meeting room and I began to pray in my prayer language as I touched each seat. I sensed in my spirit that staying on the surface wasn't going to help these entrepreneurs experience the success that they craved, and I didn't want to be another coach in the marketplace blowing smoke.

So, I yielded my vessel in surrender and allowed my spirit to take over. As I was praying in my spiritual prayer language, around the third seat in the third row, the doors to the meeting room flung open. I looked up to see an attendee enter the room. I glanced at the clock. It was around 5:30 a.m., so I know she wasn't there to get a jump start on the day. We weren't scheduled to start for another three hours. As she entered the room, she rushed in my direction, and without even saying good morning, she started to speak with urgency.

"I have a word from the Lord for you, Darnyelle."

That immediately got my attention. Up until this point in my business, my relationship with God was separate from my business. I moved in her direction, bright-eyed and bushy-tailed because the unction I had gotten in my spirit that morning was the Holy spirit telling me that I needed a shift to do what I truly desired to do for my attendees.

As I looked up at her, she'd now reached my side. "Good morning," I said.

"I'm sorry. Good morning. Girl, I was just woken up by God with this message to come deliver to you," she said.

"No worries," I said. "What is God saying?"

"God says that He is pleased with your heart for Him and your attendees. He knows that you desire to serve them more deeply and the way to do that is to take a bold stand for Him in your work. He says that if you take a bold stand for Him, He will make it easy."

Immediately, I felt every goosebump on my body erupt into the most life-affirming chill. I knew instantly that this woman was a prophet speaking to my soul and spirit what I had been feeling but couldn't articulate.

"Oh my goodness," I said. "You have no idea what this means."

She looked up at me and continued, "God says you have the influence and the results. His people are looking for the results to show them that living His principles is the way to experience the reward of lives and businesses at the next level. And unfortunately, many aren't getting what they need in traditional churches. So, your work will be looked upon as the 'church' that will give them the principles and the process to experience God more deeply as their businesses grow exponentially. There is an anointing on your life, Darnyelle. I figure you already know that, but in case you weren't sure. God intends to use you as you take this bold stand for Him by showing others what is possible if they do the same."

I took a deep breath. In five minutes or so, this woman, this prophet, just solidified what I needed to do. I needed to step out there and become more vocal for the role my faith and relationship with God was beginning to play in my business.

I got excited and I also got loud. I started to make shifts in my messaging immediately to put my spirituality on front street. While I didn't take a religious stance and shift my work into being "Christian," I did clearly spell out my beliefs and the role they played.

I was clear because God was clear. Religion is a divider and God was seeking to bring people together. My call to entrepreneurs and business owners wasn't about setting up another denomination but actually teaching the principles that are universal, the keys to unlocking the abundance for which He sent His son.

Let's fast forward to early 2014, I was preparing for my next live event. Through no additional marketing efforts or budgets, with a surrendered heart, a bold stand for God, and in full alignment with the way God saw me, we noticed a substantial shift. The most outwardly thing we did was tweak our message to focus on combining faith and business. As a result, our attendance skyrocketed to more than two hundred people. God was doing what He said. I took a bold stand for Him and marketed my event as a spiritual alignment incubator for entrepreneurs ready for their next level, and He was filling the room easily. We never spent any money on advertising; yet 265 people in total from all over the world, including Muslims from Saudi Arabia, were on their way to my event.

My sweet spirit of surrender, despite my best efforts to regain control, positioned us for massive success. Surrender doesn't have to be overt in order to work. It just has to be executed. The conditions behind why surrender will yield what is for your highest good aren't predicated on man-made thought.

The result is always determined by the Creator of the Universe and the Lover of Your Soul. Once I realized that God is always God, and He never changes for anyone, regardless of religious affiliation, like man would lead you to believe, my surrender increased. The reason the 2014 event created more than 130 clients and $1,300,000 was because I surrendered and lived into the decision to take a bold stand for God without knowing what the results might be. He literally made it easy to generate $1,300,000 in three days. My surrender allowed God to enroll more than 265 people to my live event with no marketing budget. My surrender made me a million-dollar CEO in a few days.

In his book *The Surrender Experiment*, Michael Singer shares a simple business model based on surrender and how he used almost exclusively the principle of surrender to build a widely successful company, while focusing on alignment. His premise was simple. When opportunities were presented to him, his response would be to surrender to them.[30]

As I read Singer's book, I noticed a theme, and as a result, I started to live by the premise that anything that was introduced to me was done so at God's request. Because of that, I would respond to it with all my heart and soul. This thought has changed the way I conduct my business. I resolved to surrender because everything put in front of me was put there by God. I know that. I feel that and I live that.

So again, I ask what if I told you that making and moving millions was less about strategy and more about surrender?

As I started working on this book, and looked back to 2014, I noticed a few keys that created the shift to surrender. These keys are the guideposts that I now teach to my clients to help them preside over their companies from the seat of surrender:

- Surrender doesn't make you helpless; it makes you powerful.
- Surrender is a leadership principle that creates ease and flow in your company.
- When you are clear and surrendered, there is consistent flow in your business activities toward your goals.

You'll know that you are running a surrendered company when you start each day by detaching from any outcome to achieve a specific result or goal. Interestingly, doing so doesn't negate the goal or make you work without purpose; it allows for the goal to be achieved in an accelerated fashion because there are no limits to what can be achieved. You're literally free to flow in the direction of your desire.

Recently, I had the pleasure of attending, speaking, and participating in my client Jasmine's first three-day live event. In preparation for the event, I coached Jasmine through the many moving parts and agreed to be onsite to help to make sure that her event went as we surrendered it to. Jasmine, who'd never held a three-day event before, was a little nervous. I mean, who wouldn't be? She was expecting nearly one hundred people in Atlanta for three days. Like any event host, she was more concerned with serving her attendees than anything. She wanted to make sure that each attendee got the value they had invested to receive.

As a part of the event, I prayed with Jasmine each day. Purposefully, my prayers were for her surrender. That she would yield any expectations and outcomes to God and trust that He would do just as Ephesians 3:20 says, "exceedingly abundantly above all that we ask or think, according to the power that worketh in us."

And Jasmine did. And so did God.

First and foremost, her event had the sweetest spirit. On multiple occasions, attendees were led to take to time to pray and praise God. With no attention on her sales goals or how many people she enrolled, she massively exceeded her goal and generated nearly $500,000 in sales in three days.

You can say what you want, but her commitment to surrender solidified those results for her business. She literally tripled her business in one year because we focus on helping our clients live this principle in our Move to Millions Mastermind.

I invite you to try it. Start surrendering to any and all outcomes and focusing only on making sure that you get into alignment with your Creator and have faith that He will exceed all of your thoughts, goals, and desires. My clients and I don't have to be the only ones living this principle and seeing a massive shift in every area of our lives.

If you give it a try, here are some of the benefits you can expect:

- Peace as you run your business. You will literally watch stress dissipate and confidence show up.
- A quantum leap in your business results, like my client Dr. Angela, who grew her business from $250,000 in 2020 to $750,000 in 2021.
- Confidence in your products and services that allows you to market more consistently.
- An understanding of your value in the marketplace so that you stop undercharging, comparing, and overdelivering to justify your rates.

I believe that surrender is the new strategy. If you have millions on your mind, I invite you to create your own "surrender experiment" so you stop controlling and start yielding.

Chapter Action Plan

As you move forward, here are a few questions to ask yourself:

1. What would it look like to add surrender to my favorite business growth strategies?
2. What would I have to give up in order to allow surrender to become a primary strategy in my life and business?
3. What might I gain if I focus on surrendering consistently in every area of my life?

Remember: Information without action is a complete waste of time. Decide now to spend the time setting up your surrender strategy so that you can yield your way to the million-dollar mark in your business.

Part 3:

Vision

CHAPTER FOURTEEN

Vision Point vs. Vantage Point

"The fastest way to reach your next level is to focus on it from where you desire to be, not where you are right now. This small act will pull you toward what you envision."

—DARNYELLE JERVEY HARMON

One of my absolute favorite movies is *Vantage Point*, starring Forrest Whittaker and Dennis Quaid. In the movie, several versions of the same events are depicted, each different based on the vantage point of the person watching what happened. Interestingly, while each spectator saw something different, no one person's vantage point completed the puzzle; but all of the visions together told the story of what really took place. It was from watching this movie that I realized that your vantage point is always skewed. *Always*.

When I was a little girl, I was often accused of having my head in the clouds. What was happening around me forced me to always look ahead to where I wanted to go. Looking at my life from where I was, well, it was borderline depressing. I'm still not sure how I knew to look at where I desired to be instead of where I was. But that skill has served me extremely well. As I reflect, I realize that even at such a young age, I understood that no matter what I was looking at, if I looked at it from my perspective with my limitations and beliefs, I was always going to be looking at it as if something was missing.

For example, more than likely at this moment, you have a million-dollar company. From your vantage point, you can't see it because you know how hard you're already working, how many systems are lacking, that you don't have the right team, and of course, your bank account or receivables don't reflect it either. However, if I showed you how it actually exists right now from my vision point, you might have the courage to shift your perspective. By borrowing my confidence as your own and moving in the direction of the business you already have, your vision could become clear. It is likely hard for you to see your million-dollar business because, at this very moment in time, it's not packaged, priced, or positioned to make you millions *easily*. That is why I can see it and you can't. As Kathy Kolbe says, "It's hard to read the label when you're inside the jar."

To see the millions that are already locked in your business, you'd likely have to change your viewpoint. You'd have to decide that the view from where you are now isn't serving you and decide to shift to see things differently, to see things from a higher level. To think big, and play bigger, you have to look at everything from your vision point. One of the most critical skills for a millions-minded entrepreneur to master is the skill to shift their vision. Getting to the million-dollar mark and eventually becoming a millionaire will require that you see not from where you stand in the moment with the limited view but from where you *desire* to stand.

As a million-dollar CEO in the making, everything in your path must be filtered through your vision point (where you desire to be) instead of your vantage point (where you stand at that moment). When you operate from your vantage point, you will always experience skewed results. I intend to use this chapter to offer practical insight and strategy to live into the shift that accompanies thinking, seeing, deciding, and acting like a million-dollar CEO right now. Yes, you have to be the million-dollar CEO version of yourself before you will actually live that reality. Remember, millions are mental *before* they are material.

For my company, which had been stuck at the million-dollar mark for more years than I care to count, this shift was pivotal to me doubling my business from $1 million in 2020 to $2.1 million in 2021. This shift is also what led to us hitting the Inc. 5000 list of fastest growing companies. In 2022, we grew the business again because I consistently showed up at my vision point. And I assure you that doing so is at least a little scary, but so is staying the same.

For as long as I can remember, I have had a vision board. My vision board has always been a synopsis of what I desire to bring into my life experience in the next five to ten years. I realized that setting my vision ten years in the future would allow me to back into it so that my big audacious vision became palatable, and I wouldn't back down from it. At the top of every decade for the last two, I created my vision board. I took great care and time to do so. First, sitting with the vision and writing it down. Then, finding the visual images to personify every desire, and lastly, speaking the vision out loud over myself and in covenant with God so that I could bring each into my life experience.

What I used to do just for me personally morphed into the creation of a company vision board. Starting to look at my business like I looked at my life changed everything. Where my life's vision board had my dream house, my company vision board had my dream headquarters. Where my life vision board had pictures of the boy-girl twins I desire to have one day, my company vision board had pictures of my team who would help to expand my vision without compromising my values.

Looking at my vision board as I write this chapter reminds me of when I first became fascinated by the thought of one day having a dream home. I was in Mary Kay, and I was doing a skin care class for the homeless-looking woman I met in the grocery store. The fact that I approached her at all was an act of obedience. God kept nudging me to "warm chatter" her. Today, I'm glad I did. Even though I was obedient, my vantage point believed there was no way this woman could afford Mary Kay skin care products. The woman was easy to talk to and we set up the skin care class.

Once I got inside of the breathtaking foyer of her Toll Brothers home, I swallowed hard. This home took my breath away. I couldn't stop glancing around at the crown molding, the well-decorated rooms. It was truly a dream that my vantage point didn't even know existed, *but* it stirred up my vision. In addition to pampering those ladies, I also had a new vision. I was going to live in a Toll Brothers home one day.

For years, I had that picture of the Toll Brothers logo on my vision board, never sure when it might materialize. Several years later, after brunch, my now husband Bernard and I were driving. We saw a new development that Toll Brothers was building not far from my current house. For fun, we went to look at the model. It was very nice. However, the main bedroom was a letdown for such a big house. My vision had always been to have a primary suite retreat, almost like a home within our home. I casually mentioned the main bedroom to the sales agent. She told us that there was another Toll Brothers development twenty minutes away. She encouraged us to go look at the model home in that development. She felt that what we were looking for in terms of the primary suite retreat would meet us there. We happily headed to the other development, and she was correct. This is why it helps to tell others who can add value and hold space for your vision about where you're going.

The Duke model was exactly what we envisioned as our dream home. We went on to build that dream home, and up to the moment we started living there, it was just what my vision point saw. Once we got settled in, I realized that this home was now our vantage point. We started thinking bigger to arrive at the next home for our vision point. Similarly, in business your vision point must be a moving target.

Once I started to keep this company vision board, it became my vision point. It's the 30,000-foot view of my multimillion-dollar enterprise. By taking the time and care to write the vision and make it plain, I opened myself up to understanding the long-term value, strategic direction, and intentional implementation for this company. Now, I will be honest. Taking the time and energy to think this big can be exhausting! It requires a serious dose of longevity and vision casting that is not for the faint of heart. You will be forced to think so big that it scares you, which, by the way, is how you know that you're thinking big enough. Your vision will start as a construct and become a set of goals that make the knot in the pit of your stomach leap for joy. Your vision point is about the biggest view of your company you can muster. That's why it must accompany significant mindset support.

You have to see it to see it so you get to experience it!

The mindset shift will allow you to do the hard work of voicing the vision into a mission so that you and your company stand for something besides making millions. It's seldom about the money. When you understand your big why, and you can channel that into a vision, it gives what you do more impact. Oh, and this isn't for the entrepreneur in you. This is for the CEO burgeoning to come out. You're going to have to put your big girl panties on for this one (guys, a nice clean pair of boxer shorts will do). In order to shift from my $1,000,000 company's vantage point, and operate from my $10,000,000 vision point, I had to do each of the following steps. This will become your blueprint for your million-dollar vision.

Visualize

First, as Ephesians 3:20 says, I had to think exceeding, abundantly, above all that I could ever imagine. To achieve this, I started by dreaming and visualizing my company's next major milestone. I set the goal to achieve eight figures in three years. While I was dreaming, I began to back into how we would get there. In order to be at eight figures in three years, where would I need to be in two years? And in order to be there in two years, where would I need to be in one year? If I am going to get there in one year, where do I need to be today?

In order to answer these questions for myself, I took anything that might hem me up off the table, including money and access to resources. I made them a nonissue. They'd be available on this journey however and whenever I required them. As I sat and visualized the Incredible One headquarters, I saw myself driving into the complex and the automatic gates opening to reveal the beautiful campus. As I drove into the complex, my eyes were immediately met with magnolia trees lining the driveway and an education center off to the right. The building looked modern and sleek, as if it had just been built. The marquee read Incredible One Enterprises on it in what looked like amethyst.

As I pulled into my parking space and grabbed my purse from my back seat, I smiled at the gardener as I walked through the double doors into the education center. The first floor held various meeting rooms—one for three hundred attendees, an executive boardroom, and a classroom for fifty attendees. I only leaned briefly to my left to say hello to our front desk agent before hitting the button to take the elevator up to the executive offices floor. Once off the elevator, I stopped into my COO's and CMO's offices just to say hello. I smiled at my assistant, who was holding out a bottle of Core water and my calendar for the day. Someone was booked to record in the studio, so I kept walking into my office. My vision has been refined, but I still remember the first time I saw all of this. It seemed crazy that a brown girl from the projects of Wilmington, Delaware, might dream so big that only God could make it happen. I would just see it, then write it down. It didn't have to seem possible at first. It was just about me taking the time to dream about where this company was headed.

Inspect

Once I locked in on the vision, and I started to share it with people, and they sat listening intently instead of laughing, that's when I knew that my vision was strengthening. From here, I went on to define the team that I would need to create this vision. The next step after the vision becomes clear is to inspect it. Is it realistic with a stretch? What will achieving the vision require? Who might you need to engage to fulfill the vision? When you back into the vision and dismantle the big vision by breaking it down into smaller goals and objections, how doable is it in the timeframe you've decided? The inspection process is often the longest process because you have to assess the current situation, determine the impact of the vision, and the needs payoff. Taking the time to inspect what you expect will serve your vision and your process well. The inspection process should culminate in a new vision statement for your million-dollar and beyond company. To formulate your vision statement, I recommend each of the following:

- **Project your vision ten years into the future and then back into it.** In order to arrive at your vision point in ten years, where must you and the company be in seven years? In order to be there in seven, where must you be in five? In order to be there in five, where must you be in three? In order to be there in three, where must you be in the next twelve months? As you think through your vision for the next decade of your company, you also will have the makings of your first three-year strategic plan (which your company should be run on, by the way).

- **Always speak about your vision in positive, present tense, as if it has already taken place.** Remember that your subconscious mind takes everything you present to it as if it is the truth. So, you get to tell your subconscious what you are building. It has to yield if you show up consistently to do so. When you naturally speak as if it's happening right now, you also accelerate the pace with which it does. No matter who I was talking to in the early years when I was our only employee (not including my fake employee Regina), I always spoke as if there were five to ten of us in the company. I was making space for my vision to become my reality. When you get in the habit of doing this, it will make a big difference in the amount of time it takes for your vision to become your reality.

- **Use easy-to-understand language and avoid your internal jargon.** One of the biggest mistakes I now know I made when I first started IOE was using the Incredible Factor as a key message. While it sounds cute, it also needs to be defined and is, in fact, jargon. Every time I said it, people would look at me like a deer caught in the headlights. They had no clue what I was referring to. Keep in mind that if you have to define it, it can't inspire others quickly. Your vision needs to inspire others and yourself. I'm not sure if you could say the same, but I tend to overcomplicate things. When it comes to vision, it needs to be simple. That was a big part of the reason Incredible Factor never took off. It wasn't simple to anyone but me. And if it's not simple, it will be challenging to get others onboard with it. As you decree and declare your vision, use simple-to-understand concepts. Just as with any other messaging, it should be easy for a fifth grader to understand.

- **Think big and define success for yourself and your company.** This is your vision; that means you alone get to define the parameters of success. Mr. Remsburg, one of my high school teachers, told me that my vision should be so big that in and of my own strength it's not possible. If I can do it by myself, then I am thinking too small. So, I pass Mr. Remsburg's words on to you. If you can do it yourself, it's not a vision. If there is no knot in the pit of your stomach, you're not thinking big enough and you will settle back into the mediocrity of your current level instead of shifting into the significance of your next. This is why being in masterminds and groups where you are not the smartest person in the room is important. You need a room that requires you to stretch to feel at "home."

Strategize

Once the vision has been inspected, it's time to strategize. Scaling your business to the million-dollar mark and beyond will require an amount of strategy. As the co-CEO and lead service provider (for now), you'll have to build time into your strategy so that you begin to remove yourself from the day-to-day management of the company. However, that will take time. When you begin this journey, you're likely hiring for your weaknesses. To be successful at scaling based on the vision you've set, you'll have to start hiring for your strengths. That means that you will be spending more money and bringing in higher caliber team members. A big part of the strategy will include defining the team your vision will require. Getting to the million-dollar CEO status you desire will not happen overnight. No one goes to bed a blunder and wakes up a wonder. As a result, it will take a team effort to accomplish your vision. As I shared in the chapter about your talent suite, there will be levels to this strategy. You should honestly expect it to take a few years to enact your vision in your company. We typically help our clients develop a three-year plan to the million-dollar mark in a way that is sustainable. It is not just about the money because, yes, that can be done in one year. It's about the sustainability of the company. That is going to take time to get into place. Your vision needs to strategize for this in advance of moving in the direction of it. You'll start with a broad view of the company based on your vision and deepen that view by continuing to back into it.

Interpret

The best way to interpret your vision is to tell it to someone else and see what they say back to you. Doing this will require transparency. You'll have to become vulnerable and express your goals, dreams, and your big reason why. In the interpretation phase, you can also confirm that all key players are all in on achieving the vision. When my financial advisor recommended that I talk with my team about my vision for the company as a part of my succession plan, I was amazed at their interpretation of the vision. Because of my vulnerability and transparency, they unanimously decided that the vision would have to live on. As a result, we are in the process of putting a plan in place that would sell my company to my employees when I am ready to retire or my sun sets. I wouldn't have known that would even be an option had I not been willing to enter the interpretation phase of my vision. We often think that our vision is just for us, and that is disrespectful. Our vision is for the collective we support with our companies.

Another important part of the interpretation phase is to conduct a SWOT analysis. SWOT, which stands for strengths, weaknesses, opportunities, and threats, is a great way to truly inspect what you expect. We typically have our entire team complete a SWOT on the company from their vantage point as a part of our end of year checklist. It's a very powerful exercise. I'd love to give you a copy of our checklist. Visit https://www.movetomillions-book.com/resources to download your copy.

Organize

Once you have spent time visualizing, inspecting, strategizing, and interpreting, you're ready to start organizing your vision. By now, you have a first draft of the SWOT analysis and some clear actionable steps to make your vision your reality in the next ten years with checkpoints at one year, three years, five years, and seven years. Now it's about evaluating the systems and infrastructure that will take you there. Your team will play an important role in this phase. Organizing will include crafting the vision plan and assigning specific people to specific components of the vision. After you have determined the objectives that are most important in a particular phase of the plan, you'll assign team members to organize that facet of the vision project. Delegating to the team will allow you to have an exact due date and time and put accountability measures in place. Your vision will be useless if organization and execution aren't happening on a consistent basis. Because you have taken the time to get team buy-in, it's no longer *your* vision. It's the *company's* vision.

Network

The last phase of the vision process is to get feedback from others on your company's strategic vision to and beyond the million-dollar mark. I always recommend that you start with your business coach and mastermind community. In our Move to Millions Mastermind, twice each month, we create an environment for our clients to get peer feedback and support for their goals and initiatives. It gives them confidence and support on the journey. Networking for feedback will make the written vision come alive and cease to exist only on paper. In order for your vision to manifest, it will have to become a living, breathing possibility for you and your team. Those you share your vision with outside of your core team will also help you to test the validity of the vision itself and the steps required to make it a reality. Your feedback should challenge your vision, not to make it wrong but to solidify it. The shift from six-figure entrepreneur to million-dollar CEO is real. It will require a series of breakthroughs in your vision. The right community can enhance your vision and help identify your blind spots and gaps so that you actually get to experience your vision in the near future. The Move to Millions isn't meant to happen in silos. It is meant to happen in communities that see you and the vision you hold to make, move, and leave millions.

Chapter Action Plan

1. Journal about your current vantage point. How is it serving you? Where is it not serving you? What do you envision instead?
2. Set your vision point by looking ten years ahead, then backing into what would need to happen for you to be living that vision ten years from now.
3. Craft your million-dollar company vision statement.
4. Share that vision with your team (where applicable) and your network.

Remember: Information without action is a waste of time. Set a plan right now to implement and watch your vision come into fruition.

CHAPTER FIFTEEN
Navigating the Millions Messy Middle

"When your best times are colliding with your worst times,
you are defining the Incredible in you."
—DARNYELLE JERVEY HARMON

I n late 2015, I hated my business. I had actually hated it since late 2014, but the thought of saying that out loud kept me from owning my truth. My business, by all accounts, had become a monster. A big, fat, hairy, time-sucking, breath-stinking, unrelenting monster. And I hated it. Every part of it. I hated the responsibility and the overwhelm associated with leading a company that grew almost overnight, even though that was what I prayed for. I hated that I was sought after, and I lived in hotels. I spent so much time on airplanes that I kept an ear infection and never unpacked my suitcase. I hated that no one felt sorry for me because I was living the dream, making more money than I knew what to do with and achieving big goals on my vision board. Even though others would have killed for this, I hated it.

I seriously had to find a way to kill the monster. I feared that if I didn't, it might kill me, or worse, it might prevent me from truly experiencing what I claimed all of this to be for. I used to tell myself that I was working hard today so that, tomorrow, I could chill. However, that wasn't the truth. I was working hard because I believed that was the route to success. I am so glad that I figured that out to be a bold-faced lie! Committed to finding myself again, I set out to kill the monster my business had become. Even though I knew that doing so would mean that I would have to lay off, or fire, my team that didn't quit on their own, reduce my client count, and say goodbye to millions of dollars in revenue, I had to do it. My business wasn't serving me. Money isn't validation; money isn't the most important thing in life. The truth about money is that I was clear that I could create it whenever I wanted. So, I set out to break some hearts by reducing the team and client count because I chose me. I was willing to give it all up in order to gain a business that would serve me completely.

So, I did. In 2016, 2017, 2018, and 2019, I didn't run a million-dollar business. I went from nearly $3,000,000 in 2015 to less than $600,000 in 2018, before resurfacing in the vicinity of a million-dollar business in 2019. I'm sharing all of this in full transparency so that you can see how this journey can go, especially when you don't have access to the right support, community, and methodology. There was no *Move to Millions* book for me. There was no Move to Millions Mastermind. There were a lot of tight-lipped people keeping the secrets to a business that serves you to themselves, or they didn't know either! Of course, because you're reading my words right now, we know that won't be your story. This book will become your blueprint to the million-dollar mark in your own business. It will position you to become a million-dollar CEO. A CEO, by the way, who balances all of the moving parts in a way that serves and supports you so that you never feel like you have to sacrifice your family, freedom, faith, finances, or fun.

Some might say that during this season in my business, I was in the "messy middle." The millions messy middle is the chaotic corridor between your vantage point (where you are) and your vision point (where you desire to be instead). In a lot of ways, the messy middle is that time in your business that no one ever talks about. This period is filled with sleepless nights, long days, constantly questioning your business, your relevance, and your purpose, looking for a job despite having income coming in (yes, I really did that), consistent doubt and overwhelm, disappointments, and client complaints because you're growing but haven't shifted your infrastructure to support the growth. It's the highs and the lows. It's the mental and emotional drain. It's the failed launches, the broken systems, the feast one minute and famine the next. It's the team members who are being paid but don't get results. And don't forget the team members who are just as burned out and overwhelmed as you. Your income goes up (sometimes), but your capacity goes down. There are delays and fears, and lots of them. Every delay causes you to break your business, your mindset, your strategy, your sales, your systems, and your support.

One of the biggest things I did in the years between my last stint at the million-dollar mark and now was focus on setting up a business that would be sustainable. You see, you can hustle your way to seven figures. You can grab your calculator to see how much hustle you'll need to get there. It's not hard; it's math. Except, you don't want to be a mathematician. You want to be a CEO of a company that earns through systems and support so that you can strategically preside over and do *only* the parts of it that bring you an immense amount of joy. My joy, at that time, wasn't joyful; it was a nightmare. It's not about hustling to seven figures; it's about creating a business that supports and sustains you. Yes, I know that hustle culture is attractive, but it's not sustainable. We have to once and for all break this generational belief that you have to work hard to enjoy success.

In that season, I also stopped chasing the number. I focused on my purpose and running my business with God. Chasing money is tiring! It was during this season of business that I stopped setting revenue goals and instead focused on setting tithing goals. The way I saw it, the more I earned, the more I could give. Tithing goals freed me from the need to focus solely on money. Tithing goals helped me to set an infrastructure that would support the business in every way. Tithing also took the focus off of me and put it on the people I could serve and help. Tithing made the messy middle palatable. The truth is, as you continue to elevate and evolve, you will always be in a middle. But it doesn't have to be messy.

The time off from chasing millions taught me a lot of things. It also gave me the space to prepare my heart for the season I would enter just after I agreed with God that it was time to reestablish my million-dollar company. This time, however, I was ready. I was clear, and I was determined to erect a foundation for my company that would make my millions sustainable. I had become a leader during the break. I had also become a surrendered vessel and yielded my company to God. I won't lie. Deciding to fully surrender my life and business to God was a challenge for reasons I have already shared. And some days, I had to recommit to surrender because before noon I had already taken whatever I had given to God back over and was actively working on finding a solution. I look at it like this: Committing to surrender is like committing to bathing. You have to do it daily. That meant I had to change up my morning routine and give myself time to commune with God and release any fears, doubts, insights, and strategies to His care. I also had to be willing to take the time to listen to what He was saying in order to move forward in the next step. These acts made the climb back to the million-dollar mark feel like I was attending my sweet sixteen. It was warm and fuzzy, and I felt like the prettiest girl ever.

By the time we hit 2019, I was starting to itch about playing a bigger game. After five arbitrary people stopped me at varying times that year to tell me that I was "understated," "playing small," or "leaving my brilliance on the table," I was ready. And yes, someone did actually tell me that. It turned out to be the straw that broke the camel's back. I knew that being a millionaire (which didn't dissipate when my million-dollar company imploded) was only part of the equation. I had become a millionaire in 2015, just shy of my fortieth birthday. I also wanted to be a sustainable million-dollar CEO, not just for the title but to be a living, breathing blueprint for the others who would be called to millions and follow in my footsteps. As my friend and colleague Shameca Tankerson says, "I am the prototype."

As a woman of color founder and CEO who loves God with a company that today makes, moves, and will leave millions, I am the blueprint. I am the prototype others will look to in order to be able to make the move with grace and ease instead of hustle and grind. With revenues that others would still love to enjoy in the years between 2016 and 2019, it wasn't about the money. For me, it was about setting up the infrastructure to support the business that I would run in the near future. I was willing to lose it all to gain it back in a way that would sustain. It was about the Move to Millions Method. It was about clarifying, confirming, and creating the strategy, sales infrastructure, systems, and support, and cultivating the success mindset required to run a sustainable million- or multimillion-dollar company. It was about doing exactly what I have shared with you in this book.

So in 2020, as we finished our first million-dollar year in four years, we re-entered the millions messy middle: the place where many businesses get lost because the demands and costs are high and commitment to get to the other side often wanes in the throes of disappointment, failures, and confusion. Our messy millions season is designed to take us from seven to eight figures. Yours will be designed to take you from six to seven.

Regardless of where your messy middle ends, it will look and feel the same. You will want to turn back, abort, and abandon the whole thing at least every other day, if not every hour! This is not a fun time; but it is a necessary time. The only way to the other side is through. Through the fear, through the overwhelm, through the doubt, through the team, through the CEO decisions, through the failed launches, through the constant questioning if you're really meant for this. You are. Stay the course.

PRESS: persistently run expecting supernatural success. It will surely come if you keep moving in the direction of the mandate.

In 2019, we started the Move to Millions with me, a part-time marketing manager and a full-time executive assistant. I meant it when I said that you can get to the million-dollar mark without a huge team. You will also likely find that you get way more done. No messy layers of people to go through in order to enact change in your company. My EA, at the time, was instrumental in helping me to get a lot of the systems that got our company to millions in place. With the help of my now operations manager, those systems are being updated and expanded.

As a measure of accountability, she is helping to make sure we actually use them to move the company forward. In preparation for returning to a million-dollar company, I spent a lot of time thinking from my vision point and not my vantage point that year. For the first time in the history of my business, it wasn't "hard." Sure, there were decisions to make, CEO-ing to do, work to accomplish. But it honestly felt like we were meant for it. We were meant to show up bigger and occupy more space in the marketplace.

We were meant to be an example, a prototype, of what is possible in your business. A big part of feeling less striving and more flow was of course because I had decided to stop chasing the number and to start surrendering this business to God. Sitting in the significance of my surrender changed everything. The difference was that this time I was different. I was ready. I was focused. I was surrendered. I was, as John Assaraf says, "willing to do whatever it took." The heavy lifting that I did in 2019 positioned us well to cross seven figures again in 2020. As a result, I knew I had a business that I could sustain.

There is a chaotic corridor between a six-figure business that's generating between $200,000 and $500,000 and having a business that generates $1,000,000 to $3,000,000 a year. In this corridor, everything will be called into question, personally and professionally. During this time, you might experience marital struggles that may include miscommunication, which causes more strain and pressure. This often leads to problems with your children acting up or acting out. It can culminate into all of you feeling unsupported. This is in addition to the challenges that your business causes. This corridor is where things tend to get more challenging and often very messy, especially if the foundation for your company hasn't been laid before you started to pass through. Inside the corridor, you might find yourself experiencing struggle that just doesn't make sense. One of the first things to do when you are scaling is to hire. However, as you hire, it often gets harder to track results and get things done. I know that sounds counterintuitive. But trust me it happens, especially if you scale too fast. The team that you bring on requires time to learn the ropes and become productive.

You will get hella frustrated in this part of the middle. Looking at payroll, but not seeing a return on the investment you're making in people is daunting. It will make you question if it's worth it. It might even make you start to imagine one of those businesses that you see Facebook ads for where they are walking the beach with their laptop, spouting how easy it is to hit seven figures. Scaling your business is no beach walk. Scaling is about replication and duplication, not time or freedom, especially at first. The only way to replicate and duplicate is through taking the time to create all of those systems we discussed in the system suite chapter. You're going to hire and pay a lot of people to work a little harder in the messy middle. Removing yourself too far from the day-to-day too soon will cause a rift that can intensify your challenges in the middle. The middle will call everything you think you desire into question. Go forward anyway.

When you're in the messy middle, you might notice that your profits slow down or disappear altogether. Your team will start to get bigger, as described in the talent suite chapter. Your responsibilities as the CEO start to feel much harder to bear. Seriously, you are technically the CEO. However, you're also the training department and the quality assurance department. And you might not like it. You might decide that you don't really want to be the CEO. All these people coming on need to be developed by someone. You are *someone*. This is the time when your business will tell on you. If your systems aren't tight, you'll start to break your business every few months. If you haven't properly trained your team, you will start to feel remorse for hiring them because they aren't performing and growing the bottom line; but you're still paying them twice a month. As you look to level up your client counts and onboarding, you'll find more problems than you might be prepared to solve. This is the millions messy middle. This is where you have to leave your entrepreneurial self behind and become a leader, a CEO. And your messy middle version of CEO might not fit the picture you had in your mind when you started to develop your team.

You'll likely go from being in almost all the departments in your company—marketing, sales, customer service, fulfillment, operations, and retention—to strategically presiding over the company as a whole and spending time in a few areas, but not all of them with the help of key team members. Remember, however, you won't start there. You will go from being all the things and every department head to being all the things as you train the person or people who will become the team and department heads. This will require more of you.

I recommend that before you start your middle, you over communicate with your family. Take your family to your favorite restaurant, tell them what's coming, and what you'll need from them. Tell them that they might have to fend for themselves at dinner. Tell them that you may not make it to all of their games or recitals. Tell them that this is temporary, but it's necessary so that you can get to the other side. Have them all participate in the plan to achieve the million-dollar goal.

I have long believed that people support what they help to create. So, give them the opportunity to help you and give their thoughts or opinions on the goal. Remember that everyone is looking to answer two questions: "What's in it for me?" and "Will this work for me?" Answer those two questions for them. Have them designate their reward when you hit this goal. This creates buy-in, and it will give you something to remind them of when you have to work late or can't be present. I did this with my husband. I made him an amazing dinner to tell him that this was the last time I'd be cooking for the foreseeable future. We created a plan of how he'd still eat (we hired a chef), but that I would be doing the things necessary to scale this company. As I hired, I would be spending time developing the team, which meant that some of my work would have to be done after work hours. He wasn't ecstatic, but he understood. We also determined what would be in it for him when we achieved the goal.

Once you get past the messy middle, it feels like euphoria. It's as if it's always sunny. The focus and time dedicated to the goal will pay off, and the team will show up fully and take things off your plate. There are days when I am traveling, and I never have to worry if the clients are being served. That took work, but it was all worth it. The ultimate goal for you as a million-dollar CEO is to go from implementing the systems to managing the people who implement systems and, eventually, to manage the people who manage the people who implement the systems. This is not a warm and fuzzy place because what got you to six figures won't get you to seven. You need a whole new set of skills to manage in the middle. If you're not careful, you'll get stuck in the messy middle.

Here are some additional symptoms of the millions messy middle:

- You experience hiring challenges and delays.
- You find the shift into a bigger vision uncomfortable.
- You learn that you have to start thinking about alignment at the company level.
- You start breaking your business every few months.
- Your fear goes up as you level up.

- You struggle with raising your pricing to accommodate for the new team while not being the primary service provider for your clients.
- You get frustrated over the growing pains that accompany stepping up as a leader.
- You struggle with the lack of results despite the increasing expenses.
- You have an identity crisis because you no longer see yourself as the most important person in your business.

The middle is messy, but it will stretch you into the leader you were destined to become. As a part of the middle, you'll have to journey back to the basics when things were simpler to find success as you navigate this new corridor. There is no right or wrong way to move through the middle. You'll experience the highs and lows of figuring it out as you move. There will be lots of reevaluation, but that's okay. Just remember that you're built for it because the messy millions will blossom into the company of your dreams. Although there is no right or wrong way to move through the middle, we have been successful at helping our clients navigate this time with lots of mindset support and by keeping them focused on their big reason why and their vision point instead of the vantage point of all the chaos that is surrounding them.

When you find yourself in the middle—and trust me you will—here are the steps that I most recommend that you take to navigate the middle and successfully get to the other side.

Remember your why.

As I quote often, when you know your why, you are reminded of the potential impact coming your way if you keep showing up. I will be the first to admit that the middle is ugly. However, even as I am in my own version of the middle, my why is giving me courage and comfort to keep saying yes to myself and God because this work matters. The people waiting for us to show up matter. Even though some days, I don't want to get out of the bed, and I want to go all the way back to simpler days, I think about the amazing people supporting my efforts and the lives we have already changed. That gives me the strength to get up again. I know it will do the same for you.

Look for opportunities to streamline your efforts by going back to what you did previously that worked for you.

While everything won't translate in this middle environment, there are a few things you can use and build upon to manage the middle. When we start to grow, we think we need to change everything, and that isn't true. There's solace in the basics.

Map out next steps as best you can.

Start where you are and employ the help of a coach or mentor, if necessary. Remember to work the middle from your vision point, not your vantage point. Just lifting your head up will shift your perspective and the energy around whatever challenge you're facing at the moment. Taking the time to evaluate where you are and where you are going will help you to determine the next step. Remember, as inspired by Rumi, the path emerges as you walk it.

Over communicate with your team.

By communicating consistently, you will maintain buy-in for the big goal and uncomfortableness of the middle. Your team is going to be leery, nervous, and maybe even scared, especially if you're not communicating with them every step of the way. Remember that your team believes in you. They want to be included, and as a result, they will support what they help to create. It's a huge burden to shoulder all of the hard stuff when you have people capable of lightening your load. Overcommunication will strengthen your bond, culture, and your team's commitment to remaining in the vineyard with you.

Find the gratitude in the middle.

The highest emotions are faith, love, gratitude, appreciation, and trust. Any time spent in any of these emotions will allow you to vibrate at a higher level. A high vibration is necessary to shift from the mediocre into the magnificent. Even when it's tough, there is always something to focus on that will change your perspective. Start there. For as long as we have been holding weekly team meetings, I have been keen to start each meeting with every member of the team sharing something they are grateful for. Every team meeting isn't warm and fuzzy. Sometimes I have to share the not-so-good and even ugly with the team. I have to hold them accountable for the role that they play. This simple exercise keeps them in a state of gratitude throughout the entire meeting, which lessens the fears or overwhelm.

Decide to enjoy the middle.

The middle is limited. It won't be around forever, so enjoying it can help it to move more quickly. As with most things, it's a decision. The truth is that the messy middle is the space between what used to be and what is coming next. So, it's actually a space to be excited about! I love knowing that everything I desire is on the other side of the middle. It puts pep in my step to get up and get moving to solve the problems, fix the challenges, and find new ways to achieve the goals. Enjoying the middle gives me so much energy. If you rush it, you won't get to see the beauty of your next level unfold. Truth be told, although you desire to get out of the middle as soon as possible, change is perpetual, which means we are technically always in a messy middle. When you look at it that way, you have to find a way to enjoy every minute of it!

Get community so it doesn't feel so lonely.

I may be biased, but I believe that if you're desiring to have a million-dollar or bigger company, you should never be without coaching and community. Even the Bible talks about having a multitude of advisors. This is one of the big reasons for our two community-based programs, Move to Millions Mastermind and the Legacy Collective®. They are community-based coaching experiences so that millions-minded entrepreneurs have the support they need to navigate the journey. Sometimes it's just about knowing that you aren't alone and other people are going through the same thing that gives you the courage to keep moving forward. And sometimes it's about having a wealth of knowledge around you to give you ideas to maximize the middle.

Chapter Action Plan

1. Journal about the other side of your messy middle. Be sure to include what you're grateful for and what your business will be like when you arrive on the other side of this season in your business.
2. Determine what you need to focus on getting back to the basics of in order to navigate this season.
3. Map your next best move during this season in your business.
4. Find a community for support as you navigate (try ours).

Remember: Information without action is a waste of time. Set a plan right now to implement so that your middle becomes less messy, and you get one step closer to your million-dollar goal.

CHAPTER SIXTEEN
The Move to Millions Manifesto

"To make and move millions, it's going to take mastery,
operational obedience, vision, and execution."
—GOD

When I was a little girl, I was lucky enough to be introduced to entrepreneurship through my paternal grandmother, Sylvia Jervey, or Nanny, as we called her. She sold freeze cups out of her South Bridge project. I'd watch her make a pitcher of Kool-Aid, usually the red kind, pour it into white Styrofoam cups, and place them in her freezer. When the neighborhood kids came knocking, she charged them twenty-five cents for one. Once a week, she'd have several flavors for the neighborhood kids to choose from. Nanny didn't play about her freeze cups business. Even though we were Nanny's grandchildren, she never gave us free freeze cups. *Never*. She was the first person to teach me, without me even realizing it at the time, that you had to have respect for your own pricing. In business, we solve problems for profit. The problem Nanny was solving was a sweet cool treat for the neighborhood kids on a hot summer day.

I learned many things from watching Nanny work. One of my favorite lessons was understanding the value of your product. I recall so many times when the neighborhood kids would try to get over on Nanny, coming to the back door with fifteen or twenty cents. They might have come that way, but trust me, they left empty-handed. Nanny didn't play that. You could try to hustle her if you wanted. You were usually the one who felt hustled when all was said and done. She was the first person to teach me about fiscal responsibility. Anyone who's come to any workshop I hold where I cover pricing has to recite several axioms as a result of what my Nanny taught me (I shared each of them in the offer suite chapter).

They were just a few that I can totally admit to having learned from watching Nanny.

You can blame Nanny for me not offering discounts! Nanny was serious about her coins. She made no apologies for it. It's definitely a principle we can all leverage today to move our businesses forward. One of the biggest challenges I see our clients and prospective clients face and attempt to work through hinges on their pricing and the belief that something is better than nothing. This lack-minded pricing philosophy has stifled many businesses. Price is an indication of value by the consumer. When I see something that is priced low but promising a massive result, I run in the opposite direction.

When God gave me each word for MOVE, I remember immediately thinking about how I learned about mastery. Another time, I was at Nanny's for the weekend, and I got into more trouble than usual. It was so bad that my dad was called in to intervene. While I can't recall exactly what I did, I can recall the pain I felt from the experience. While I wasn't a stranger to getting a beating, this pain wasn't from my hands hurting. My dad was not a violent man; he was a practical one. He wasn't above the belt, but he used it as a last resort if he thought there was a better way to teach you a lesson. Bob wanted better for his kids than he had. So, often, the lessons or punishment we received came in the form of something to aid us on our journey to adulthood. It's actually a lesson I plan to take into raising my own children one day.

When I went to live with my dad after my mom went to jail, I learned the importance of mastery. My dad was a former teacher turned industrial engineer who was known for being a devout disciplinarian. I was grateful to my father for handling his responsibility when my mom went to jail. He could have disappeared, but he didn't. I will always thank him for that. My dad is also the reason that I value education more than material possessions.

I believe that, when given a choice between material possessions and an investment to further your development, career, and livelihood, the answer is simple: invest for the knowledge. My dad taught me that.

My dad was very strict; it was his way or the highway. He also didn't show much emotion. He let it be known that he loved us as evidenced by the roof over our heads, the food on the table, and the clothes on our backs. My brother Dar couldn't keep up, so he ended up leaving and the streets became his family. So before long, it was just my sister and me. My dad was traveling a lot for work back then, so we were left with my stepmother a lot.

When my dad was home, he resumed his post of disciplinarian. Any time we did anything he didn't like, he sought to teach us a lesson. The lessons that he used were always designed to make us better. He wanted us to think logically instead of responding emotionally. When I started to think about sitting down to write this chapter, I instantly saw my dad standing over me with a stern look and a command to write one thousand sentences. He believed that, by the time you were done, you'd have mastery of the lesson he meant for you to learn so that you wouldn't make that mistake again.

He was usually right.

Call it what you want, but the man had a point. Because of my sentence writing skills, I didn't go through half of what my younger sister did. I was the first of my dad's kids, and the only of my mom's, to actually graduate from high school. Getting out mostly unscathed and scandal-free was a plus by itself. Don't get me wrong. I did my fair share of dirt, but it wasn't the kind that you couldn't wipe off.

When I got in trouble at Nanny's that time, my punishment was to write five thousand sentences. I had until midnight to do it. The edict came down around five o'clock that evening. One thing for sure, and two things for certain, was that my dad was after the best from us. Even though I had blisters on my hands when I was done, I had learned a lesson that day. As I reflect some thirty-five years later, that lesson was about mastery. Master your mind so you make decisions that advance you. My dad was clear. At least one of his kids was going to be something in the world. Although he had never been able to overcome his own demons, his goal was that we (it really felt like *I*) were going to make something of ourselves. Dad was tough; he was after mastery. Now, at the time, it sucked. As I look back today, I'm grateful to my dad for teaching me a valuable lesson about mastery, especially since we lost him while I was writing this book. This lesson warms my heart, and I am grateful to be able to share it with you.

By definition, *mastery* is a comprehensive knowledge or skill in a subject.[31]

When I first started my business, I was the master of nothing. In fact, if you used to watch *Good Times* and you remember episodes that featured Lenny (pronounced lenn-naaay), I was like him. I had plentaaay.[32] If you recall, you could find him at any time with tons of goods—from toothbrushes to watches and everything in between. Lenny was more of a generalist. When I first started IOE, I was, too. I would speak, facilitate, consult, coach on anything—seriously, anything. I had coached clients who had relationship issues despite the fact that I couldn't keep my own man. I coached people on whatever they needed because I just needed to make money. I had bills to pay.

Being a generalist in those early days was a matter of survival. It kept me fresh because I had to know a lot of things. However, the challenge is that when you know a lot, you are a master of *nothing*. That reflects in your ability to get clients and to earn at a level to prevent you from having to go back to work and end up filing bankruptcy like I did.

When I wasn't being a generalist, I was creating generic content. I spent the first nine months creating content based on what I thought my clients would like to receive from me instead of conducting some market research so that my time wouldn't be spent in vain. As a part of those nine months, I created tons of "good" content; but it turned out not to be desired by the marketplace, which is why I ended up running out of money and, ultimately, filing bankruptcy and going back to work. To this day, I never recommend that anyone create before they sell; that is not mastery.

Mastery, on the other hand, is validating that the problem you solve is one that those with the problem are willing to make an investment in a solution, both financially and emotionally. These days, I like to call this the universal law of business. It is when we are masters of the solution to a problem that our most ideal clients have that we can get them to invest in the solution to solve the problem. People in pain will always be seeking a pain killer. The master can stop the pain.

As a result, I have mastered my craft. That is why I have won so many awards, had clients renew multiple times to work with us, and am known for changing lives in masterful ways. Mastery, according to Malcolm Gladwell in his book *Outliers*, is considered having ten thousand hours of "proven" knowledge and experience on the topic you want to be known for.[33] At this point, I have more than twenty-five thousand hours in, and that is why we also have five hundred testimonials on our company website. As Toni Childs from *Girlfriends* used to say, we specialize in results.[34]

After God gave me the acronym for MOVE, I quickly realized that it was a double entendre. It works in life and in business. I love acronyms. There is only one artform I love more than acronyms: writing manifestos. A manifesto is a public declaration, historically tied to politics.[35] I got excited when God spoke Move to Millions because it meant that I was finally going to have my own movement, and that meant I would need a manifesto.

I remember years before when a brand influencer named Warren Carlyle, whom I had met at my friend Aprille Franks' event, asked me, "What's your movement?"

I looked at him with that deer-in-the-headlights look as I said to myself under my breath, *What in the devil is a movement?*

You see, I didn't build my business to seven figures online. My business was built leveraging tried and tested offline marketing strategies, like speaking and live events. So, I wasn't used to all of this online business lingo. I had struggled with the "tempermentalism" of online marketing. It seems like it could go away in an instant. I remember those times in recent years when Facebook or Instagram went down, and the whole world panicked. Well, probably everyone but me because my business never hinged on the internet or social media.

He went on to school me. "To stand out online you need a movement, a shared purpose and reason to bring people together. When you have a movement, it will galvanize people, create a shared purpose, and meet a substantial need. Everyone is looking for a place to belong, a place that feels safe for them to discover who they really are. That's what your movement will do for others."

I'll admit not only did I love his definition, but I loved the energy with which he expressed it. I wanted a movement, and I wanted one bad. In that moment, as I stood there thinking about how to answer his question, I had nothing.

Nothing.

For years, I racked my brain, trying to come up with a movement. I even asked my clients and small team if we had one. They, too, looked at me like I had looked at Warren.

We were movement-*less*.

Probably because movements aren't "come up with." They are inspired. They are purpose personified. I now believe that a movement is a natural extension of who you are and the work you were called to do. In the early years, I felt that my work mattered. However, I hadn't really taken the time to hear the purpose in my work until I decided that I was going to stop chasing the million-dollar mark. It was just such a shallow goal to live for. Until I stopped setting revenue goals and started to set tithe goals instead, I was just meandering, one step above mediocrity. Shifting my focus is what allowed my movement to come into my life experience. God was able to speak, and I was able to hear and then act because I was open, in alignment, and able to focus outside of myself. Focusing on tithing and, therefore, giving was the beginning of my Next Level Everything.

Movements don't just spring up out of nowhere. Until I was grounded in something bigger than myself, I couldn't live into my ultimate purpose. My purpose brought this movement right to my proverbial front door. What I tried to "come up with" for years came to be just like that. Just like God said, "Let there be," there was Move to Millions. Just like that, I had a movement, which meant I needed a manifesto. In order to create a manifesto, the mission had to be clear.

The Move to Millions mission is to eradicate small business poverty (a low six-figure business) and create CEOs that normalize wealth, scale a sustainable business, establish a financial legacy, and shake the planet. We believe that wealth and abundance are your birthright. We believe that you came into the earth realm as abundance personified. Then, your family introduced you to fear, lack, and uncertainty. Don't get us wrong. We believe that your family did the best that they could with what they had. We believe that their best was not *the* best, God's best. We believe that God is calling you back to your birthright. We believe that it's time. We believe you deserve to get everything God earmarked for you. We believe that entrepreneurship is the vehicle God created to bring wealth into your life experience. We believe that when businesses make more, the impact is felt by millions. We believe that if you didn't come from millions, millions should come from you.

I love that it's *Move* to Millions because, if you desire to generate millions of dollars in your business per year, it will require consistent movement—action—to make the journey. In fact, I typically go so far as to say that there are seven *M*'s that are essential to making, moving, and leaving millions: mindset, messaging, marketing, money, methodology, metrics, and movement (action). Since getting to the million-dollar mark doesn't happen overnight, it's important to remember that no one goes to bed a blunder and wakes up a wonder. There has to be consistent action happening to produce millions. It's about the principles and the process. The move is a marathon, not a sprint. Our manifesto reflects our vision and mission. I am excited to share our manifesto with you:

> I am wealth. I am abundance. I am blessed. I am grateful. I am loved. I am surrendered. I am an entrepreneurial leader who was made to move millions.
> I came into the earth realm as abundance and now I am stepping back into the light.
> I am an Incredible One and millions are my birthright.
> I'm ready to get what God has earmarked for me so I am ready to MOVE.
> I make millions. I move millions.
> And because my business serves me financially, spiritually, and sustainably, I'm going to leave millions.
> My legacy will be financial.
> I am prepared for rain, and I am changing the game.

I am my ancestors' wildest dream.
It's my time. It's my turn.
I didn't come from millions, but millions will absolutely come from
me.

Along with the manifesto I created, the inspiration kept flowing. So, I also created what is now the Ten Commandments of a CEO on the Move to Millions:

- Thou shalt stop stressing and start surrendering.
- Thou shalt forgive every day so that nothing keeps you from more abundance than your hand, heart, and bank account can hold.
- Thou shalt not be all the things; thou shall be the co-CEO and thou shalt know that God is the real CEO of your company.
- Thou shalt know that you deserve a business that serves you financially, spiritually, and sustainably.
- Thou shalt make decisions from your vision point, not your vantage point.
- Thou shalt work the business from the top, not the bottom.
- Thou shalt not base your prices on your time, but instead on the result you provide to the problem clients can't solve on their own.
- Thou shalt set strategic sales goals and put the systems and processes in place to achieve them with grace and ease instead of hustle and grind.
- Thou shalt be confident at all times. Your confidence will close more deals than your skills ever will.
- Thou shalt focus on strengthening your strategy, systems, sales, support, and success mindset.

Chapter Action Plan

1. Journal about your own movement's manifesto. What would you want to share with those who are part of your movement?

Remember: Information without action is a waste of time. Set a plan right now to implement so that you have the right words to speak over your life and business on your way to the million-dollar mark.

CHAPTER SEVENTEEN
The Leverage + Scale Legacy Suite

"The Move to Millions is about leaving an inheritance to your children's children and scaling your business in order to do it because legacy is financial."
—DARNYELLE JERVEY HARMON

I purposely left this Million Dollar Asset to the vision section of this book because creating a legacy is absolutely a vision play. This chapter really has three objectives. First, I want to share exactly what should be included in your legacy suite. Next, I want to reinforce the need for financial advice and building a team to substantiate the real reasons you will have a million-dollar company. Lastly, I want to help you determine which vision point decisions are impacted as you begin to build this asset.

Before I walk through what is included in this asset, I need to state the obvious. I am not an attorney or certified financial advisor, and I don't play one on TV. Nothing I share here should be construed as or taken as advice. Please talk with your professionals about anything that I share here. Also, because I am not an attorney or a certified financial advisor, I will not be going super deep into any of the concepts. What I'm sharing is just for your basic knowledge, so you'll know what to ask for and create with your chosen professionals.

As a million-dollar CEO, your legacy suite will include several things: intellectual property protection, a wealth plan, an investment portfolio, an insurance portfolio, an estate plan, and a business succession plan. I will go into each of these shortly. However, before I do, there are some questions I need you to answer:

- What does legacy mean to you?
- What are your legacy milestones?
- Fast forward to age sixty-five. What will you have in place?
- What will retirement mean for you? What will you have to have in liquid and assets to be able to stop working?
- What are your short-term financial goals?
- What are your long-term financial goals?
- What is the number you want to have in place to leave to your children and grandchildren (or designees)?
- What will it take to be the parent and grandparent to leave your children and grandchildren money to buy their first house, start their first business, or go to college and graduate debt-free?
- Have you given any thought to your business's exit plan?

Each of these questions are important now because they will determine what you do to continue to live out your vision. If you started your business just to make more than you did at your job, that needs to be taken into consideration. Somehow though, since you are reading this book, I doubt that is still the case, even if it was when you first quit your job. For the record, I am not judging you. When I first started this company, I was just trying to keep my house and car. As I started to do meaningful work, things shifted. It became less about me and more about the impact I could make.

I give you permission to take your time to answer each of those questions. They are serious and shouldn't be answered off the top of your head. Instead, you should TTT: think things through. Maybe even consult with your spouse if you are married. I will be honest. I struggled with a few of the questions. I had never thought beyond where I was in my business initially. My goal was singular: to have a million-dollar business. So, once we started making and keeping millions, I had to shift my vision. I had to start thinking about what I desired that my financial legacy be. Honestly that is hard to ponder in and of itself.

At the time of writing this book, my husband and I have been trying to start a family for four years. When we got married in 2017, we promised to give ourselves a year to enjoy one another and travel and see the world. We did. Once the calendar struck year one married, we immediately started trying to get pregnant. After three months, we saw a fertility specialist. When we started, I had just turned forty-three. When I started writing this book, I had just turned forty-seven, and we are still waiting for our miracle. We've tried everything: IUI, IVF, changing our diet, and enrolling in fertility coaching. You name it, we have done it. So, asking myself questions about legacy when I have no heirs is just hard. Therefore, I have avoided it. Well, I *had* avoided it until I started to accumulate an intense amount of wealth, that is. Now, it's just not responsible to not think about all of the things that make up the legacy suite. So, I have had to decide what will happen to my company when either I decide to retire or my sun sets. I realized that I didn't just want the business to die with me. That is why I started working on the first part of my legacy suite: intellectual property protection (IPP).

Your IPP portfolio will need to be managed by an intellectual property attorney. They will help you to assess what you have and create a plan to manage and protect all of your assets. When I speak of assets in this way, I am referring to your registered trademarks, frameworks, and methodologies. Everything you do and have created must be assessed. From your company name (and your name) to your signature system, key messages, frameworks, training content, and everything in between, they likely should be protected. Each of these has value that could be licensed or sold outright. They should add money to your estate. Your IPP portfolio will also include a plan for licensing once all of your assets are determined and protected. There is so much money in licensing. It's a great way to extend your paydays and start to earn six figures or more per client. Also included here are your copyright registrations for each framework, your program content, and curriculum. If you write articles and create video content, and all that entails, all of that should be protected, too. It's all an asset that will create income.

After you assess your intellectual property, you'll want to meet with a certified financial planner to create your wealth plan. I recommend meeting with them after you meet with the IP attorney because the attorney will help you to determine more assets to be included in the plan beyond any retirement accounts and investments that you have. Together, they can help you to determine your net worth. When working on your wealth plan, you should complete your money map very early in the process. You can download the money map at https://www.movetomillionsbook.com/resources. They'll help you to determine your lifestyle maximization number, which includes what you need to live now and at retirement as well as what you'll have to leave to heirs. They'll likely have you do a spending audit if your ability to get to the numbers you want are hindered in any way. They'll also give you a savings plan, an investment strategy based on your goals and risk tolerance. They will evaluate your full financial picture, including a valuation of your company. From there, they will help you to determine/start an investment portfolio.

I started working with a certified financial planner in my twenties. As soon as I started my first full-time job, I was clear: I was going to do what white people did. In my mind, all white people had a financial advisor. As a result, I got into investing very early, from my 401(k) to some stocks outside of that like Microsoft and Apple, and later, Amazon and Tesla. I got into each of those stocks early. That's the reason I became a millionaire. I didn't have tens of thousands of shares of those early stocks, but I had enough for it to add up. In your investment portfolio, they will likely tell you to diversify. You should have some real estate, turnkey businesses, stocks and bonds, an IRA or SEPP, and maybe even some crypto. They'll also likely get you involved in both long-term and short-term investment strategies based on your risk tolerance. Another thing I want to share here is that an investment portfolio is a long game. It builds assets over time, so keep that in mind.

I also highly recommend that your legacy suite include an insurance portfolio. You'll be able to talk with your certified financial planner about this. There are lots of insurance types that a million-dollar CEO needs to have in their portfolio, including term life insurance, whole life insurance, disability insurance, general liability insurance, professional liability insurance, health insurance, home insurance, and car insurance. When you start building out your real estate portfolio, you might even have some landlord insurance.

Next, you'll want to build your estate plan. This one could be tough because no one wants to think of their sun setting. But here's the thing. Every one of us will have a sun set moment. We recently lost my father to liver cancer—stage four, inoperable—out of nowhere. Within thirty-three days of being rushed to the emergency room, he was gone. My younger brother Paul and I barely had time to get a basic will and power of attorney in place. And not even six months later, we lost my stepmother unexpectedly. Sadly, most people think they have more time. Your estate plan will include a living will, healthcare directives, and a power of attorney, your last will and testament, financial power of attorney, trusts, beneficiary designations, and a letter of intent.

Lastly, you'll need a business succession plan. You'll work with all of your professionals on this, including your estate attorney, your small business attorney, your certified financial planner, and possibly even your intellectual property attorney. There are more questions to consider for this one:

- Will you be able to voluntarily let go?
- Do you have children who could run the company?
- Are you grooming someone to run the company in your stead?
- Are you offering profit sharing to your employees so that they own your company over time?
- What is your financial goal at sale?
- What is the business's vision for the future?
- What will need to be in place at the time of the sale? What will the sale include?
- Does your succession plan reflect your business goals?
- Does the succession plan align with your personal objectives?
- Who are the potential successors, and do they have the requisite skills—and interest—needed to lead the company?

Once you have the answers to these questions, you'll be able to get some great guidance to establish your succession plan. Your business has a bigger purpose than making money and just crossing the million-dollar mark. Your business is the key to a financial legacy. By starting to ask yourself these tough questions today, you'll be better positioned to leave a financial legacy and have a team that can help you expand your mission without compromising your values.

Chapter Action Plan

1. Review each area of the Legacy Suite.
2. Craft your Legacy Vision.
3. Get referrals for key professionals to help you: a small business attorney, an estate attorney, an intellectual property attorney, and a certified financial planner.
4. Start thinking about your business as the key to your financial legacy.

Remember: Information without a plan to implement is just a waste of your time. Decide now how you will put this suite to work for you. Also remember: If you didn't come from millions, millions should come from *you*.

Part Four:

Execution

CHAPTER EIGHTEEN

Move to Millions Accountability & Implementation

"Acquiring knowledge is not where your power lies; implementing acquired knowledge gives you power."
—DARNYELLE JERVEY HARMON

When I was in college, a friend and I were having lunch with our mentor. During that lunch, he encouraged us to finish a project that we had started together as a part of one of our business administration classes. Without even realizing it, he gave us *the* idea that would turn the project into something transformational and, honestly, the start of an amazing business concept. As I listened, I got goosebumps all over my body, which were always a sign of God's presence for me. Whenever I felt God, I knew that I was in the presence of a God idea.

God ideas have always felt like God winks to me, those not-so-subtle indicators that God has kissed something that would change my life. As our mentor spoke, I could hear myself thinking through the next few steps to get the project done. I turned to my friend to ask her how she felt about continuing to work on it. She said she needed to think about it but if I wanted to, I should get started. I could tell that she was over the idea, and I was fine with that. For me, this idea was something I definitely intended to follow through on. As she looked at me, I could read between her words. She just didn't want to turn the project down in the mentor's face. I figured that would be her response because the entire time we were working on the project she came up with excuse after excuse as to why she couldn't work on it. So, I already knew what was happening. I was fine with it. After all, I was used to doing things alone.

When we left that lunch, the idea was still percolating. I felt my excitement increase. I couldn't wait to get back to my dorm so that I could lay out my next steps. I knew they were the key to finishing the project and getting the recognition that would accompany it. So, I got to work. It took me another two months to finish it. When I presented in class, it was met by a resounding level of excitement and praise. More than that, there was a ton of interest in participating in the project as an investor. Both the students and the professor were interested in adding value that would accelerate the project. When class ended that day, you know my friend rushed over to me to express her disdain for the fact that I proceeded without her. Suddenly, she was interested in the project because she was now aware of the results.

"It doesn't work that way," I smirked at her.

She rolled her eyes.

And I continued, "You were the one telling me to move forward if I wanted to, and you told me you would let me know. It wasn't my responsibility to follow up with you to see if you decided you wanted to keep working on it. So, I moved forward on my own. Now that you hear how well it's being received, you want a share of the success. It doesn't work that way. I am not giving you any credit for something you didn't do."

Upset, she pushed past me, purposely hitting me hard on my left shoulder. Although I wanted to go after her and punch her in her face, I didn't. It wasn't worth it. I realized something important that day. Something that I still leverage and has served me well. All the knowledge in the world is useless if you don't take action on it. She heard our mentor tell her the same thing he told me. Yet she allowed the information to go in one ear and out the other. I, on the other hand, took that information and ran with it. The difference was in the implementation.

You know the saying there's nothing to it but to do it? That's kind of how I live my life. For years, my friends, co-workers, and clients have acknowledged that I take action. Consistently. I won't wait. I have long believed that taking action is truly how you separate the gifted from the ready. I also know that the universe loves speed. When we sit with an idea longer than necessary, God will often give your God idea to another messenger because your delay can't delay the message.

We have gotten to the point in this book where I'm the mentor sharing an idea with you over lunch. You have a distinct opportunity to decide if you'll take action and implement, or if you'll think about if you want to continue the journey we started together. Either choice is yours, but the consequences for choosing not to take action on all you've consumed could derail your own journey to and beyond the million-dollar mark. I have laid out the entire framework that I, and many of my clients as evidenced in the case studies shared in this book and at https://www.movetomillionsbook. com/resources, have used to move closer to, or actually beyond, the million-dollar mark. It's called the *Move to Millions* for a reason. In order to achieve the goal of leveraging and scaling your business to the million-dollar mark, consistent moves must be made. That means that you have to work toward mastering the million-dollar assets, living the principles of operational obedience, and setting the vision. The final part of executing the physical, spiritual, emotional, and financial tasks allows the whole framework to come alive for you, your life, and your business.

When God made the *E* in MOVE execution, I got very excited. What I lack in talent, I have always made up for in execution. Remember that pneumonic device I shared earlier: if it is to be, it is up to me? That is the very reason why I stay in action. I also think about the verse in James 2, which says, "Faith without works is dead." That's the reason that I like to say, "We have to give God something to bless." It's time to give God something to bless.

When you re-read and study this book, you'll realize that what it will take to achieve your goal of becoming a million-dollar CEO is here for you. I didn't tell you how I did it without telling you how you can, too. Each chapter unfolds nicely to give you divine insight into exactly what you'll need to do. With consistent action, in one to three years, you could have a million-dollar company. I say one to three years because it really depends on where you are starting. It depends on what you already have and what you'll need to get in place. It's not just about hitting the number, although hitting the number is essential. It's about setting up the systems and infrastructure to sustain the work you are doing. That is why the first time my business did millions (notice I said business, not company—there is a difference), it didn't stick. I couldn't sustain it because I didn't have the proper foundation in place.

Right now, as you hold this book (or listen to the audio), you have a distinct opportunity to be able to say something altogether different. This could be a defining moment for you. The moment that you took a firm grasp of your decision to make the move to millions. The book is a complete blueprint of the proven framework. The book could also be the start to coming to work with me and my team to get the accountability and support required to become a million-dollar CEO. In this book, I have shared the proven framework with you. It takes all five components working together to make the move with grace and ease, and not hustle and grind. *All five*. If just one is missing, you threaten a delay, a disconnect, or a distraction that is not for the good of your company.

If you have a sound strategy, but your sales infrastructure could implode if it is pushed to the limit, your systems haven't been set up to support the strategy. If there is no one on the team but you, you won't actually be able to see the results of your strategy. If you have the right sales infrastructure but your strategy is lacking, your systems are nonexistent and you're the only person on the team, you won't actually increase your sales enough for it to make a difference. If you have the right systems, but no clear strategy and sales process, it won't matter if you have a team. If you have a team, but you haven't set the strategy, created, and tested the sales infrastructure, and the systems aren't fully operational, well you will create a mess that you're overpaying for. The Move to Millions Method is tried, true, and tested. The Move to Millions Method is *how* you become a million-dollar CEO.

THE MOVE TO MILLIONS® METHOD:
A proven formula to scale to 7 figures and BEYOND

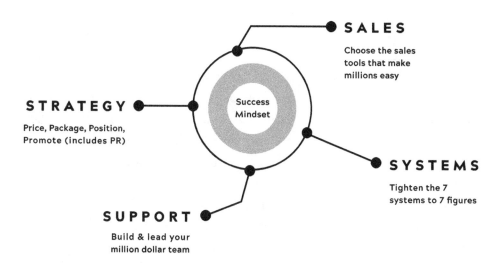

SALES
Choose the sales tools that make millions easy

STRATEGY
Price, Package, Position, Promote (includes PR)

Success Mindset

SYSTEMS
Tighten the 7 systems to 7 figures

SUPPORT
Build & lead your million dollar team

I am clear. The Move to Millions is a journey, not a sprint. Getting there too fast prevents sustainability. Scaling isn't about speed; it's about replication and duplication over time. In your hands at this moment, you have the blueprint for a sustainable million-dollar company. It all boils down to whether this was good reading, filled with witty anecdotes from my life, or if this was exactly what you've been praying for.

If this book has been the latter for you, then the only thing left to do is to get accountable and implement.

So right here and right now, it's time to decide. Are you a million-dollar CEO in the making? If you're answering with a resounding yes, then you must decide why you want a million-dollar company. Your why will ground you enough to become accountable to your own goals and desires. Your why will get you into action so that you get on a trajectory to achieving this big goal.

When working with our clients in our Move to Millions Mastermind, our work begins with them taking an assessment of their business. We look at each of the seven areas of their company to identify the successes and the gaps. Once we identify the gaps, we can create their custom roadmap for shifting their company by turning each gap into a gateway to their next level. It takes time. It's why we often see clients enroll in the mastermind for three years. During their program tenure, they are supported by our team for the duration of their move so that their million-dollar company is one they can sustain if they decide to offboard working with us once they have achieved it. Sometimes, clients leave too soon. As a result, they delay getting their company to this mark, or they don't sustain the move into the next year. There is something to be said about community and accountability that aids implementation. When people think they will implement on their own once they leave, often they don't because the demands of implementation without support, coaching and consulting, community, and mentorship cause delays and distractions.

It's why I encourage our clients to not unplug from what is working. You might think you can read a book like this and make it happen. Some of you will set a goal and start your timer to begin implementing what is in this book. But the vast majority of you won't. You will put this book down and go right back to what your life and business looked like before you picked this book up. You will talk yourself out of the next step because it feels too hard.

I am not trying to be funny or disrespectful. The truth is most people don't even set goals. But even those who do don't actually achieve them. Why? Because it takes community, outside accountability, coaching and consulting, and implementation *together*. Just like missing any one part of the Move to Millions Method will delay the results. The same is true when it comes to these five. You need community, consulting, coaching, and accountability support in order to actually implement. If we use the logic of the 1979 Harvard study[36] on goal setting, 75 percent of you will give up next week. Seventy-one percent will give up the week after that. Sixty-four percent will make it a month focused on making the move to millions, and 46 percent of you will make it to six months before you give up. Community, accountability, coaching and consulting, and implementation together is the key to you being successful with everything I've laid out in this book.

We just so happen to have a place where you can get the community, accountability, and coaching and consulting support to implement all in one place. We would love to be community, coaching and consulting, accountability, and a place for implementation for you. As you sit here, book in hand, contemplating what to do next, if you're looking for more support, we'd love to be that for you.

Ready to Go Deeper?

SURPRISE: You didn't just buy a book! This book is your key to unlock a whole suite of valuable resources for building your business. We have thousands of dollars' worth of valuable resources waiting for you at https://www.movetomillionsbook.com/resources. I am going to mention a few of my favorite resources here for you:

- **Resource One:** Subscribe and listen weekly to the *Move to Millions Podcast*. Each week, listen in for insightful solo episodes, guest interviews and spiritual principles combined with business growth strategy.
- **Resource Two:** Order our Move to Millions 90-Day Planner. I designed this planner to support our clients on their own move to millions. It's the perfect companion for this book.
- **Resource Three:** Join us at our next Move to Millions Live Event Experience. This three-day event for million-dollar CEOs and million-dollar CEOs in the making will allow you to experience the content of this book in the flesh (as well as new content that you haven't even begun to envision yet). The whole event will feed your soul.

We'd love to help you:

- **Set your Move to Millions goal so that it is clear, specific, actionable, measurable, and you're clear of your Move to Millions timeframe.** It's not enough to say you want to move to millions. You'll have to drill down and say when you want to move to millions by and *why* moving to millions is the next best move for you. You'll have to take the time to get clear. We can help you with that while also identifying what may need to be modified so that you can achieve the goal.

- **Confirm your *real* reason why you're going to become account-able to the goal of making, moving, and leaving millions.** Start by declaring the reasons so that you can walk into the answers. It's like Matthew 7:7 says: Ask and it shall be given you. The reason(s) why you are desiring this level of achievement in your business is your ask of God and the universe. Without taking the time to clarify your reason why, you'll eventually get fed up and quit, just like the Harvard study shows us. It might be one week, or it might be six months. But not being tied to a reason that is bigger than you will position you to drop the ball and forget about moving millions. You might become like me, who eventually said that I really didn't need a million dollars. (This was my way of giving myself permission to quit and back down from the real goal in my heart because it was easier.)
- **Create a real, customized, and actionable plan.** This is where the rubber often meets the road. This is where my team and I create magic. We look at your gaps and turn them into gateways. Without a plan, one thing is for sure. You will not make the Move to Millions. The other thing to keep in mind is you don't know what you don't know. That could cause problems. While this book is an amazing blueprint, it's not a *customized* blueprint.
- **Take strategic, inspired, and massive action.** The plan is the start, but no plan guarantees results without action. Because making the move to millions is your goal, it means you'll have to show up fully for the goal daily. Taking small and large steps, but taking them consistently, is the key to achieving the goal. As I have shared via our case studies, we have some clients who do it in one year. We have some clients who take two to three years. It all depends on the level of action and commitment to the decision.
- **Determine KPIs and track, review, and adjust the goal accord-ingly.** This is something else that we can help you to do when we work together. Having a plan is the first step. Understanding what you should track and what the numbers are telling you is a whole other thing. This is accomplished by taking that plan and breaking it down into daily or weekly subplans so that you are focusing on

the right activities consistently. There will be some busy work, but there is also some work that leads to opportunities and revenue. We want to make sure that you are spending time on those so that you are strategic every single day. We will also help you to set up automations and the right software so that this isn't a manual effort. We clarify your revenue generating activities from your awareness generating activities because you do need both.

- **Become the best version of yourself so that you can lead a team committed to helping you make, move, and leave millions.** You were not meant to be a one-trick pony. You were born to lead while also deepening your impact and income. We can help you refine those skills so that you don't find yourself overwhelmed or spin your wheels on mistakes that take many people out in the messy middle.

- **Get in community with like-minded entrepreneurs also making the move to millions so that you can escape the loneliness and feel supported during your journey.** Jim Rohm says, "You become like the five people with whom you spend the majority of your time." When you spend your time with us, you'll become a better version of yourself! We've watched so many long-standing relationships form as a result of this community. Your next joint venture partner is waiting for you. Join us!

We've placed several options for support beyond this book at https://www.movetomillionsbook.com/resources for you so that they are all together for easy access.

Chapter Action Plan

1. Determine your implementation path on your own or through taking advantage of one of the resources we propose to make sure that this book doesn't become just another book that you read.
2. Confirm the plan you'll be following to achieve this million-dollar goal for yourself.

Remember: Information without action is a waste of time. Set a plan right now to implement all you've learned in this powerful book so that you get one step closer to your million-dollar goal.

CHAPTER NINETEEN

The Move to Millions Charge

"Million-dollar CEOs are made in the actions they take."
—DARNYELLE JERVEY HARMON

One of my favorite movies that I watch every time it's on TV is *Sister Act 2: Back in the Habit,*[37] starring Whoopi Goldberg. If you love musicals like I do, this movie will give you all the feels. There is one scene in the movie when Whoopi's character, Sister Mary Clarence, is waiting for Lauryn Hill's character, Rita, near Rita's home. It's just after Rita and Tanya (another student in the choir) were singing in the chapel, and Sister Mary Roberts walked in on them. (I told you I love this movie!) Rita and Tanya were singing, and when confronted by Sister Mary Roberts, they stopped cold. Sister Mary Roberts convinced Sister Mary Clarence to pay Rita a visit.

When Rita walks past Sister Mary Clarence on the street, she got her attention and left her with these words from Rainer Marie Rilke's *Letters to a Young Poet:* "If when you wake up in the morning, you can't think of anything else but singing, you're supposed to be a singer, girl."

Now, I say the same to you. If you can think of nothing other than getting your business to the million-dollar mark, not just for the money but to live your why, to deepen your connection to God, and to impact the lives of those you love and desire to bless, then you are supposed to be a million-dollar CEO. If the desire to make, move, and leave millions is in you, it's there because that is what God desires for you.

When I read Psalm 37:4, "Delight thyself also in Jehovah and He shall give thee the desires of thy heart," I have always believed that God is saying if you have the desire, it is because I *gave* it to you. The desire to make millions isn't arbitrary. It's what God desires for you. It's your birthright; it's what God saw for you before you were formed in your mother's womb. God has told us so many times in His word that we are to have access to wealth. Your business is the vehicle God is using to bring wealth into your lineage.

There's nothing wrong with desiring a million-dollar company. You don't have to apologize or downplay your desire either. You don't have to say it out loud or share it to appease others. Just say it in your soul. Just confirm it in your spirit. Just take the next step you know to take so that the path can emerge. You don't need anyone's permission to desire making, moving, and leaving millions either. Nor do you have to explain why you're moving to millions. It's your decision alone. If you want it deep down inside, you have to claim the desire as your own. That is how the path emerges. Decide first.

In another one of my favorite movies, *Facing the Giants*,[38] I love the scene where Mr. Bridges, a local man who comes into the school weekly to pray over the students' lockers, confronts Coach Grant Taylor. You see, Coach Taylor was having his own Moses Moment. Some fathers of the football players were trying to get the principal of the school to let him go because he'd had six losing seasons. Coach Taylor walked in on the fathers talking with one of his coaches and the principal, and the little courage and confidence he had dissipated. Coach Taylor started to lose heart but knew where to look—to the Father. He started praying, but the feelings of inadequacy weren't vacating. So, in walked Mr. Bridges one day with a message. He told Grant to bloom where he was planted. Grant, enamored by the message, went after Mr. Bridges for clarity. When Grant expresses his uncertainty to Mr. Bridges, he shared the story with Grant that I now want to share with you. The story goes (I'm paraphrasing a bit here):

There were two farmers who were praying for rain, but only one went out and prepared his fields for it. God will send the rain when He is ready, but He won't send the rain if you're not prepared.

We've come to the end of this book, Incredible One. I have shared everything that God has told me to tell you. Now you have a decision to make. Are you going to prepare your business for the million-dollar rain as you pray, or are you going to pray without preparing to give God something to bless?

Only you can decide what you will do now, so I am leaving this Move to Millions charge with you:

Tighten your strategy, sales infrastructure, systems, support, and success mindset. Develop and *master* your Million Dollar Assets. Become *operationally obedient* by way of surrender, alignment, forgiveness, and confidence. Hold the *vision* for your next level with a commitment to do whatever it takes to manifest, and by all means, go forth, *execute*, and make millions.

I am so grateful to be at this point in the book with you. I answered the call God gave me to start this movement, rebranded my company and podcast, and wrote this book. I did it, despite my own Moses Moments, for *you*. It was more important for me to give you the blueprint, light the torch, and chart the path for your next level than it was to let my own fears consume me. I am so glad that I didn't let my fear win. Instead, I saw it for what it was: an indication that my next level was present. Writing this book is the catalyst to my next level. As a result of this body of work, I am now ready to step into leading the Legacy Collective and hosting God Girls Making Millions®, not just because I am one but because I know how to create others. As I already shared, we have added thirty-eight million-dollar CEOs to our list over the last few years. I have to admit that it is poetic justice because I am finishing the writing of this book just days before the inaugural GGMM is set to begin. I love it when God winks at me! And now He's winking at you.

You might be the first in your family to make millions, but you won't be the last. Most have the desire but have no idea how to make it a reality. So, they talk themselves out of their birthright.

You will not talk yourself out of your birthright. I wrote this book for you. It is my hope that I answered your prayer to learn *how* to make the Move to Millions in a way that serves you, glorifies God, and doesn't turn you into a number-chaser. I feel 100 percent confident that I did my part.

Now, it's your time to MOVE.

Your Move to Millions starts here.

Let's go!

PASS THE BLESSING ON

"True joy and fulfillment are found when you
focus on being a blessing to others."
—DARNYELLE JERVEY HARMON

One of my favorite songs is Patti LaBelle's "When You've Been Blessed (Feels Like Heaven)." What I love the most about this song is that it fosters a mindset to help others even when there's nothing in it for you. In his book *$100M Offers*, Alex Hormozi says, "People who help others (with zero expectation) experience higher levels of fulfilment, live longer, and make more money."

Has reading *Move to Millions* blessed you so far? If you are shaking your head unequivocally yes, then I have an ask for you.

Would you do me the honor of sharing how *Move to Millions* has blessed you by passing the blessing on to others in the form of a book review? I promise that it will only take you a minute or less to share your thoughts via the platform (Amazon, Audible, etc.) you used to invest in yourself through this book.

I have a mission that many may think is elusive. I want to impact five million entrepreneurs through my work. To impact this volume of entrepreneurs and small business owners, I must expand my reach. To that end, I need your help. Your review will help others learn about and read this powerful book for themselves.

Think of the difference book reviews and recommendations have made for the books currently lining your nightstand and bookshelves. By sharing your review of *Move to Millions*, you will offer the same feeling of confidence and excitement to others.

By taking the time to do me this favor, you will be helping another entrepreneur or small business owner learn how to become a million-dollar CEO with grace and ease instead of hustle and grind. You'll be instrumental in the transformation of another life because of what they learn in order to leverage and scale their business.

Thank you in advance for passing the blessing on.

CONNECT WITH DARNYELLE ONLINE

We absolutely must keep this party going! Remember, you didn't just buy a book, you've unlocked a vault of resources to aid you on your *Move to Millions*. I invite you to join me online to continue to deepen our connection. You can find me by searching Darnyelle Jervey Harmon on all online platforms, including Facebook, Instagram, LinkedIn, YouTube, and TikTok.

Remember that, throughout this book, I have shared additional worksheets with you that are waiting for you online at https://www.movetomillionsbook.com/resources. Once you opt in, you will be able to download each worksheet for your professional library. Additionally, you'll have information about our programs and other products and services created with your Move to Millions in mind.

ABOUT THE AUTHOR

Dr. Darnyelle Jervey Harmon is the award-winning Inc. 5000 recognized CEO of Incredible One Enterprises, LLC, which specializes in transforming six-figure service-based entrepreneurs and business owners into CEOs who make, move, and leave millions. Harmon and her work have been featured in *Inc., Success, Essence, Forbes, O*, and *Black Enterprise* magazines and on a host of podcasts and other media outlets. With a mission to change the lives of others through words, when she is not writing or creating content, you can find her keynoting on stages around the world or hosting her podcast, *The Move to Millions with Dr. Darnyelle Jervey Harmon*. The Delaware native lives in New Castle, Delaware, with her husband, Bernard, and their puppy, Lady.

Learn more about Darnyelle at www.drdarnyelle.com or her company website, www.IncredibleOneEnterprises.com

ACKNOWLEDGMENTS

I am so excited to present to each of you the book I was born to write. This book wouldn't have been possible without those I mention here.

My creator, God: Thank you, God, for choosing and using me. I accept the call to be your modern-day Moses to teach your children how to master the little things so that they can live and experience what you desire for them.

My mother, Regina: I'm so grateful for how our relationship has blossomed. To my late father, Robert. I am grateful for every conversation leading up to this book.

My husband and best friend, Bernard: Thank you for allowing me to miss date nights and work on this book in bed. You are truly the wind beneath my wings, and because of your support, my light gets to shine. Thank you for never doubting, asking questions, or dismissing my greatness. Thank you for being my biggest supporter and gracefully standing beside me so that I can be the impact God created me to be.

My editorial team: Tenita Johnson and Melissa Stevens, you have been instrumental in making my words come to life. To my advanced readers who took the time to read every word I wrote and give me valuable feedback. Thank you so much for lending your time and talent in an effort to help me to turn this book into a masterpiece.

My sister-friends who have been cheering me on as I've navigated life and business. Thank you for letting me cry on your shoulder, praying big prayers for me, reminding me that I can do it and holding my hand through writing this book. I love each of you to life: Janice Anderson, Lucinda Cross, Aprille Franks, Natasha Joan Haughton, Shawndra C. Johnson, Nina Parker, Doreen Rainey, and Linda Denise Williams.

My Incredible Factor University® clients, past and present: Thank you all for trusting your Incredible Factor® to me and being an important part of my journey. Thank you for encouraging me to play bigger so that others would know what you do and that my work changes lives and businesses. A special thank you to the clients highlighted in this book: Attiyah Blair, Bridgett Battles, Christine Cambrio, TerDawn Deboe, Herman Dolce, Dr. Pamela Ellis, Dr. Angela Grayson, Althea Hearst, Keira Ingram, Lindsey Jones, Dr. Erica Jordan-Thomas, Kim Kendall, Dr. Madeline Lewis, Marissa Q. Paine, Crystal Perkins, Marquel Russell, and Jasmine Womack.

My Incredible One Enterprises LLC team: Thank you for supporting the vision and mission of the company and taking things off my plate so that I could write this book. I am grateful to each of you and the role you play in helping me to shake the planet.

My future babies: I get excited thinking about you reading this book one day and knowing that what created your financial legacy has shaken the planet.

ENDNOTES

1   American Express, T*he State of Women-Owned Business Report*, New York: American Express, 2019, https://ventureneer.com/wp-content/uploads/2019/10/Final-2019-state-of-women-owned-businesses-report.pdf.

2   American Express, *The State of Women-Owned Business Report*, New York: American Express, 2019, https://ventureneer.com/wp-content/uploads/2019/10/Final-2019-state-of-women-owned-businesses-report.pdf.

3   Godlewski, Nina, "Small Business Revenue Statistics: Annual Sales and Earnings," Fundera (website), last updated January 23, 2023, https://www.fundera.com/resources/small-business-revenue-statistics.

4   Godlewski, Nina, "Small Business Revenue Statistics: Annual Sales and Earnings," Fundera (website), last updated January 23, 2023, Fundera (website), https://www.fundera.com/resources/small-business-revenue-statistics.

5   Godlewski, Nina, "Small Business Revenue Statistics: Annual Sales and Earnings," Fundera (website), last updated January 23, 2023, Fundera (website), https://www.fundera.com/resources/small-business-revenue-statistics.

6   American Express, *The State of Women-Owned Business Report*, New York: American Express, 2019, https://ventureneer.com/wp-content/uploads/2019/10/Final-2019-state-of-women-owned-businesses-report.pdf.

7   Sincero, Jen, *You're a Badass at Making Money*, New York: Penguin Books, 2017.

8   Nee, Sean, Paul H. Harvey, and Robert M. May, "Lifting the Veil on Abundance Patterns Model of Abundance," Proceedings: Biological Sciences 243, no. 1307 (1991): 161–63, https://www.jstor.org/stable/76714.

9   Harvey, Andrew, The Way of Passion: A Celebration of Rumi, New York: Jeremy P. Tarcher/Putnam, 2001.

10   Dweck, Carol, *Mindset: The New Psychology of Success*, New York: Ballatine Books, 2007.

11   Fuller, Andrew, *Your Best Life at Any Age*, Indianapolis, IN: Cardinal's Publishers Group, 2021.

12   SBA Office of Advocacy, *2022 Small Business Report*, SBA.gov (website), accessed February 28, 2023, https://cdn.advocacy.sba.gov/wp-content/uploads/2022/08/30121338/Small-Business-Economic-Profile-US.pdf.

13   Google Dictionary, "Definition of Asset, provided by Oxford Languages," Google, accessed February 28, 2023.

14   Phillips, Kristine, "'They Had Us Fooled': Inside Payless's Elaborate Prank to Dupe People into Paying $600 for Shoes," *The Washington Post* (website), posted November 11, 2018, https://www.washingtonpost.com/business/2018/11/30/they-had-us-fooled-inside-paylesss-elaborate-prank-dupe-people-into-paying-shoes/.

15   World Population Review, "2023 World Population by Country (Live)," World Population Review (website), accessed February 28, 2023, https://worldpopulationreview.com/.

16   Intelligent Change, "The Benefits of Positive Language," Intelligent Change (website), accessed February 24, 2023, https://www.intelligentchange.com/blogs/read/the-benefits-of-positive-language.

17   Kennedy, Dan, *No B.S. Time Management for Entrepreneurs: The Ultimate, No Holds Barred, Kick Butt, Take No Prisoners, Guide to Time, Productivity, and Sanity*, Bellingham, WA: Self-Counsel Press, 1996.

18   Kennedy, Dan, No B.S. Time Management for Entrepreneurs: The Ultimate, No Holds Barred, Kick Butt, Take No Prisoners, Guide to Time, Productivity, and Sanity, Bellingham, WA: Self-Counsel Press, 1996.

19   Internal Revenue Service, "Self-Employment Tax (Social Security and Medicare Taxes)," IRS.gov (website), accessed February 24, 2023, https://www.irs.gov/businesses/small-businesses-self-employed/self-employment-tax-social-security-and-medicare-axes#:~:text=The%20self%2Demployment%20

tax%20rate,for%20Medicare%20(hospital%20insurance).

20   Harmon, Darnyelle Jervey, *Market Like a ROCK Star*, Newark, DE: Incredible Factor Publishing, 2012.

21   Hawwa, George, "How many brand touch points do you need with an audience before they purchase/enquire?" Attention Experts (website), accessed February 24, 2023, https://attentionexperts.com/many-brand-touch-points/.

22   Hendricks, Gay, *The Big Leap: Conquer Your Hidden Fear and Take Life to the Next Level*, New York: Harper Collins, 2009.

23   Williamson, Marianne, A Return to Love: Reflections on the Principles of a Course in Miracles, New York: Harper Perennial, 1996.

24   Bhardwaj, Kinjal, "The Ways Women Shrink at Work," Medium.com (website), September 19, 2019, https://medium.com/@kinjalpike/the-ways-women-shrink-at-work-32607e1aa878.

25   Carranza, Eliana, Chandra Dhakal, and Inessa Love, *Female Entrepreneurs and How They're Different*, Washington, DC: International Bank for Reconstruction and Development / The World Bank, 2018, https://documents1.worldbank.org/curated/en/400121542883319809/pdf/Female-Entrepreneurs-How-and-Why-are-They-Different.pdf.

26   Buffington, S. D., *The Law of Abundance*, Dallas, TX: QuinStar Publishing, 2009.

27   Hebel, Bruce, and Toni Hebel, *Forgiving Forward: Unleashing the Forgiveness Revolution*, self-published, Regenerating Life Press, 2011.

28   Dictionary.com, "Surrender Definition and Meaning," Dictionary.com (website), accessed February 24, 2023, https://www.dictionary.com/browse/surrender.

29   Duke, Bill, dir., *Not Easily Broken*, Hollywood, CA: Screen Gems, 2009.

30   Singer, Michael, The Surrender Experiment: My Journey into Life's Perfection, New York: Harmony Rodale Books, 2015.

31   Dictionary.com, "Mastery Definition and Meaning," Dictionary.com (website), accessed February 24, 2023, https://www.dictionary.com/browse/mastery.

32   Monte, Eric, and Mike Evans, creators, *Good Times*, "Character Looting Lenny played by Dap Sugar Willie," CBS, 7 episodes, 1976–1979.

33   Gladwell, Malcolm, *Outliers: The Story of Success*. New York: Little Brown

and Company, 2008.

34   Akil, Mara Brock, creator, *Girlfriends*, "Character Toni Childs played by Jill Marie Jones," Paramount Network, 137 episodes, 2000–2008.

35   Definition of Manifesto. Dictionary.com, "Manifesto Definition and Meaning," Dictionary.com (website), accessed February 24, 2023, https://www.dictionary.com/browse/manifesto.

36   Wanderlust Worker, "The Harvard MBA Business School Study on Goal Setting," Wanderlust Worker (website), accessed February 24, 2023, https://www.wanderlustworker.com/the-harvard-mba-business-school-study-on-goal-setting/.

37   Duke, Bill, dir., *Sister Act 2: Back in the Habit*, Burbank, CA: Touchstone Pictures, 1993.

38   Kendrick, Alex, dir., *Facing the Giants*, Culver City, CA: Samuel Goldwyn Films, 2006.

A free ebook edition is available with the purchase of this book.

To claim your free ebook edition:

1. Visit MorganJamesBOGO.com
2. Sign your name CLEARLY in the space
3. Complete the form and submit a photo of the entire copyright page
4. You or your friend can download the ebook to your preferred device

Morgan James BOGO™

A **FREE** ebook edition is available for you or a friend with the purchase of this print book.

CLEARLY SIGN YOUR NAME ABOVE

Instructions to claim your free ebook edition:
1. Visit MorganJamesBOGO.com
2. Sign your name CLEARLY in the space above
3. Complete the form and submit a photo of this entire page
4. You or your friend can download the ebook to your preferred device

Print & Digital Together Forever.

Snap a photo

Free ebook

Read anywhere

Printed in the USA
CPSIA information can be obtained
at www.ICGtesting.com
BVHW040242100823
668393BV00002B/12